A Southern Garden

Elizabeth Lawrence

A Southern Garden

University of North Carolina Press

Chapel Hill and London

This edition reproduces the text of a special edition published
in 1991, on the occasion of the fiftieth anniversary of the original
publication of *A Southern Garden.*

Library of Congress Cataloging-in-Publication Data
Lawrence, Elizabeth, 1904–1985.
A southern garden / Elizabeth Lawrence.
p.   cm.
Includes index.
ISBN 0-8078-4930-8 (pbk.: alk. paper)
1. Flower gardening—Southern States.   2. Flowers—
Southern States.   3. Flowering woody plants—
Southern States.   4. Flower gardening—North Carolina.
5. Flowers—North Carolina.   6. Flowering woody plants—
North Carolina.   I. Title.
SB405.5.S68 L38   2001
635.9'0975—dc21   00-056362

05   04   03   02   01   5   4   3   2   1

First paperback printing

Original watercolors by Shirley Felts, Garden Studio.

For *Ann*

Contents

Illustrations

116   "The fall-flowering, red-and-white-striped crinum of old gardens in East Carolina is called, as are all those of this type, the milk-and-wine lily."

132–33   "In midsummer I always watched for the bright flowers of the coral-tree, *Erythrina Crista-galli...*"

140   Fall: A witch-hazel blooms by the front door of Elizabeth Lawrence's Charlotte home.

145   "The dark color of ox-blood lilies [*Hippeastrum advenum*] shows to best advantage against small white flowers."

157   "In the copse a bright patch of bottle gentian, *Gentiana Andrewsii*, blooms under a strawberry-bush [*Euonymus americana*] all through November."

164   Chinese bamboo (*Polygonum cuspidatum*): "The shoots grow to fifteen feet by September, producing great sprays of fine, rosy red flowers."

177   "*Crocus laevigatus* 'Fontenayi' blooms on sunny days all through the winter."

179   The flowering plum (*Prunus Mume*): "The Chinese say that the three friends of winter are the pine, the bamboo, and the flowering plum."

182–83   *Clematis cirrhosa* has "greenish creamy flowers that bloom steadily from early October through February..."

191   Poet's laurel (*Danaë racemosa*) and butcher's broom (*Ruscus aculeatus*): "The year begins and ends with evergreens."

Publisher's Note

*D*ear Mr. Couch, I have written. a garden book for the Middle South based on my own records which I have been keeping for a number of years with a book in my mind, for there is no book for gardeners in our section, and there is need of one." Thus did Elizabeth Lawrence, a landscape designer and writer in nearby Raleigh, begin her letter in March 1941 to William Couch, director of the University of North Carolina Press. They met the following week, and Couch, after consulting with such local gardening authorities as H. R. Totten and William Lanier Hunt, agreed to publish *A Southern Garden.*

In her typically self-effacing style, Lawrence entitled the preface to her book "An Apology for Myself as a Gardener." In fact she had little to apologize for. A graduate of Barnard, Lawrence was a trained landscape architect, the first woman to complete the course in landscape design at North Carolina State College (in 1930). But the wealth of information in this book was not the result of her formal education. Early in her studies Lawrence had discovered that "a knowledge of plant material for the South could not be got in the library, most of the literature of horticulture being for a different climate, and that I would have to grow the plants in my garden and learn about them for myself."

The first edition of *A Southern Garden* appeared in the spring of 1942. Most of the reviews politely applauded the book for its aptness for southern gardeners. A few reviewers, though, discerned something special here and pointed out qualities in her writing that readers now regard as hallmarks of Elizabeth Lawrence's style. Lester Rowntree, writing in *Golden Gardens*, a magazine for California gardeners, noted that the book was the work of "a born experimenter and one who lives intimately with her plants and writes of them as she would her personal friends. It reads very much like a letter from one gardener to another." In the *New York Herald Tribune*, Robert S. Lemmon included *A Southern Garden* in his roundup of the season's gardening books. "You will find here no vague theorizing, no pseudo-scientific posing, no wavering sentimental flights of fancy." Lawrence's work, he said, was "straightforward, sensible, informative, pleasantly readable."

Good notices notwithstanding, the book enjoyed only modest sales over the next fifteen years and in 1957 went out of print. Lawrence, meanwhile, had moved to Charlotte with her mother, leaving the Raleigh house and the garden she had chronicled in the book. In her new home she quickly went about creating a new garden—and writing. *The Little Bulbs* was published in 1957, followed soon after by *Gardens in Winter*, in 1961. (Both are still in print.) Lawrence had also begun, in 1957, to contribute a weekly gardening column to the *Charlotte Observer*, a practice she continued for fourteen years. (A selection of these columns, edited by Bill Neal and entitled *Through the Garden Gate*, was published in 1990 by the University of North Carolina Press.)

In the 1960s copies of the original printing of *A Southern Garden* had become collector's items, jealously guarded and lent only to best friends and trustworthy relatives. In 1967, at the urging of William Lanier Hunt and others, the University of North Carolina Press published a revised edition of the book, with a new introduction and an updated list of nurseries. Hunt wrote a foreword for the edition. "Gardening books written in elegant style and filled with information are rare indeed," he wrote. "*A Southern Garden* is to American gardeners what the best English books are to the Britons." Katharine White took note of the new edition in her *New Yorker* column, writing, "*A Southern Garden* is far more than a regional book;

it is civilized literature by a writer with a pure and lively style and a deep sense of beauty."

The book was reissued in paperback in 1984, and in a new preface, Lawrence looked back over the more than forty years that had passed since she wrote the book. "I am always and forever being asked to bring *A Southern Garden* up to date. It can't be done. I could no more rewrite the book than I could remake the garden that it was written about, the garden that I left behind when I came to live in Charlotte; that garden is gone, and so are many of the friends who helped to make it. When Mr. Krippendorf died, and then Mr. Morrison and Caroline Dormon, I thought gardening as I knew it had come to an end. Gardens are so perishable; they live on only in books and letters; but what has gone before is not lost: the future is the past entered by another door."

The renewal she spoke of was near at hand. Old friends and correspondents had died, but not before passing on to their sons and daughters and nieces and nephews an appreciation for gardening and for Elizabeth Lawrence. "Soon after Mr. Krippendorf died," she wrote, "I went to an annual meeting of the American Daffodil Society . . . and there I found his daughter, Rosan Adams, and his granddaughter, Mary Nelson, both full of enthusiasm for daffodils and everything else that grows." After her death in 1985 friends discovered among her papers materials for two posthumous works, *Gardening for Love* (1987) and *A Rock Garden in the South* (1990).

Of the several thousand books published in 1942, few are still in print, and many gardening books published as recently as last year can already be found on the bargain tables in bookstores. Yet *A Southern Garden* endures. Reissued now for the third time, it stands as a testament not only to the book and its author but to the dedication of her many admirers who sustained her and the book through the years. To William Lanier Hunt; to Caroline Dormon; to Carl Krippendorf; to her vast network of friends and correspondents, named and unnamed; to William Couch, who had the wisdom to publish this book; to members of the Press staff who nurtured the book through its various editions; to a new generation of gardeners who are just discovering the pleasures of reading about and digging in the garden; and to Elizabeth Lawrence and her memory, we dedicate this fiftieth anniversary edition.

For the 1967 and 1984 editions, Lawrence made a few minor changes. Except for correcting typographical errors, we have not departed from the original text in any other respect.

Foreword

*D*o you know *A Southern Garden*?" That question was asked of me fifteen years ago by clients intent on finding a source for *Allium flavum*, a charming flowering onion described within the book's pages. I found *A Southern Garden* on the shelves of a local bookshop in Chapel Hill, and my reading of it set me on a path of gardening adventure that is the most rewarding part of my life.

Though written over fifty years ago, *A Southern Garden* never grows old or outdated. I have copies of every edition published. My treasured first edition was inherited from the great-aunt for whom I am named. I turn to an office copy whenever I need inspiration, help with identification, or clarification of a point about the history of a plant. Yet another copy occupies a place on my headboard bookshelf for nighttime pleasure reading. When I was studying at North Carolina State University, J. C. Raulston, conducting a class on plants in the landscape, showed us the ten horticultural books he would not be without. Heading the list was *A Southern Garden*.

Elizabeth Lawrence wrote eloquently and genuinely about the adventure of gardening. Although *A Southern Garden* is a regional book—her books and garden columns primarily tell of personal gardening experiences in piedmont North Carolina—gardeners everywhere have much to learn from it. Few garden writers combine her skill with words, classical education, botanical accuracy, and keen perception of color.

She writes with the courage of one who knows her subject well—a knowledge born of careful and accurate long-term observation. Hers is the voice of experience.

When we share in Elizabeth Lawrence's experiences, we share in her triumphs. We also share in her failures, such as the crocus in perfection of bloom that was crushed by ice. Or the *Cyclamen coum* that never made itself at home in her garden (and won't make itself at home in mine either). I am comforted by her failures as well as encouraged by her successes. A friend, Doug Ruhren, says he always checks through *A Southern Garden* when he acquires a new plant to see if Elizabeth Lawrence grew it. If she did, then he feels fairly sure it will grow for him. But when reading this book, remember that Elizabeth Lawrence was aware of the environmental differences among gardens—and the temperamental differences among gardeners. She recounts her experiences, and those of others, but she would be the first to counsel us all not to judge our gardens by hers. Plants that fail in one person's garden are often successful in another's.

The classics of garden literature, botany, history, and poetry infused Elizabeth Lawrence's consciousness and her writing. There is no pretension in her quotations, only the genuine enthusiasm and appreciation of a fellow lover of words and of growing things. She can transport us from her Raleigh garden back to that of Addison in eighteenth-century England, or take us off to the flower stalls of Barcelona to enjoy cut clouds of sea lavender (*Limonium latifolium*). I am grateful to her for introducing me to *Elizabeth and Her German Garden*, to Sir Herbert Maxwell's *Memories of the Months*, to dozens of poets, botanists, and gardeners. Through the pages of *A Southern Garden*, we can visit not only the vanished gardens of great horticultural writers but also those of Elizabeth's personal friends. With her, we meander down Bill Hunt's hillside to see his cyclamen and sternbergias, or travel to Caroline Dormon's "Briarwood" in northern Louisiana.

The quality that best characterizes Elizabeth Lawrence and her writing is accessibility. In her lifetime she carried on a lively and rich correspondence with gardeners from every walk of life. She welcomed visitors to her door and answered their questions if she could. If she couldn't, she made every effort to find an answer, which led to more correspondence. Hers was an inquisitive and retentive mind. Writing about *The Little Bulbs: A Tale of Two Gardens*, she says, "I wrote this book, as I write everything that I write about gardens, to answer my own questions." In answering her own questions she answers ours, though perhaps we did not know what to ask.

Some of what Elizabeth Lawrence wrote about is of the past. Several of the cultivars she describes are no longer readily available (though I hope they still remain in someone's garden and that I may one day see them). Many of the nurseries from which she ordered no longer exist. And yet the past has a way of repeating itself. The local farmers' market I shop at is filled with cut flowers and potted plants, some of them the old and treasured varieties described by Elizabeth. Every day I learn of another specialty nursery where willing gardeners work to spread the wealth of plants. I believe that if I continue to search, I'll find the phlox cultivars and the Korean chrysanthemum hybrids named mostly for planets and constellations that she described in *A Southern Garden*.

Through the pages of this book, we share in her enthusiasm for the plants that made up her garden, and it is easy to note that Elizabeth Lawrence was a fine plantswoman. But, as she wrote in the introduction to the 1967 edition of this book, "I do not mean to lay undue emphasis on plants. Plants are the material from which the garden is created." Still, it was her passion for plants—and for finding out all about them—that made her a rare and gifted designer of gardens.

A visit to her Charlotte garden left no doubt in the visitor's mind that her garden design was brilliant. Entering the house, one passed into the living room; at the end, three windows were curtained from the outside by bamboo. In *Gardens in Winter*, she writes that the idea of planting bamboo near the house came to her from Elsie Hassan, who "borrowed it from the Chinese poet, Po Chu-i: 'I love lying near the windowside' he said, 'to hear in their branches the sound of the autumn wind.' All winter the green leaves rustle outside my window, and the low winter sun sends slender shadows into the room." The effect is magical.

Out of the back door and across the upper terrace flowed a garden that represented a masterly synthesis of various styles of garden making. Broad stone steps, planted with tiny treasures and flanked by a rock garden, led down from the terrace's edge to a wide walk of fine crushed gravel. On one side of this walk, Carolina cherry laurels (*Prunus laurocerasus*) pruned up high gave the illusion of a row of olive trees. Moving from the terrace to the path, I felt that I had journeyed from an alpine meadow to the Mediterranean. The path proceeded further between borders of flowers and evergreens, eventually leading to a low stone wall whose curved arcs enclosed a second terrace. In the heart of the terrace was a circular reflecting pool. Beyond this terrace the wide gravel path resumed, leading into a lovely woodland of stewartias, pines, and magnolias. The ground was clothed with choice perennials, among them hellebores, epimediums, and *Iris japonicum*.

In this edition, the frontispiece and the full-page illustrations for three of the four seasonal sections are newly commissioned paintings based on images of Elizabeth's Charlotte garden. (We have no photographs of the Raleigh garden.) The illustration for summer represents a section of the Elizabeth Lawrence Border at the North Carolina State University Arboretum in Raleigh. The spot illustrations are paintings of plants described in the text.

A few botanical names have changed since Elizabeth Lawrence last updated her manuscript. (Taxonomists do, after all, have to make a living.) The oxblood lily is once again *Hippeastrum advenum*. Miss Edna's Chinese bamboo is now *Polygonum cuspidatum*. The Double Japanese aster that Elizabeth got from Catherine Taylor in Greensboro can be purchased under the name *Asteromoea mongolica*, though its exact identity still remains clouded in mystery. *Amarcrinum Howardii* is now × *Crinodonna howardii*. The lacy moss verbena (formerly *Verbena erinoides*) is now *V. tenuisecta*.

The names in this text are those last updated by Elizabeth. More recent nomenclatural changes and current horticultural usages have been noted in the index. In addition to plant name changes, the American Amaryllis Society is now the American Plant Life Society.

Although names change, as do fashions for plants and styles of gardens, the information contained in *A Southern Garden* still remains useful and relevant. Elizabeth Lawrence, because she wrote so elegantly and accurately about the plants she grew, is my frequent partner in forays to identify mysterious occupants of the garden. Among the mystery plants I identified with her help are *Verbena bonariensis* and *Heliotropium amplexicaule*. A part of the beauty of *A Southern Garden* is the sense I have of sharing in a dialogue with Elizabeth about her garden and all its occupants.

Like Elizabeth Lawrence, I eat lunch in my garden as often as I can (whenever magnolia leaves or pods are not crashing down onto the terrace). I try to make daily rounds and remember to get down on my hands and knees to check tiny blooms for fragrance. As yet, I have not come to follow Elizabeth's advice with regard to record keeping, but I am grateful for her notes. The chart of blooming dates she prepared for *A Southern Garden* is still an accurate source of information for the plants included in her list.

When I visited Elizabeth Lawrence during her last summer in her Charlotte garden, she was still actively thinking about the garden and planning for its future. "Do you know where I can get seeds of *Verbascum olympicum*? I've lost mine and would love to have it again." She told me that of all the boltonias she had grown, her favorite was a soft pink one bought from a Japanese nurseryman, which did not persist in her garden. She would be pleased to know that the following summer I found a pink boltonia seedling in a nursery in eastern North Carolina. It was introduced in 1988 to the horticultural trade under the name of *Boltonia asteroides* 'Pink Beauty', by Montrose Nursery in Hillsborough, North Carolina, and is now widely available. Today it grows in the Elizabeth Lawrence Border, backed by white *Lespedeza japonica* (another garden choice of Elizabeth's). From late summer through fall, its flowers create a pale pink haze in the border. In front of the *Boltonia asteroides* 'Pink Beauty' is a planting of blue salvias, purple lythrum, and pale pink trumpets of × *Crinodonna howardii*, along with a soft yellow daylily from Elizabeth's Charlotte garden.

When *A Southern Garden* was published in 1942, Elizabeth Lawrence lived in Raleigh. She continued to live there for another six years before moving to Charlotte to build a new house, starting a new life and garden. Little of the original garden remains, but thanks to the efforts of the members of the Farm House Fraternity, who now own and occupy the property and periodically clear invading poison ivy, we can still enjoy its remnants.

The copse she described in *A Southern Garden* is now carpeted in late winter by the flowers of *Crocus tomasinianus* in every tint and shade of silver lilac, lavender, and deep glowing violet, woven with the silver-marbled heart-shaped leaves and yellow flowers of *Ranunculus ficaria*, the "lesser celandine" beloved of Wordsworth. Here winter aconite still lift their glistening yellow flowers surrounded by a green ruff of sepals. In spring the grass is carpeted with blue star flower (*Ipheion uniflora*) and in late spring and summer with clumps of pink and white *Oxalis crassipes*. Foliage and flowers of the lady tulip (*Tulipa clusiana*), colchicums, *Scilla peruviana*, and *Crinum* 'Cecil Houdyshel' persist. The outlines of paths are still evident, lined with hundreds of pink magic lilies (*Lycoris squamigera*) in July. Red spider lilies (*Lycoris radiata*) abound in August and September.

This book is a wonderful companion and guide for the garden maker. The information contained within its covers is of the best sort: that gleaned from the actual experience of growing the plants described. Elizabeth Lawrence was an artist with words. She wove her and her fellow gardeners' experiences with those of the gardeners of literature and history into a rich narrative. The plants appear on the pages of this book as fully developed characters as complex and fascinating as any in a novel. Such are her descriptive powers that we not only see the plants but frequently smell (and even taste) them as well. It seems that the reader is by her side in the garden as she examines the "dead white, crystalline, very thick petaled flowers of *Cooperia pedunculata*" and smells their "strange, disturbing sweetness." Her writing went beyond simple description and the performance of various plants in her own garden to cover details of horticultural history, poetic and philosophical references, and the practical recommendations of other gardeners. For Elizabeth Lawrence, gardening was an adventure, a challenge, a romance, an act of love. And her writing still conveys her enthusiasm and passion for growing things.

In reference to the twenty-fifth anniversary edition of *A Southern Garden*, she wrote, "Rereading what I wrote so long ago makes me want to start all over to grow some of everything that grows." I hope that what she has written will inspire other gardeners, as it has me, to grow some of everything that grows. My garden, like that of Elizabeth, "demands every single moment that I have to spare and every single ounce of strength that I have left in me." As Elizabeth observed in her first column for the *Charlotte Observer*, the world of gardening is "a world as old as the history of man, and as new as the latest contribution of science: a world of mystery, adventure, and romance; a world of poetry and philosophy; a world of beauty; and a world of work. Never be deceived about the work. . . . But I do not need to tell you, if you are a gardener, that no other undertaking will give as great a return for the amount of effort put into it."

The Elizabeth Lawrence Border

Doug Ruhren and I, who are garden makers by profession, volunteer our time to design and care for a series of borders at the North Carolina State University Arboretum in Raleigh. Among these is a mixed border of small trees, shrubs, grasses, perennials, annuals, and bulbs that is dedicated to the memory of Elizabeth Lawrence. We know that her Raleigh garden contained a border that she described as pink, and we have designed ours around that theme. A pink gravel path leads through the border to a bench set against a fence. Over the bench is a bas-relief by sculptor Alice Pohl. A climbing China rose, 'Old Blush' (propagated from one given by Elizabeth to a friend), and the evergreen *Clematis armandii*, clothe the fence. The path turns left and leads through the border. Here clumps of the Japanese iris with violet-ribbed flowers are backed by the chartreuse blooms of *Thalictrum glaucum* (now *T. speciosissimum*).

I am pleased that we were able to find the 'White Duchess' rose that grew and died in Elizabeth's Raleigh garden. It is *Rosa* 'Mrs. Joseph S. Schwartz' and grows in the Lawrence Border with the red urn-shaped flowers of *Clematis texensis* threaded through it. Miss Edna's Chinese bamboo (now *Polygonum cuspidatum*) also grows in the border; around its feet are red spider lilies (*Lycoris radiata*) transplanted from Elizabeth's Raleigh garden and the crystalline red flowers of oxblood lilies from her Charlotte garden. The polygonum stems provide shade for Lenten roses (*Helleborus orientalis*) transplanted from both gardens.

Elizabeth's beloved *Prunus mume* frames the east end of the border. Early blue *Scilla sibirica* and crocus occupy the ground beneath it. Huge dusky mauve flower heads of the tall purple-stemmed *Eupatorium purpureum* var. *atropurpureum* mingle with cannas and white-striped miscanthus. The towering stalks of variegated *Arundo donax* rise above the yellow and orange flowers of *Buddleia x* 'Sun Gold'.

A river of yellow oenothera weaves its way in spring through clumps of *Phlox*, purple-leaved *Setcreasea pallida*, and variegated sweet flag. Verbenas of every sort and hardy heliotrope edge the border. Atamasco lilies bloom in spring, and *Zephyranthes candida* in fall. On late summer afternoons, the lavender flowers of vesper iris (*Pardonopsis dichotomum*) unfurl amid tufts of lavender-pink flowers of the tall-stemmed *Verbena bonariensis*. Then it seems that a haze of lavender extends over the border.

The Elizabeth Lawrence Border contains many of the plants described in the pages of *A Southern Garden*. It includes plants that Elizabeth gave to us herself: *Asteromoea mongolica* (her "double Japanese aster"), two colors of Korean chrysanthemums—pink ones and white ones—and a sturdy pink-eyed white phlox that she rescued from a neighbor's trash pile. And it has been greatly enriched by gifts of plants from friends and admirers of Elizabeth. I would like to acknowledge the generosity of the Farm House Fraternity, who allowed Tony Avent, M. K. Ramm, and me to collect bulbs and plants from that garden for inclusion in the border. I also wish to thank Lindie Wilson, who lives and gardens in Elizabeth's Charlotte home. She has supplied us with a wealth of plants from that garden. Doug and I are interested in hearing from others who knew Elizabeth and the plants she grew.

But like Elizabeth Lawrence, both curators of her namesake border find that the lure of new plants is irresistible. Thus, new species and varieties grow in Elizabeth's border—plants she may not have known in addition to a large selection of those familiar and dear to her. (For example, *Kalimeris integrifolia*, a recent introduction from Japan with large single white flowers, grows near Elizabeth's *Asteromoea mongolica*.) As Elizabeth would be the first to acknowledge, every garden is different. Although she regretted giving up on *Chrysanthemum uliginosum* and aconitum, with its deep blue spires, both plants grow side by side in the Early/Late Border of the North Carolina State University Arboretum.

An endowment to perpetuate the Elizabeth Lawrence Border at the North Carolina State University Arboretum has been established. For more information about how you can participate, write to the NCSU Arboretum, P.O. Box 7609, Raleigh, NC 27695-7609.

Gardens, by their very nature, are ephemeral, but *A Southern Garden* (though written over fifty years ago) possesses a timeless quality. Within its pages one can catch glimpses of the long and ancient story of humankind's fascination with growing plants and making gardens, interspersed with stories of contemporary gardeners and gardens. Most importantly, one meets the author, a very special person who charms, intrigues, and inspires as she coaxes the reader to try new plants and plant combinations. Through the pages of *A Southern Garden*, Elizabeth Lawrence became my mentor, guide, and friend—long before I actually met her. No one I know of has ever written so well or so warmly about gardening. *A Southern Garden* and Elizabeth's other books are the map by which I have plotted my own course as a gardener.

Many years ago, I sent a copy of *A Southern Garden*, then out of print, to a British friend as a thank-you for the time we'd spent together in his garden. He wrote to thank me in return: "*A Southern Garden* is one of the treasures of this life I thought never to possess." How fortunate we are that the University of North Carolina Press has chosen to reissue this classic garden book. May it never again go out of print.

Edith R. Eddleman
Durham, North Carolina
1990

An Apology for Myself as a Gardener

*P*raise a gardener for abundance of bloom, and he will say modestly, "I don't know how it is, but flowers just seem to grow for me."

Flowers do not just grow for me. I have no green or growing hand. Nor do I believe what old-timey people say, that flowers grow for those who love them. On the contrary, I believe that gazing upon them too fondly and too intently is the death of many. For this reason (and others) the failure of a plant in my garden does not mean that this plant will languish in all gardens in these parts. In fact I have only to say that a plant will not grow in the Middle South, to have a dozen people come forward to prove that it will—for them. When it became obvious that delphiniums do not grow as vigorously in North Carolina as in Maine, Mr. Jacques Busbee (that excellent gardener and perverse citizen) took delight in confounding his neighbors with the height and fullness of his blue spires. They did not know that he bought new plants of Dreer each and every spring and set them out in the dead of night. Of course, only Mr. Busbee's special magic could have raised them to any height even then.

Although I have gathered as much information as I can from all sources reliable and unreliable, which "I gin ter you as gun ter me," one learns about gardens from gardening, and I must necessarily depend upon my own records for what I write about plants. Any one person's experience can be taken only as an indication of what plants will do in a given locality. Thorough knowledge must be accumulated from the recorded experience of many gardeners. Therefore I offer mine with an apology.

I mean to state at the outset the sort of gardener I am. I am interested in gathering from all parts of the world plants that find to their liking the conditions in the part of the country where I live and garden. I am not interested in acquiring rare and difficult specimens merely because they are rare and difficult. However, I see no reason for excluding a good plant that grows and blooms and fills a need because it is not generally grown, or because it has a name like *Campanula Portenschlagiana*. I am not of the school which says, if it would grow here we would have grown it. There is still too much of the spirit of "it-cannot-be-done,-it-never-has-been" in the South. The world is full of good things that we could grow and do not grow.

I do not believe in pampering plants. If they are miffy, let them go. There are plenty of others just as lovely and far more amenable. It is garden value that interests me rather than rarity—or even beauty. I consider of garden value in this climate, those plants which grow easily and lustily when their requirements are met in so far as is reasonable to do so. If a plant that cannot abide excess moisture will grow presentably in porous soil on top of a wall, it is reasonable to give it those conditions. If it can be saved only by the "protection of a handlight" (a great phrase with the British who think nothing too much trouble where any plant is concerned) in wet weather, I consider that very unreasonable. If a plant can survive periods of drought only when it is planted in the shade and given a soil rich in humus and a cool root-run, I give it those conditions. I am even willing to water it in very dry weather—if I can remember, and if I am at home. But I did not mean to construct a system of leaking pipes to supply the moisture that the heavens withhold to alpines loath to leave their mountain tops to summer in the piedmont. In these parts one learns to be wary of plants whose cultural directions include the familiar and treacherous phrases: "likes moisture at all times, but must be well drained." In the case of doubtful hardiness it seems reasonable to give the plant in question the warmest and most protected situation that the garden affords (only in mine, warm and protected spots are already overcrowded), and to cover it with leaves and coal ashes until it becomes established—but not indefinitely. I do not want plants that must be taken up and stored in sand in winter.

Of course, a variety of plants will require a variety of growing conditions. Plants from woods, swamps, and mountain tops cannot be expected to grow equally well in the same soil and under the same conditions. Even a small garden can afford raised borders for plants from arid regions, some low spots for moisture lovers, shade and leaf soil for flowers from the woods, and a sunny place for those from the fields.

One hears a great deal about "dirt" gardeners. When a gardener has identified himself as the dirt variety he feels a marked superiority. But dirty fingernails are not the only requirement for growing plants. One must be as willing to study as to dig, for a knowledge of plants is acquired as much from books as from experience. One must know something about a plant, the part of the world it comes from, and the conditions under which it grows naturally, in order to cultivate it. One must know its proper name. I do not go as far as Mr. Jacques Busbee, who says that he takes no pleasure in a nameless flower; nor do I hold with the shoe clerk who pressed me to come to see his rock garden: "I think we gardeners ought to visit each other's gardens," he said, "we'd learn a lot. You ought to see my ferns . . . *there's* six varieties out of the woods—all different. You'd be surprised at all of the things I've got—and I don't know the name of a one of them." I wondered how I was going to learn anything by viewing the six ferns from the woods (all different), in which I am very much interested and of which I knew nothing, if he could not name them.

We all have plants whose names did not accompany them. "What!" Mrs. Totten said when I asked her about one of hers, "don't you know anasent?" "Anasent?" "Yes, we call it that because Anna sent it!" I have grown and enjoyed a number of anasents for many years, but I should enjoy them more if I could find some one to tell me what they are.

I mean to write in English, not in Latin, and I use common names as much as possible. Some of them are so pretty. But common names do not serve as well as scientific ones. A plant may have a different common name in every section, or several in the same section. Or the same name may be applied to several plants. There is a great deal to be said for the botanists. *Lepachys pinnata* may be difficult to remember, but is "grey-headed coneflower" any easier, particularly when *pinnata* describes the way the foliage is cut, and grey-headed describes I do not know what? In general I have followed the nomenclature of L. H. and Ethel Zoe Bailey's *Hortus Second* (New York: Macmillan Co., 1941). Where I have not been consistent, it is because I considered it less confusing to give the name more commonly known. In checking colors of the flowers I have used Robert Ridgway's *Color Standards and Nomenclature* (Washington: The Author, 1912).

It is also important to be sure that one has the right plant for the name. I started out blithely with the assumption that all plants came into the garden correctly labelled, and that my part was to see that the labels were not lost or misplaced. I soon got over that. Now I assume that all plants are wrongly named until proved otherwise. Not even the genus, let alone the species, is to be accepted for what it is said to be. Once, after searching in vain for *Pancratium illyricum*, I came upon it in print, not in a description of someone else's garden, but in a dealer's list. It was sent for, planted, and watched eagerly for eighteen months. When the green tips pushed up the second spring I was delighted, for pancratiums are tender. When a bud appeared, I held my breath. The flower opened. It was an hymenocallis, and not a very good one. Another time, having pondered the resemblance a plant acquired as *Draba verna* bore to *Ajuga reptans*, I realized that it was *Ajuga reptans*. And too often a jasmine offered under a new name will prove to be the one that has to be pulled off of the back fence, or a new poppy turns out to be another form of the inevitable *Papaver rupifragum*. Alliums are the worst. The same allium may appear under a dozen names, or a dozen under the same name. A gardener must not only know a plant when he sees it, but know where to find it under its proper name.

I am writing, then, not for those who want to grow rare and difficult plants, but for those who want to grow a variety of plants in an average garden, giving them a reasonable amount of care and spending a reasonable amount of intelligence upon them. And I think that I may say, without undue self-praise, that I am the very best person to encourage other gardeners to go farther afield for their plant material. If a plant grows for me, it will grow for anyone. If you read that Mrs. Wilder—one of America's best gardeners of all time—has had success with a plant, you need not think that you can go and do likewise; but if you hear that I have grown it, you may rest assured that you can do even better.

One thing more. I do not mean to lay undue emphasis on plants. Plants are the material from which the garden is created. I think of a garden not as a manifestation of spring (like an Easter hat), nor as beds of flowers to be cut and brought into the house, but as a place to be in and enjoy every month of the year.

Elizabeth Lawrence
Raleigh
North Carolina

his is a book for gardeners in Virginia, North Carolina, South Carolina, Georgia, Alabama, Tennessee, and parts of the Southwest. It is based upon the records of a garden in piedmont North Carolina, and applies generally to the territory known as the Middle South. In this part of the country there is much variation in the character of the vegetation. In North Carolina alone it changes from the boreal forest of the mountains to the subtropical verdure of the coast. A planting guide for the piedmont does not apply equally to all sections.

How far north of its native habitat a plant will survive is one of the most fascinating questions for searchers of new plant material, particularly for those in this part of the country. "Hardy to Washington" is a magic phrase to a gardener south of the District of Columbia. It means that much that is rare and beautiful will grow here. For the Middle South is the northern limit of hardiness for a multitude of shrubs, vines, perennials, and bulbs native to warmer regions. Wherever winters are mild there is the temptation to borrow from places where winters are milder. That this is a reasonable field of experiment is proven by Dr. Orland White's ten years of research at Charlottesville, Virginia, and ninety miles farther north at the Blandy Experimental Farm of the University of Virginia. Even at Blandy many tropical species have come through severe winters safely, for plants native to warm countries do not necessarily perish in cooler ones.

Plants looked upon as tender may not be half so tender as we think. A Mexican lilac (*Duranta repens*) that I brought back from my great-aunt's garden in South Georgia has proved root hardy in North Carolina, blooming and fruiting for three summers, and even coming back after last winter, though not with the same vigor. It is described in the catalogues as "rather tender, but planted as far north as northern Florida." An oleander that Dr. Coker brought to Chapel Hill from South Carolina came through the severe cold of last winter without dropping a leaf, while shrubs considered hardy were cut back to the ground, or killed outright.[1] The casualties of last winter are a reminder that plants survive much colder weather in places where they are blanketed with snow from fall to spring than in those where they are left exposed to the winds.

In climates similar to ours gardeners have been surprised at the endurance of plants from tropical and subtropical countries. The French horticulturist, M. Noter, grew supposedly tender exotics in his garden in Paris, and the correspondence of shrubs and bulbs hardy with him and with us is very interesting. The English, too, have long felt the fascination of half-hardy plant material, as is evident from their horticultural literature. Reports from the south and west of England serve as a guide for us, since the winter temperature of Charlottesville—where the thermometer may drop below zero but not to stay—is similar to that of the Royal Botanic Gardens at Kew. This means that we can turn to the pages of Colonel Grey's *Hardy Bulbs* and Mr. Bean's *Trees and Shrubs Hardy in the British Isles*, for information about the plants that we ourselves can grow.

The caprices of the climate are a problem to Southern gardeners. In the Middle South the difficulty is not that it is too

---

[1] Dr. Coker comments that this oleander was chosen because of the hardiness of the individual plant. It had lived when hundreds of others died. He showed me the oleander, which has now lived through its second winter, and a gardenia which has gone through many winters unscathed while others near it were killed back in part or to the ground. Dr. White has a story of an Englishman who tried four thousand sequoia seedlings before he found one hardy on his estate. The one grew to a tree.

hot or too cold, or too wet or too dry, but that the changes from one extreme to the other are so frequent and so sudden. In summer we cannot depend, as in England, on steady moisture, nor, as in our Southwest, on continued drought. Instead, weeks when no rain falls are followed by weeks when it rains every day. In winter we cannot depend, as in the northern states, on cold and snow, nor, as in the Far South, on warmth and sun. One day the air may be like spring, and the next the ground may be covered with ice. On the other hand we have the advantage of being able to establish many of the hardy perennials of northern gardens that will not thrive in the heat of the Far South, and many of the half-hardy bulbs of Florida gardens that cannot endure New England winters. But we must learn which of the plants to the north of us and which to the south will flourish here. There is too much good plant material that is congenial to this climate for us to waste time with any other.

In the South there is bloom for every month in the year. But keeping a garden in bloom for four long seasons is different from keeping one in bloom for three short ones. Succession of bloom depends upon the characteristic plant of each period of the year, in combination with others in bloom at the same time. After winter bulbs and shrubs there are daffodils, then tulips, then the long season of iris. Summer begins with day-lilies,[2] and ends with other members of the amaryllis family. In September, gardens filled with red spider-lilies are as gay as in spring, and from October until frost there are chrysanthemums.

But what other plants bloom in the South with tulips or chrysanthemums? Not the ones that bloom with them in other places. When I read of white camassias and scarlet tulips in Miss Jekyll's English borders, I know that I cannot repeat the combination in mine. For white camassias, the latest to bloom, are not open with me until the last red tulips (Feu Brilliant in my garden) are past their best. And I have learned that I will fare no better with the combinations worked out by Mrs. Wilder for her garden in New York.

[2] Classed under *Amaryllidaceae* in *Herbertia*, Vol. V (1938), p. 112.

From dates for the North we are told to subtract according to our position in the path of spring. Here we are said to be about a month ahead of New England. But records show that plants do not fall in as neatly with this mathematical maneuvering as we have been led to believe. Having long suspected as much, I sat down with Mrs. Sedgwick's invaluable book *The Garden Month by Month* and my own files, comparing plant by plant (insofar as the material is the same) her very complete records of the bloom of perennials in the vicinity of Boston with their bloom in my garden.

While it is true that many plants do bloom just a month earlier with me, there may be ten weeks difference in some, and practically none in others. Here the tawny day-lily blooms a month in advance of Mrs. Sedgwick's date, and the very early day-lilies a month to the day, but the golden day-lily blooms here in mid-April, and there in July. Here *Iris reticulata*, recorded for the middle of March in Boston, rarely blooms more than two weeks ahead of that date. The Florentine tulip and the lady tulip move up to mid-March from early May, *Dianthus arenarius* and *Salvia pratensis* to late March from early June. *Campanula garganica*, on the other hand, blooms in May in both sections, but in New England it continues all summer. Other perennials bloom only in spring in the North, but with us repeat in late summer or fall. Many of the fall flowers of the North are the summer flowers of the South. Boltonia, for example, blooms from late August to mid-October in New England, and in July and August in North Carolina. But *Sedum spectabile* comes in September whether set out above Mason and Dixon's line or below it.

From the records of my own garden and those in the neighborhood I have gathered an account of the succession of bloom in the South. The dates will not be exact for every one; they vary from garden to garden, and from town to country, and from year to year. "Elizabeth," Isabelle Henderson accuses when she meets me in market, "you said that Cheddar pinks would be in bloom on the thirteenth of April, and in my garden they are not." Gardens in town may be ten days ahead of those in the country, just as town dogwood, which has the warmth of wall and pavement to bring out the buds, is always earlier than that in the woods. And there is as much as a month's difference in the appearance of the first single hyacinths in an early season and in a late one. Blooming dates also differ from the mountains to the coast. From Asheville to Wilmington there is almost as much variation in the season as from Raleigh to New York.

In the South the progress of the season does not follow the accepted pattern of spring, summer, fall, and winter. Spring, when spring should come, has already been with us at intervals throughout the winter. Summer lasts into fall, and fall into winter. The garden year has no beginning and no end. There is not a time when everything is in bloom at once, nor is there a time when the box is wrapped in burlap and the borders covered with pine boughs. There is not time for the gardener to take a rest before beginning again. To follow the tradition of bloom in three seasons only is to miss the full meaning of gardening in a part of the world where at all times of the year there are days when it is good to be out of doors, when there is work to be done in the garden, and when there is some plant in perfection of flower or fruit.

Two Months of Winter

inter, in my garden, takes up December and January in ordinary years. Even in those months there is a breath of spring in good years, though in bad years the cold encroaches upon February. Perhaps it will seem contrary to begin the garden year with winter, but to me it begins with the flowering of the first paper-whites and sweet violets after heavy frost has cut down the last chrysanthemum. We do not have to wait for spring to start the new season. After the slimy stalks of fall flowers have been cleared away, the garden assumes its winter aspect, and winter flowers begin to bloom.

The Garden in Winter

During our open winters we have some of the most delightful weather of the year. There are times when we have the "little snatches of sunshine and fair weather in the most uncomfortable parts of the year" that Addison describes in his essay on *The Pleasure of a Garden,* and we have frequently days that are as "agreeable as any in the finest months." During the false spring that almost invariably comes in December or January—sometimes in both—the weather is mild enough to permit finishing up chores that were left undone in the fall, and even pulling a long chair out of the summer house to sit in the sun. If a garden faces the south and is protected from the north by a hedge or wall, it is surprising to find how many days it is pleasant to sit there out-of-doors. Yet we turn our backs on our gardens after Thanksgiving and leave them unvisited until the daffodils appear.

Certainly we should consider the appearance of the garden in winter as well as in summer, particularly in the choice of shrubs. I have often wondered with Addison that "those who are like myself, and love to live in gardens, have never thought of contriving a winter garden, which should consist of such trees only as never cast their leaves." Addison "so far indulged himself" in the thought of a winter garden as to set aside an acre to be planted in evergreens. Most of us have not room for an acre, but, as Bacon—also a lover of color in the landscape on grey days—suggests, we can have a few "such things as are green all winter: holly; ivy; bays; juniper; cypress trees; eugh; pine-apple trees; fir trees."

The beauty and variety of the broad-leaved evergreens is most apparent in winter when their foliage—varying from the pale jade of mahonia to the dull purple of yaupon—is contrasted with grey stems; when hollies, cotoneasters, and firethorns are scarlet with berries; and when the sweet olive is fragrant with creamy flowers. I like at least one evergreen tree, a magnolia or a holly or a pine, so that there will be something more than bare branches against the sky after the bright leaves have fallen. But too many evergreens become oppressive. The winter effect is gayer if the shrubs that hold their leaves are planted with deciduous trees and shrubs with colored bark. Crape-myrtles are especially lovely in winter, particularly when they are old and their smooth trunks are mottled with a warm grey and tan. The bare trunks and branches of the sycamores are so beautiful that we should be willing to overlook the untidy summer and fall litter of dead leaves and broken twigs.

Further delights of a garden in winter are the grey of lavender, the frosted green of santolina, and the dull olive of rosemary. These aromatic herbs from the Mediterranean are very much at home in sunny, well-drained situations in Southern gardens. This is a fact that we should remember when we abuse our climate, for rosemary, lavender, and santolina are not very hardy in the Northern states. A gnarled rosemary is one of my chief treasures. I treasure it for the charm of its irregular outline, for the pale blue of its flowers in very early spring, and for the refreshing odor of its foliage as I brush against it in passing. These three herbs need a poor light soil and lime. Santolina will stand any amount of drought, but no excess moisture. All must bask in full sun.

Some of the smaller foliage plants are important for winter color. In the crevices of stone walls and steps, and between flagstones, thyme and the evergreen sedums have an all-season charm. *Sedum album, S. acre*, and *S. reflexum* take on a warm reddish color in cold weather. They are good sedums for the South for they are able to adapt themselves to our humid summers and our changeable winters.

As companions to sedums the thymes are dark green in winter, and fragrant as soon as the sun warms the stones that they cover. If there is a place in the garden for a sun-catch, where there is warmth and a shelter from the wind, and a paved footing, nothing could be nicer for growing between the paving stones than the pungent, creeping thyme, *Thymus Serpyllum*, and the citron-scented lemon thyme, *T.S.* var. *vulgaris*. In a garden, sun is to be courted in winter as shade is courted in summer, and all sun-loving plants that have any winter advantage in foliage or in fragrance are particularly desirable.

By the end of November when the gradual destruction of frost has finally ended the season for most flowering plants, when the dead stalks have been cleared away, and the garden made tidy for the winter, greys and greens are restful after the final burst of autumn color. The quiet greens of hedges, ivy, and evergreen edging plants, the fresh color of the winter grass, the arching leaves of the lily-turf and red spider-lilies, the decorative rosettes of the yuccas, and the greys of santolina and lavender take on new importance. Winter foliage is almost as pleasing as winter bloom. Particularly if it comes up fresh in the fall, and dies down in the spring, and is not something that you are accustomed to seeing the year around. The newly unfurled leaves of the Italian arum, *Arum italicum*, held fresh and crisp above the foliage of plants cut down by frost, are broadly arrow-shaped (to eight inches across), dark green, and prettily marbled in a silver grey. All through the winter they furnish the otherwise denuded borders, keeping their freshness even in bitter weather. Another spot of green that I enjoy in this season is the rosette of the Peruvian lily, *Scilla peruviana.*

I cannot think why the yuccas are so little used. Once in midwinter I went into a little garden that had no claim to distinction in any season, but acquired the charm of simplicity when it was reduced by frost to a pattern of brick-edged walks accented by the stiff rosettes of yuccas and framed by a clipped hedge. The wide-leaved yucca seen in country gardens, and native in the eastern part of this state, has more character than the commonly planted Adams-Needle, *Yucca filamentosa*, which is the only species to be found in the nurseries. Sometimes you can get the former from farm women in the market. They have many interesting slips and plants and flowers tucked in with eggs and sausage. The western *Y. angustifolia (glauca)* is a very narrow-leaved species, a variation from our own natives.

Gardens planted for winter green and winter bloom have an air of spring when warm days come and redbirds flash into the open. This year we had our fine weather before Christmas. Roses bloomed into December, and I went out in the snow on Christmas Eve to pick the last frost-bitten buds with a big bunch of paper-whites. But January was unusually bitter, with the ground frozen; the pearly buds of the snowdrops in their green sheaths were waiting for a little warmth to bring them out.

Another year, in January, I came back from south Georgia with a box of greenhouse camellias to find them blooming here in the open. Twenty other flowers were in bloom in my garden or in the neighborhood. There were pansies, sweet alyssum, violets (the variety Governor Herrick—the Prince of Wales had been blooming furiously in Augusta), white Roman hyacinths, winter aconite, two types of polyanthus narcissus, and the Christmas rose. In addition a few buds had opened on the earliest spring shrubs, the Japan quince and the January jasmine, spiraea, forsythia, and Christmas honeysuckle. The mahonia was in bloom too, with spikes of daffodil-colored flowers.

That winter was an unusually mild one. Horticultural magazines were full of reports of winter bloom. At Port Washington, Long Island, January jasmine, Japan quince, and Christmas honeysuckle bloomed in January for the first time in fifty years. A list of plants in bloom in an Irish garden included winter aconite, snowdrops, veronica, aubretia, roses, the Algerian iris, winter heath, wallflowers, primroses, January jasmine, and the Christmas rose. In a Scotch garden jasmine, snowdrops, witch-hazel, primroses, double arabis, and wallflowers were in bloom the first of the month.

Although that winter was milder than most, the list of plants in bloom in my garden is about the same as that for the previous five or six Januaries, with the exception of 1936. The winter of 1935–36 was the only one in my lifetime when there was snow on the ground for two months, and I hope there will never be another.

Flora Hyemalis

Where winters are mild, all sorts of flowering plants burst into bloom in "unseasonable" weather, particularly in warm and sheltered situations. But flowers out of season are the least of January and December bloom. The most intense moments of gardening are those when one finds among dried leaves that drift into the borders the wintry flowers which, as Conrad says, "blossom in the dead of winter, emit a sort of faint perfume of adventure, and die before the spring sets in." You will find the literary gardeners of England, from Elizabeth's time to the present day, very much preoccupied with them.

For the latter part of January and February, Bacon thought a garden should have "the mezereon tree, which then blossoms; crocus vernus, both the yellow, and the grey; primroses; anemones; the early tulip; hyacinthus orientalis; chamairis;

fritillaria." Sir Herbert Maxwell in his charming paragraphs on
flora hyemalis in *Memories of the Months*,[1] sixth series—and
if you do not know them, let me commend to you for delight
to the mind and benefit to the garden the beautiful writing
in these volumes—describes his adventures in this season in
his garden on the southwest coast of Scotland, where winter
weather is at times deceitfully mild. He rejoices in the cold-
endurance of the blossoms of the Chinese witch-hazel and la-
ments the severity of a night in January that caused the winter
jasmine "to shed its golden veil, and turned the crimson flush
of Rhododendron Nobleanum to ill-colored ashes," adding that
the rhododendron "always keeps plenty of flower-buds in re-
serve, for the return of mild conditions."

The chance that tender blossoms will escape the rigors of
winter is to most gardeners a chance well worth taking. And if
the flowers come into perfection only to be whipped to shreds
by icy winds, the only harm done is that we must wait for another season and hope for more clement weather. Ever since I
first shared Billy Hunt's enthusiasm for winter bloom, I have
been collecting January and December flowering plants for my
garden. I still have the buttery list that I made as we talked and
lunched, and I pictured myself as living henceforth in a sort of
Hesperides of perpetual spring, perfumed with sweet olive and
gay with camellias—both *Sasanqua* and *japonica*—winter
heath, winter-heliotrope, and in particular the white cowslip,
Saxifraga ciliata. I have yet to see, except in Mr. A. W. Darnell's treasury of *Winter Blossoms from the Outdoor Garden*,[2] any mention of this saxifrage, but I still tear open every
list of rare plants that arrives in the hope of finding its name
among them. It has "heads of large pure white blossoms, with
their pale green calyxes and brightly colored stems," and is
found "in the Himalayas, on the Mussooree and Suen Ranges."
In cultivation "in warm sheltered localities, it flowers early in
the New Year."

Darnell's book and the notes of British writers in the winter

[1] London: Edward Arnold, 1919.
[2] Ashford, Kent: L. W. Reeve, 1926.

numbers of *Gardening Illustrated* are maddening to gardeners in our part of the world. Not only because we cannot get the plants in this country, but because the plants that we can get do not bloom so late or begin so early for us as for them. With envious incredulity we read Darnell's full and optimistic account of "exotic trees, shrubs and herbaceous plants that flower in the outdoor garden in the British Isles during the months of December, January and February" (with a few that bloom in October, November, March, and April for good measure). Here, and in the notes of other gardeners in the British horticultural papers, we gather that November to March is the normal season for January jasmine which rarely reaches perfection here before February; that *Cassia corymbosa*, gone here by the end of October, continues through November; and that leadwort, which September sees an end of here, lasts well into the winter. Even our own chrysogonum, with few blossoms in North Carolina after August, is reported as "frequently seen in flower from March to Christmas." If it were not for the fact that other gardeners less prejudiced in favor of winter bear him out—and often go him one better—I should wonder whether Mr. Darnell's versions of the extent of the blooming season were not as highly colored as his delightful illustrations.

Even allowing for that, there is much for us to look forward to in our own gardens in winter, especially as we are able to grow so much of the half-hardy material from countries where the warm winters are a foretaste of spring. We have even a few plants for this season that have escaped Mr. Darnell.

The first flower of winter is the paper-white narcissus, *Narcissus Tazetta*. This season has been an unusually good one for it. The cold came upon us gradually, and the buds were hardened so that there was still bloom in the border in the freezing weather after Christmas. Early in December there were enough of them to perfume the garden and to give it an illusion of spring. We always set out the bulbs of these and the little Roman hyacinths after they have done blooming in a bowl in the house. It takes a season for them to recover, but after that they will bloom normally. The hyacinths bloom in January (some years not until February) with an occasional spicy stalk in December. Both should be planted where their decaying foliage can be hidden in the spring, for a patch of dead leaves among the fresh foliage of the spring-flowering daffodils will spoil the effect. Occasionally there are a few January buds from the Grand Monarque, another of the sweet-scented tazetta group of narcissus. Dr. Carrick, in High Point, has praise for the yellow-flowered Soleil d'Or which has never done much for me in the open. He sent me some bulbs this fall, so it is having another test.

Often in January a few campernelles, *N. odorus*, come into bloom, and in mild seasons the first of the little early trumpet daffodils. The earliest trumpet is said to be *N. pallidus praecox*, native to the Pyrenees. I have not found it in the American trade, and it may be no earlier than our own little trumpet.

There is solid satisfaction, as well as delight, in winter flowers that flower in winter. Last year the white hoop-petticoat daffodil, *N. Bulbocodium monophyllus*, said to bloom in January, bloomed in January—not in some one else's garden but in my own. This, the real winter daffodil, is a miniature form with flowers like sea-foam, and one or several thread-like leaves. It pushes out of the ground very early in the New Year. Two bulbs produced between them three flowers. The first appeared on the twelfth of January. It was immediately followed by the second, and the two remained fresh and fair until the last of the month. In February the third flower appeared. This year the ground has been covered with sleet since the tips of two pointed buds became visible. They are waiting unmarred under the white sheet for the sun to bring them out. But it is already the end of the month, so they will not bloom in January this season. I have visited them daily, making a little hole in the sleet to be certain that they are still there and still unharmed. The pale flowers with delicately fluted, wide flaring crowns and thread-like segments are similar to the later yellow-flowered forms, but shorter stemmed and fewer leaved. They are not pure white as described, but as the poetic Mr. Bowles observes, "beautifully crystalline" when young, and in age "almost as transparent as finest lawn." It is unbelievable that anything so fragile could last through cold and rain for two weeks. It is unbelievable that anything can be so lovely.

The common little yellow crocus flowers very early on every lawn, very nearly as soon as the so-called winter-flowering species. Of these I have found only *Crocus Sieberi* to be satisfactory, permanent, and truly precocious in habit. But all of the species are delightful. They are more delicately colored and more graceful than the over-sized horticultural varieties. *C. Imperati*, from the mountains near Naples, is said to be very early indeed, but I have never been able to get it above ground at any season. Mr. Darnell considers it superior to *C. Sieberi* because the lilac flowers open wide even on dull days. *C. Tomasinianus* bloomed in the middle of January one year, but comes normally a month later. *C. etruscus*, usually classed as winter-blooming, did not put in an appearance until spring. On two occasions *C. Korolkowii* bloomed in mid-January in the New York Botanical Garden, although its regular season is in February. With me it blooms, if at all, the very first of February.

Crocus Sieberi, which occurs in the mountains along the Adriatic sea, is a vigorous species, easily established. It increases wonderfully even in one year, and a few bulbs soon make a good splash of color. A patch that Marjorie Lalor planted at Saint Mary's has been increasing for four years, and blooming profusely from mid-January to March. When the weather is mild, a few flowers open the last of December. They open only on bright days. It is a variable species with pale and deep lilac forms. Those that I have are mauve. The greyish tone merges into the silver of the stems, and is accented by the bright colors of the orange stigma and the yellow stamens and throat. The petals are grey on the reverse, delicately feathered with dark violet. The leaves are comparatively wide, and appear with the flowers.

With me, in so far as I have been able to test them, only two of the irises said to bloom before February have done so: *Iris unguicularis* and one of the early-flowering forms of the reticulata group. *I. persica*, said to bloom in winter in "warm and forward" seasons in England, does not bloom in these parts until February. *I. Vartanii* and *I. alata*, tender species from the Mediterranean region, are supposed to bloom from fall to spring. I have not had either of them. Both are difficult and probably are only for the gardener with unlimited patience. The snake's head iris, *I. tuberosa* (or *Hermodactylus tuberosus*), which Mr. Darnell says may be gathered in January in warm sheltered spots, did not put in an appearance until February in its warm sheltered spot in my garden, and in a "forward season" too.

Of all winter flowers the Algerian iris, *I. unguicularis*, is most to be desired for delicacy of texture and coloring, and for fragrance. In general it is one of the most dependable bloomers, although Mr. Busbee has found it freakish, blooming one year in October and another not until March. With me it does not bloom until the first of the year, and not at all until the plants become well established. On the other hand Miss Jekyll counted on flowers from November to April, and Billy Hunt reports the same season for Chapel Hill. One bleak day in January I saw Billy's patch in full bloom under bare-branched oak trees. It was as if a wand had been waved. I wonder now if I am telling the truth. But there they were, dozens of them, enough to pick handfulls and still leave a bed of tender lavender. This shows what comes of judging a flower by what it does in one's own garden. For I would have said from my experience that it is a very shy bloomer.

The flowers of the Algerian iris are large for so dwarf a plant, and sit on short, slender stems said to be from six to twelve inches, but scarcely more than four, that do not hold them above the narrow, yellowish, and never very flourishing leaves. They are a charming color, Ridgway's lavender-violet veined with a deeper violet. The falls are three inches long and over an inch wide, the standards as long and very slender. I like to think of the grey morning when I found one in bloom for the first time in my garden, in an otherwise desolate border. The plants had been flowerless for so many seasons that I had not only ceased to hope, but had forgotten their very existence. I can think of nothing else so bright and fragile as this iris, nor so fragrant when it is brought indoors to warmth. It has been

described as smelling of violets, and again of primroses. To me it smells of spring.

Iris reticulata histrioides major occurs in Asia Minor. Mr. Darnell says that it is easily established and the most robust of the group, but I cannot be sure that it will prove so here. The first season it bloomed on January the twenty-first. This, its second season, being "unusual," it has only now—at the end of the month—shown a tip above the frozen earth. In spite of being so robust and easily established, I gather that this little iris is even more dependent than others of the group on drainage and all possible sunshine. The flowers that bloomed for me were nothing like the size claimed for them, the flowers of *I. histrioides* being described as five inches across, and those of the variety major as more. Nor have I been able to detect the odor of violets when the flowers are brought inside. But I have never seen anything, except a blue jay, so brilliant on the wintry landscape. A single flower catches the eye the minute one enters the garden. The color is said to vary, but in this case it checked with Ridgway's greyish blue-violet, a very vivid color with a very dull name. The bulbs that I set out bloomed a month ahead of the catalogue date, and the flowers lasting for over a week stayed bright and fresh through freezing weather and heavy rains. They were almost stemless. Except for the characteristic horizontal position of the falls, giving them a winged look, the flowers are similar in form to *I. reticulata*. Mine were about the same size. The linear foliage is like that of the other irises of this group, but it is very scant.

European snowdrops, *Galanthus nivalis*, require cool slopes, shade, and a more moist, but no less well-drained, soil than the sun-loving Eastern species. Sir Herbert Maxwell calls them children of the mist and rain. Here, in a less congenial climate than his Scotch coast, they are apt to dwindle from year to year. When I first came to this garden, there were a few under the hedges. They bloomed in the mild intervals between the first day of the year and the first day of spring. Now they are gone. Last year a fresh start was made, with rather poor results except for the variety *Scharlokii*. This was planted in moist shade at the foot of the rock garden where the characteristically green-tipped flowers appeared to advantage against the grey background, and where two bulbs increased in one year to sizable clumps. Perhaps I have found the right place at last. I have known the European snowdrops to bloom in January, but they are apt not to start until February.

The earlier Eastern sorts are more truly winter blooming, and are thought to take more kindly to our climate, especially Mr. Elwe's giant snowdrop, *Galanthus Elwesii*, which is the one to acquire in quantity, for to my way of thinking there is not enough difference in the various kinds to warrant a collection. It is the handsomest species and is supposed to produce the largest flowers. Mr. Darnell says that it is variable in size, but that the expanded flowers of a good form measure fully two inches across. It is nothing like that in my garden, but the entire plant, bulb and leaf and flower, is much more robust than the fragile—and more graceful—European snowdrop. The very white drooping flowers are prettily marked with lettuce green. Last spring it made its first appearance in my garden, the first flowers opening on the seventh of January. This year January has passed and the buds are still waiting under the snow for soft days. A patch at Saint Mary's has bloomed for years in January, or even at the end of December.

I wanted the Byzantine snowdrop, *Galanthus byzantinus*, because I had heard that it would bloom on Christmas day. A bud did appear in mid-December. I watched it hopefully from day to day, and hour to hour, but buds have a way of standing still in cold weather. Christmas passed with the pearly drop still hanging on its slender stem. It did not open until the last day of the year, but at least I can say that it bloomed in December. By the second year there was no sign of bloom early or late, nor of the pretty plaited leaves. The Byzantine snowdrop has a bad name in gardens for being capricious and susceptible to snowdrop diseases. Said to be a natural hybrid between *G. Elwesii* and *G. plicatus*, it has the markings of the one, and the plaited foliage of the other. It occurs in Asia Minor.

Two things are essential with snowdrops: early planting and neglect. The first is easier said than done if the bulbs are imported stock, but they should not be held out of the ground any longer than necessary, or planted later than August if it can be avoided. To be of real value in the bare winter garden, they should be planted in masses, and once established should not be disturbed. The Eastern sorts are said to like sun and a sandy soil, but Mr. Moncure insists that they like their roots in moist shade. He says that some of them have been in bloom in his garden since November in the cool, damp shadow under the edge of a board walk. They must be well-drained, and Mr. Darnell thinks that they are likely to die out without a yearly dressing of old manure. More robust than the European snow-drop, they cannot do with a lean diet. The bulbs should be planted three inches deep.

The Christmas-rose, *Helleborus niger*, with its pure white flower and poisonous black root, has an aura of good and evil. The meaning of the name is lost in time, but it is thought to be "food to kill." The drug made from its roots has been in use as a remedy and a poison since the legendary days when a king of Argos rewarded, with a large portion of his kingdom, the physician who cured the madness of his daughters by this means. It was not until Elizabethan days that Parkinson taught gardeners to appreciate the Christmas flower "like unto a single white rose" as an ornamental as well as a medicinal plant. Since its appearance in the quaint and elaborate knot gardens of that age, it has been cherished in English flower borders. An established plant becomes an heirloom, for in all likelihood it will outlive the gardener who plants it.

Consider carefully the situation for your Christmas-rose, for once planted it must not be disturbed. Traditionally it belongs at the front door, but it is better not to follow tradition if the house faces east or south. This native of European woods needs a cool exposure during our hot weather. Mrs. Loudon, in the *Ladies Companion to the Flower Garden*,[3] describes it as a hardy perennial that will thrive in any common soil. This may be so in the moist climate of England, but here it needs a sandy loam with plenty of humus and a mulch to keep the roots

[3] London: William Smith, 1842.

from drying out in summer. It also needs some lime. If it must be moved, a rainy spell in the fall is the time for removal.

In Raleigh the black hellebore blooms from early December to spring, in its early blooming forms. The type does not bloom until after Christmas. The variety *praecox* is said to be the earliest, flowering from September to February. Mr. Darnell observes that the variety *altifolius* is "in our opinion the finest and most desirable Hellebore in existence." His description of this form sounds like Miss Rohde's variety *maximus*, with which he says it is often confused. These names must be confused in this country too, for I ordered *maximus*, and *altifolius* arrived. So far the plant that came to me has not produced flowers either early or superior; the stems do not approach a foot in length and the flowers are by no means four inches across. However this is only the second winter, and hellebores are notoriously slow in getting settled. The variety *angustifolius* is a small-flowered, pure white form known as Saint Brigid's hellebore. It does not bloom until spring, and who wants a Christmas-rose in spring?

One of the delightful qualities of winter flowers is that they last so long. Hellebores flattened by cold or rain come up again after the storm and appear fresh and delicate in the shelter of the dark, deeply cut leaves. The foliage dies down in summer in this section. This is a pity, for it is very decorative. Fresh leaves come up in the fall. The flowers are short stemmed, but a mulch of leaf mold encourages them to grow longer.

There is no excuse for a bare garden in winter, when a packet of seeds from the ten-cent store will make a grey wall gay with yellow, orange, and wallflower red. Last winter I drove out of my way nearly every day to pass a yard where, close to the street, a bed of wallflowers, *Cheiranthus Cheiri*, bloomed at the foot of a stone terrace. The plants, I discovered upon inquiry, were grown from a package of seeds sown in March, and nursed through the summer. They began to bloom in September, and bloomed all through the fall and winter and spring. Once or twice they were cut back by the cold, but they came out again as soon as the sun warmed the wall behind them, and were as gay as ever. (I had seen winter-blooming wallflowers in a sunny Pinehurst courtyard, but I would never have thought that they would bloom like that in Raleigh.) Somewhat biennial in nature, wallflowers should be resown (if they do not seed themselves) from time to time. A few plants may live for several years, but they cannot be counted on.

Mr. Darnell includes Venus navelwort, as the English call the creeping forget-me-not, *Omphalodes verna*, with winter blossoms, describing it as frequently in bloom throughout the winter months in mild sheltered localities. Last fall I set some out in the rock garden, and sure enough, on the tenth of December I found anchusa-like flowers among the heart-shaped leaves. Whether this little creeper of central and southern Europe will take to this climate permanently, I do not know. For the present it seems very much at home on a shady slope in a carefully prepared pocket of sand and leaf mold, where I hope its roots will find moisture under the rocks in summer droughts. The flowers are a deep and lovely shade of blue-violet.

In damp shady places in crevices between the flags of a walk, the adorable and minute crucifer, *Ionopsidium acaule*, called violet cress, or diamond-flower, will bloom during mild winters from fall-sown seeds. The seeds must be sown very early in the fall, or they will lie dormant through the cold weather and there will be no flowers before March. Frequent sowings will keep these little flowers in the paths at all seasons. A hardy annual, violet cress is said to reseed itself indefinitely once it has been brought to bloom, but I find that in my garden I must do the reseeding. Here there is not so much moisture as this native of Mediterranean meadows requires in order to become a fixture. It will not grow at all in dry, hot soil. Only lovers of the very small will ever kneel to examine the flowers that are like pale miniature bluets, suitable for an arrangement in a thimble.

Adonis amurensis is a very difficult plant to get into one's possession. Sought out and ordered at last, it did not come until May, and the weak growth soon died away. I thought I had seen the last of it. But the lovely, lacy leaves began to unfurl the following February, and among them was a flower the color of a buttercup and with a buttercup's sheen. The lateness of bloom was due, I think, to my having got the double form instead of the type which is single-flowered and early, blooming, I have read, in January. The flowers of the double form look rather like everlastings and have the same reluctance to fade. In fact one gets rather tired of them after a month of their looking exactly the same; the lacquer finish keeps then unspotted even in bad weather. The top of my plant disappeared again after flowering, this time for good. The nursery the plant came from lost its stock during a hard winter, but I have discovered a new source. It is said to bloom the first year from seeds, but I have not been able to find seeds listed. *A. amurensis* is one of those plants that must be well-drained in winter, and never allowed to dry out in summer. Perhaps in just the right spot in sand and leaf soil, and with a summer mulch, it would become established and produce in abundance its glossy yellow flowers and finely-cut reddish foliage. It is said to grow in sun or partial shade and to improve with the years.

The diminutive and precocious *Cyclamen coum* is called a hardy cyclamen, and is regarded as such in England where it is planted in quantity to brighten the winter woods. Mrs. Wilder reported that it did not persist in her garden, nor at Poughkeepsie. A tuber planted in my rock garden in the fall bloomed the second of February but did not survive for another season. The flowers are miniatures of the florist's cyclamen, perfectly proportioned to their two-and-one-half inch stems, and of a brilliant color that is almost a true purple, with violet throats. The tubers should be planted in July in a shady place and in a well-drained soil supplied with leaf mold and a little lime. They should be set two inches under ground. This cyclamen occurs from southern Europe to Persia. It improves with age and should not be disturbed.

Winter aconite, *Eranthis hyemalis*, cannot be counted upon for winter bloom in my garden, and even Mr. Darnell admits that it is not unfailing. My earliest date is the twenty-fifth of January, and it is usually February before the buds open. Even so they are ahead of most spring flowers. The shining buttercups star the bare earth in the rock garden or under trees. They should be in spots where the shallow planting of the small tubers will not be disturbed by later attention to the soil. The root stocks must be set horizontally at a depth of two inches. The winter aconite is not particular as to soil and will bloom in sun or shade.

Winter-Flowering Trees and Shrubs

The trees and shrubs that bloom in winter have a beauty that is more than the beauty of those, no matter how resplendent, that bloom later in the year. Many of them are delightfully fragrant, as is evident from the frequency of *fragrans* as a specific name: *Osmanthus fragrans, Viburnum fragrans, Petasites fragrans*, and *Lonicera fragrantissima*—very fragrant.

Buds of many of the spring-flowering shrubs begin to expand on summer-seeming winter days, particularly those of the forsythias, cydonias, and spiraeas. These and the truly winter-flowering shrubs will bloom earlier, and be less likely to be nipped by frost, if they are trained—as in England—against a sunny wall. Nearly every winter there are a few flowers on the Japan quinces, *Cydonia japonica*, especially those in sheltered positions, and more on the very early forms such as the brilliantly scarlet variety *cardinalis* and the snow-white variety *nivalis*. There is a very early form of spiraea that grows in old gardens and is almost winter-flowering. The tiny white blossoms that powder the fine branches begin to open in January. The shrub does not leaf out until it is in full bloom. It is tall, over six feet, and daintier and more graceful than Thunberg's spiraea. I have no name for it other than "the Gatlings'." It is probably not in the trade, but I am sure it could be found, if a search were made, in a neighbor's yard. It is divisible. The winter jasmine, *Jasminum nudiflorum*, bursts out in January, too, if the season is propitious, and if it is planted in the sun. This common and useful but formless shrub is much better trained on a fence or wall. Often in January the Christmas honeysuckles, *Lonicera fragrantissima*, that grow in every yard regale the passer-by with the first breath of spring. But there are better things than these for winter bloom.

Distinctly southern, for the reason that it is not hardy north of Washington, the winter-sweet, *Meratia praecox*, has been planted in this part of the country for generations. Nearly every old garden has one in bloom at Christmas. It is related to another old favorite, the sweet-Betsy, *Calycanthus flori-dus*, and was formerly classed as a calycanthus. Like the sweet-Betsy it is a wide-spreading, coarse shrub, growing eight or ten feet high, and not ornamental, but it takes kindly to shade (though preferring an open sunny situation) and can be set in out-of-the-way corners and forgotten until the delightful fragrance of the flowers fills the air with a headier perfume than that of the tuberose. This is one of the shrubs that can be counted on to bloom at the appointed time whether the weather is mild or severe. Even if sleet and snow discolor the open flowers, more buds will expand when the storm has passed. The wax-colored flowers with dark wine markings are closely set on the bare stems. They are odd and charming, but not conspicuous.

Since there is much variation in the size and color of the flowers, and since nurseries are not apt to offer selected varieties, it is better to avoid buying sight unseen. It is better still to pick out a good form in a garden and beg to have it layered. This is slow, but worthwhile. The variety *grandiflora*, if it can be acquired, is a superior form with flowers larger and brighter than those of the type. There seem to be early and late forms also, one blooming before Christmas and one afterward. I had supposed that the difference in date was due to the exposure until I saw the two side by side in Miss Janet Badger's yard. The winter-sweet comes from central China.

Like winter-sweet, the Asiatic witch-hazels produce flowers that endure much from the weather. Sir Herbert Maxwell says that "no amount of cold which they have to face in the British Isles makes any effect on their crowded sprays of blossom, except to prolong the display." The Chinese witch-hazel, *Hamamelis mollis*, is the showiest of these, and blooms before *H. japonica* and its varieties. With me it comes in January. The intensely fragrant flowers are charming in detail, with four narrow ribbon petals over half an inch long. The petals are a bright lemon chrome; the calyx is dark red. The large, coarse, round leaves turn a bright yellow in the fall. This species requires an open, sunny situation, a light well-drained soil mixed with leaf mold, and judicious pruning after it has flowered. This is not a plant for crowded quarters, for it grows in time to be a sizable shrub or small tree.

Loveliest of all is the Japanese apricot, *Prunus Mume*, so called because the delicately colored and delicately scented almond-like blossoms are prized by the Japanese for winter flower arrangements. It is not native to Japan but was introduced from China by Buddhist priests. It varies in habit from a medium or small tree to a bushy shrub. There are standard and weeping forms. The flowers are single or double and vary from deep rose to pure white. The variety known as the Bongoume apricot, with pink buds opening into white flowers, blooms in January in the arboretum of the University of North Carolina. It is considered tender north of Philadelphia. Dr. White, in the *Rock Garden Forum*—whose mimeographed sheets, as near as I can tell, Dr. White, Violet Walker, Mr. Robert Moncure, and

I compile for each other—says that it blooms in Charlottesville in February. "Sometimes the buds freeze because of their early blooming propensities, although they will stand quite a bit of cold; but at least fifty percent of the years that I have had Mumes around, I have been able to surprise my wife's tea-party guests by producing the loveliest Japanese Cherry blossom effect in early February often though the window outlook was especially cold and wintry. 'Where in the world did you find a florist that has flowers like that?' say the ladies. 'Why those?' says my wife. 'Those came out of our garden. My husband picked them for me yesterday.'"

The autumn-flowering rosebud cherry, *Prunus subhirtella autumnalis*, is a form of the Japanese cherry which is much planted in England where it blooms all winter. I have seen only one specimen in North Carolina. It was in bloom at the end of October in a Winston-Salem garden and had been too recently set out for the gardener to be able to tell me much about its blooming habits in this part of the country. The flowers are semi-double, white flushed with pink.

Some of the winter-blooming broad-leaved evergreens are hardy to Washington. One of the most pervasive scents of winter is that of the sweet olive, *Osmanthus fragrans*. In Thomasville, Georgia, there is one at every doorstep; in mid-winter the town smells like a perfume shop. Mrs. Royster's two very beautiful specimens on a terrace patterned with ivy and box fill warm and sunny mornings with their fragrance. The clusters of tiny white flowers are so nearly hidden by the glossy oval leaves that one wonders at first where the perfume comes from. In habit they are tall (to twelve or fifteen feet) and rather narrow for their height. They do best in the open.

Viburnum Tinus from the Mediterranean region is a common evergreen in England where it is said to bloom in mild parts of the island from November to March. Here, at Christmas, I have seen bright pink buds and a few wide-open white flowers on the small plant that grows under Miss Isabel Busbee's sunny front windows. However, its real season is in February and March. This is a spreading shrub that may grow to eight or ten feet in favored places but is usually rather dwarf in this climate. It will do in any soil, even a dry one, and in sun or shade.

The Oriental hollygrape, *Mahonia Bealei*, is distinct and interesting for the character of its holly-like leaves. They are coarsely pinnate, with four or more pairs of leaflets and a large terminal one. The leaf stalks are reddish. The light green leaves are long, to twelve inches, set in whorls on the stiff unbranched stems. Racemes of yellow flowers, smelling of lily-of-the-valley, bloom very early in the year, usually in January. The flowers are followed by berries in grape-like bunches. They are apple green, at first, with red stems, and turn dark blue with a heavy bloom as they mature. This is a Chinese species and is much less hardy than the American natives. Dr. White says that one has been through a winter or so at Boyce. This is a shrub for a shady place in a heavy soil rich in humus. In poor soil it is leggy and most unattractive. It grows to six feet or more. It is sometimes in catalogues as *M. japonica*.

Spring Comes in February

I do not suppose there is any part of the world in which gardens are not beautiful in spring. Travellers in other seasons are told, "you should see our gardens in spring." To which they reply, "but we cannot leave our own then."

> This is a fair and stately country
> With a gracious girdle of hills about—
> If I leave at once can I reach my garden
> Before the iris buds come out?

The special charm of a Southern spring is its earliness; it is as long drawn out as it is sweet. First a few white hyacinths appear, and then the snowflakes and violets (if they have not already begun to bloom in January), and then the early daffodils and flowering trees and shrubs. There are days in February when the sun is warm, and children play singing games in the street, when, if you shut your eyes for a moment and listen to the whir of a lawnmower as it goes over lush winter-grass, you will be shocked upon opening them to find no leaves on the trees. By the end of the month winter is in the past.

February is a month of promise (which is often more satisfying than fulfillment) and of disappointment—of the promise of flowers to come and of the disappointment of buds brought to their ruin by a few mild days. But the opening of the first buds, and the resurrection of plants that looked to be dead, fill the gardener with an enthusiasm that is as perennial as the season.

27

Daffodils in Old Gardens

Whatever the date, the first day of spring for me is the day
when the early trumpet daffodil blooms. This has been as early
as the middle of January and as late as the second of March. In
normal seasons (if there is such a thing) it is early in February.
The six weeks difference in the earliest and latest dates recorded gives an idea of our variable springs.

The "early trumpet" is one of the traditional types of the
South, and is unidentified. Mr. Wister describes it as the "common early naturalized trumpet of our Southern states." A Virginia grower lists it (characteristically as "early Virginia") with
the statement that this and *Narcissus biflorus* have been
naturalized in the state for over two centuries. This small and
charming trumpet is as pale as early sunlight and as graceful
as a wild flower. It should be sought out and planted in great
quantities to bloom with the early shrubs. I like it for planting
in grass because the sparse thin foliage withers soon and allows the passage of the lawn mower.

Other charming old-fashioned daffodils have become naturalized in the South. They come up spring after spring, to
bloom for generation after generation. If you think back to
quiet gardens in little towns passed by in modern times (you
will have to go off the main highways to find them) you will
remember the pale delicate pattern of the Silver Bells against
dark cedar trees. I have seen them in dooryards in Hillsboro,
and in drifts under the oaks and along the box-bordered terraces of Cooleemee plantation, and in gardens in the country.
They came to me from an apple orchard. To the orchard they
had come from an old colored woman who traded them for an
apple tree. I do not know their proper name, although they are
similar to, if not identical with, William Goldring, an old white
trumpet called the swan's-neck daffodil. The slender buds are
so bent, like a swan's neck, that the tips point to the ground.
They rise slowly as they expand, but they never become horizontal. The twisted sea-foam petals are held forward over the
crown. The best way to get a stock of Silver Bells is to watch
the farm markets in February when they appear among the cut

flowers brought in to add a little to the butter money. The farmers' wives are reluctant to part with the bulbs, for they are slow of increase, but they can be coaxed to sell you a few later on when the tops die down. I bought some from the butter woman this year. She said she had them from her grandmother. The fact that I was eager to buy, and she was not eager to sell, did not raise the price. In fact, she said that they would be thirty cents a dozen, and when she brought them told me that she had made a mistake, that they were only a quarter.

With Silver Bells one must plant the early single blue hyacinths. These too can be bought with the butter, and much more readily than Silver Bells for they increase well. Their fragrance is of cinnamon, and their color that of the periwinkle which usually serves as a ground-cover for them. The hyacinths and pale daffodils are a cool blue and silver that reminds one of things past.

In the same apple orchard I found another pale daffodil called Silver Star, probably the original *Narcissus Leedsii* or one of the early types. The petals are white, and the shallow fluted cups of the palest primrose.

One of the very early and very old-fashioned varieties, the incomparabilis Sir Watkin, is much beloved by me. I like the genteel pallor of its broad primrose petals and shallow cup better than the garish yellows of some of the modern types. Sir Watkin is a good bloomer and a good increaser, as is Emperor, one of the oldest and best of the trumpets. Emperor, too, is a soft yellow and a fine flower, abundant in bloom and in increase. It follows Sir Watkin in bloom.

Three of the rush-leaved jonquilla group that made their way very soon to the gardens of this country are noted for their fragrance. The campernelle, *N. odorus*, is early, one of the very earliest, sometimes even coming ahead of the first trumpets. *Narcissus Jonquilla simplex*, with polyanthus-like clusters of small, bright yellow, overpoweringly sweet flowers, blooms later, and later still—among the last—come the hoop-petticoats, *N. Bulbocodium conspicuus*, with their flaring crowns and short petals.

In old gardens there are two forms of the poets narcissus, *N.*

poeticus, the large-flowered early variety *ornatus*, and the smaller, later variety *recurvus* (pheasant's eye).

This spring I found another old form in Dr. Carrick's collection. He said he got it from South Carolina, where it has been in cultivation for more than a hundred and twenty-five years. It is the cluster-flowered type and is called seventeen sisters, probably because long ago in some favored spot and in some favored season there was a stalk with seventeen flowers. The flowers are small, the petals a very pale yellow fading to creamy white, the cups citron. It blooms very late in the season.

The twin sisters, *Narcissus biflorus*, are the last to bloom. They come with the tulips, and it is a yearly delight to find daffodils again in the garden when their season has passed. I remember the first time I saw them. We had taken an old house in the country, and when the spring came the yard was full of daffodils. After we thought they were all gone, we looked out of the window one morning to see the twin sisters in fluttering groups along the paling fence. This is another of the cluster-flowered daffodils. It is long stemmed, with two white-petaled yellow-cupped flowers to a stem. It lasts until the end of April or maybe into May, so that the daffodil season in this region lasts about three months.

White Daffodils

The cool, silvery grace of white flowers has turned my taste in daffodil collecting to the pale forms. I prefer the all-white ones, but bicolors sufficiently pallid as to the colored portion save the garden from the monotony of daffodil yellow.

The ancestor of the modern white trumpets is the slight, early flowering species, *Narcissus moschatus*. There was some difficulty in getting it, and now that I have it I am beset by doubts. Have I the *N. moschatus* of gardens or of Linnaeus? Of Linnaeus, I think, for it holds its head in a horizontal position as that plant is said to do. This small pale trumpet is deli-

cately formed and very pretty for rock gardens, but it is not to be compared with our silver bells.

When it comes to the modern forms, Beersheba is still, to my way of thinking, the best in the white trumpet class. It is the only one that I have seen that opens pure white. Some so-called white trumpets are yellow when they open, and some, like White Emperor, are really bicolors in effect. Beersheba is short stemmed for its size (a common fault in this class) and hangs its head rather badly, but the flower is clear cut and beautifully proportioned, with a slender trumpet and pointed petals. It is among the very earliest, blooming the second week in March. The flowers are of good substance and very lasting. One bloom will stay in fair condition for two weeks. Beersheba is a steady and dependable grower that is best left undisturbed. Although it is said to prefer a wet, cold climate, reports of its behavior in the South are uniformly good. Once very expensive indeed, it has never become really cheap and is still in a class in which the price quoted is for a single bulb.

Chastity is one of the whitest flowers in this class, but it is not a typical trumpet in form. It is more like a leedsii. The perianth segments are longer than the crown which flares suddenly from the narrowed neck, giving the flower a distinct and rather odd appearance.

Corinth, one of the late bloomers in its class, has an oddly square trumpet that is long and straight and unfluted. It is not a pure white, but the deep ivory of Mrs. Krelage.

The white leedsiis are more effective than the white trumpets because of their longer stems. The best I have seen in this class is one called White Pearl. It is very large, of fine form and substance, and pure white. Unfortunately it is obsolete.

Perhaps the next best is White Nile. This is a giant leedsii, praised by Mr. Bowles as hard to beat for "perfection of form, substance and whiteness." To me it was a disappointment, for it comes out definitely bicolor, and as the first flowers pale, the later ones still give the clump a two-toned effect. Eventually, when all are open, it does achieve something of the desired pallor and is one of the finest and most fragrant varieties. It has also the merit of being early, blooming about the middle of March.

Pax is really white. It comes in midseason, and is recommended by Dr. Carrick as doing extremely well in the South. Hera is a giant leedsii with a distinct but very narrow yellow rim on the shallow, fluted cup. This detracts but little from its whiteness. It is of medium size, long stemmed, and light and graceful in form. It blooms in midseason.

Silver Salver is a small-crowned leedsii that is like a small, all-white poeticus with a hint of green in the center. It is a distinct and charming variety, and very late in bloom.

In the triandrus group are the most graceful and delightful of all daffodils. They should be made much of in the South, for it is with us that they are at their best. Several of the hybrids are pure white and very similar. Of these Thalia is the best. Its flowers are a combination of delicacy of outline and good substance that is altogether lovely. The leaves are very broad and decorative. There are two or three flowers to a stem.

Early Bulbs

There are still, in a few gardens in North Carolina, patches of the rare *Iris persica* that have been handed down from one generation to another. I went to a garden-club meeting one day, and there sat Mrs. Calvert with one of the frilled, pearly grey flowers pinned to her finely plaited collar. She said the bulbs had originally been in her great-grandmother's garden in the country near Pittsboro. When the family moved into town, the iris moved with them, and later they were given to Mrs. Calvert to bring to Raleigh. She said she had only a few left, and what should she do for them. I told her that it would be better for her to tell me what to do, since hers were living and mine was dead. After years of catalogue searching I had found it at last, but the bulb bloomed only one spring and was gone. The iridescent flowers are blue-grey in effect, but they change color in every light, showing green tints and violet tints, and sometimes a hint of olive. The falls are marked with spots of dark purple velvet. To me the flowers have no odor, but like the Florentine iris they are said to have a fragrance so delicate that only an aristocrat is aware of it. I once passed one around among my friends and found that they all belonged to the aristocracy. The Persian iris is called fair maids of February, and blooms in the middle of that month. The almost stemless flowers appear before the leaves. The large bulbs, surprisingly large for so small a flower, need to rest in the summer. They should be planted where they will be as dry as possible at that time, and it has been suggested that under the eaves of a building is a good place for the purpose.

Iris reticulata is much easier to establish than the Persian iris and not less beautiful. It grows anywhere, so long as the drainage is good, and increases rapidly. The slender dark flowers begin to open as early as the nineteenth of February or as late as the seventh of March. I like to plant them where their rich purple color will be seen with the bright yellow of the sweet early campernelles.

White and purple is a combination that I am very fond of for February and early March. Single white hyacinths—followed by snowflakes, the common early white iris, and the poets narcissus—are planted along the path to bloom with sweet violets. The violets are the variety Governor Herrick. There is a small white violet in the South that I have not been able to identify. My father brought it to me from some of the Georgia relatives, and I am trying to pass it on to other gardeners so that it will not be lost. Like so many once treasured plants, it has almost disappeared with the generation that tended it.

> As long as my grandmother lived,
> The sweet white violets that grew
> On either side of the garden path
> Bloomed every spring, and when in bloom
> Made sweet the garden and the lane,
> And scented all the avenue;
> While in the house, from room to room,
> Their fragrance travelled with the breeze.
> They thrived until she died, and then
> Survived her death another spring.
> And after that nobody knew
> The words she said to make them bloom,
> When walking up and down the path
> She poked among them with her cane.

There are two kinds of snowflakes in my garden. Both were bought for *Leucojum vernum*, the spring snowflake, and one is the bulb common in the trade under that name though it does not correspond with the description of that species in Colonel Grey's *Hardy Bulbs*.[1] The other I take to be the summer snowflake, *L. aestivum*. The spring snowflake is one of the earliest flowers, sometimes flinging out a few green-tipped white bells in January. The stems are short at first, but they stretch up to eighteen inches as the warm weather comes. The spring snowflake blooms until the first of April when the summer snowflake comes into flower. The latter is a much more robust plant, with stems to two feet, larger and broader bells,

[1] Vol. II, New York: E. P. Dutton and Co., n.d.

and longer, thicker leaves. The summer snowflake is much handsomer, but one would want both for a long season of bloom. The way to get both is to order *Leucojum vernum* from several sources. I know of but one nursery that lists *L. aestivum*, and the plant sent out under that name is the spring snowflake. Snowflakes bloom very freely and grow in any situation, increasing so rapidly that they can be spread out over the garden and used to fill in awkward gaps.

I have an open space under trees to be carpeted with all kinds of little early blue-flowering bulbs to bloom with daffodils. To that end I have been tediously transferring the heavenly blue grape-hyacinths, *Muscari botryoids*, from the borders where their masses of dying foliage are like a blight for weeks after the bloom has passed. They increase with alarming rapidity. The best blue glory-of-the-snow is *Chionodoxa Luciliae*. The flowers are large with a white center. This is not so prolific, and must be bought in quantity to be effective. The Taurian form of the Siberian squill, *Scilla sibirica taurica*, the one I have found to be most easily established and readily increased, is a clear blue that can be combined with the related tones of *Hyacinthus azureus* (one of the best of the little early bulbs), the creeping forget-me-not, and the forget-me-not-flowered anchusa, *Anchusa myosotidiflora*. The last long languished in the borders, but in leaf soil in the shady copse it is beginning to produce the bold leaf pattern that Miss Jekyll used to such advantage, and that I desire to emulate. It is not, as I had thought, unsuited to this climate, but it will not make good foliage in arid soil or in full sun.

In early spring Dutch hyacinths fill the need, filled by tulips later on, for something large and showy, definite in form, and delicately colored. After they have been in the borders for a year or so they lose their stodgy, hothouse look and become real garden flowers. In late March the silvery blue of the variety called Electra blooms with pale yellow primulas and white candytuft, *Iberis sempervirens*.

Parkinson's Starre-flower of Naples, *Ornithogalum nutans*, used to be grown in southern gardens as the satin hyacinth. It is still to be found in a few of them, but a search for bulbs ended by my having to get them from California. It is hard to account for the neglect of a spring bulb so lovely and so easy to grow. It is called the drooping star-of-Bethlehem, and is said to have the spreading tendencies of its more humble relative, *O. umbellatum*. I have not found this to be true, but perhaps it would be as well to leave it to the less choice spots, since it will grow in the poorest places and bloom in deep shade, producing in mid-March large spikes of green and silver stars.

The false camass, *Zigadenus Fremontii*, bloomed one March in the heavy wet clay that suits most of the zigadenes, but it did not come back the second year. And no wonder, Mrs. Rowntree said, when I complained, for it needs light soil and drainage. I have hopes that it can be established now that I know where to put it, although its hardiness in the East has not been proved in spite of catalogue assertions. The large stalks of white flowers with mustard yellow centers are worthy of another trial, especially since they came through one winter even under adverse conditions. The botanical tulips are delightful, and I have an idea that many of the species would do well in our gardens. I wish I knew more of them. The earliest is the water-lily tulip, *Tulipa Kaufmanniana*, with enormous short-stemmed flowers, striped red and yellow, that come the first week in March.

The fragrant lady tulip, *Tulipa Clusiana*, opens its peppermint-striped flowers only in full sun. I like them in rows with red and white English daisies. Planted in light, well-drained soil in full sun they should come back year after year.

The Florentine tulip, *Tulipa sylvestris*, is bright yellow with a buttercup sheen. There may be more than one flower to a stem, and they are wonderfully fragrant. The slight stems are twelve to eighteen inches. This wild tulip of England and Europe was brought to colonial gardens when gardening was at its height in America; it was in Jefferson's garden at Monticello. Now it is not so well known. Mrs. Wilder complains that it is a shy bloomer in cultivation, but here it is very free of the long pointed buds. It endures and increases in a sunny spot in light soil, and not the least part of the pleasure in it is in planting the small bright-orange bulbs that are as pretty as the flowers. This tulip blooms in the middle of March.

Along with the early bulbs bloom the dwarfs of the bearded iris section. For some reason most of them refuse to grow in my borders. I am sorry, for their bright and many colored flowers can play an important part in the daffodil season. My only fixtures are the charming little yellow one called Orange Queen (for what perverse reason I cannot tell, for it is pale yellow), and the ugly, dirty white one called The Bride. Other gardeners in these parts seem to have no difficulty with these early irises, and I have envied them the lovely soft blues, Lobelia, Miss Owen, and Princess Louise. Lobelia is one of the best in color and size. The most effective planting of dwarf iris that I have ever seen is an edging to Mr. Jacques Busbee's borders. The borders are raised and held in place by a moss-colored shale that repeats the yellow, olive, and claret tones of the iris. There are lavish patches of the yellows and olives of Zwanenburg, Jean Siret, Harbor Lights, *Reichenbachii*, and Keepsake; and of the claret-colored Graminea (the bearded Graminea—not the species), and a little brownish one called Neola. Neola and Jean Siret are repeaters.

Shrubs with Flowers before Leaves

Everyone greets the first daffodil with the feeling that there cannot be too much sunlight or too much yellow in the world. But a few weeks of jasmine, forsythia, and the narcissus King Alfred bring the conviction that there can be too much of anything. In this frame of mind I began digging up the masses of forsythia and jasmine that had overgrown the shrub border, offering them to all those new enough to gardening to be willing to take anything offered, and going about from garden to garden to see if anyone was discarding pink. I collected a purpleleaf plum to add to the flowering almonds from Mrs. Toy's garden in Chapel Hill, and redbuds from the old colored man who sells them from door to door (garden-club conservationists do not inquire too closely into his source of supply). These, with *Spiraea Thunbergii* and an apple-blossom quince are to be a background for my white daffodils. The daffodils are in drifts along a path through what used to be Mammy's chicken yard. As modern servants do not seem to raise chickens, something had to be done with it, so I am making a combination of copse and rock garden. I am not at all sure what a copse is, but I gather from English books that it is a shaded path bordered by ferns and other woodsy things. There are peach seedlings in my copse—a legacy from the chickens—much nicer I think than the double-flowering kind. They are very lovely with the white daffodils (but, please, not with yellow).

I mean to have shadblows in the copse to give the proper woodsy effect. When I see tufts of flimsy white flowers scattered sparsely on their leafless branches in the wintry spring woods, I wonder that they are seldom or never seen in gardens. The shadblow—or, as it is more commonly called in this section, the shadbush—flowers with the late daffodils. It is just ahead of redbud, and redbud is in full bloom when the first dogwood petals uncurl. There are two shadblows in North Carolina, *Amelanchier canadensis* of the swamps, and *A. laevis* of dry woods.

One of the first flowering trees of the year is the star magnolia, *Magnolia stellata*. When the winter is mild, it blooms so early that it is sure to be frost-bitten. There are few seasons when the creamy stars reach perfection without being caught at one stage of bloom or another. When we see them coming out at the end of our street we always say we are in for a freeze. In the rare springs when the star magnolia is at its best there is nothing so lovely. The furry buds of the saucer magnolia, *M. Soulangeana*, open a little later, and the cream-colored, purple-backed flowers are less often caught by the cold. The wine-colored *M. purpurea* blooms later still and is perfectly safe. Redbud, *Cercis canadensis*, blooms before the saucer magnolia is past its best, and they are more than pleasing together, especially if the ground is covered with a quantity of moss pinks.

The purpleleaf plum, *Prunus cerasifera* var. *Pissardii*, is also very early, sometimes beginning to bloom by the middle of February, but the pale flowers are not so tender as magnolia blossoms. I remember only one spring when the bloom was really damaged by the cold. The frail pink-tinted flowers have the delicate charm of cherry blossoms, but the new leaves are a violent reddish purple that can play havoc with the color scheme of later shrubs and flowers.

The flowering almond, *Prunus glandulosa*, come in March, first the pink one and then the white one. The pink is a delicate color and the white is the snowiest of shrubs. These are rounded, medium-sized bushes to about six feet.

Ranging in color from apple-blossom to rose, and from palest salmon to deep red, a profusion of delicate and lovely tints, the Japan quince, *Cydonia japonica*, is seldom met with except in the hideous orange-red in harmony with no other color, possible only with white. Mr. Busbee and Mrs. Lay planned and planted a quince hedge on the Saint Mary's campus that begins with the palest pink and shades gradually into the deepest red. These soft and charming colors are neglected by nurserymen and gardeners alike in the vicious circle of their not being grown because there is no demand, and their not being demanded because they are not grown.

There are low-spreading forms of the Japan quince that are excellent for rock gardens on a not too small scale. I bought one in bloom last November that has scarcely been without flowers since. It bloomed a little in winter, profusely in spring, and in summer had a scattering of the small coral flowers.

Where there is room for its full spread—say ten or fifteen feet—the pearl bush, *Exochorda grandiflora*, acquires lovely symmetry. There is one that I always visit early in March when the unopened buds are like pearls, and a little later when the bush is a dazzling white. There is room even in a small garden for an almost infinite variety of bulbs and border plants, but in any garden short of an estate one must eventually call a halt on shrubs. I enjoy a number that I cannot possess, visiting them in their seasons as regularly as I visit my friends.

A broad-leaved evergreen to bloom with these leafless flowers comes before the end of February, and sometimes before the middle of the month. This is the lily-of-the-valley tree, *Pieris japonica.* It first blooms with the earliest daffodils, drooping its white sprays against dark evergreen leaves, and continues through March and into April. This oriental species is more showy, but less hardy than our own mountain fetterbush, *Pieris floribunda*, which blooms late in March. The pair that I am acquainted with (at the Greaves-Walker's front door) are less than five feet tall. They are in dry soil under oak trees. Plants in the moist leaf soil that all of the heaths prefer would probably grow to ten feet.

Tulips for High Spring

Daffodils bloom when the bareness of winter is still in the trees. Iris bloom when the borders are already touched by heat. Tulips bloom when warmth and color are returning, and when there is still an early freshness in the air. They begin when the trees show the first red and green haze and are at their best when all but the oaks are in leaf, when dogwood, wisteria, white and purple iris, and Van Houtte's spiraea bloom in every garden—when high spring has come.

The first tulips open in late March and early April. With me the very first is Avalon, a large white one with black anthers. Earliness is its only recommendation, Zwanenburg and Carrara being later and better whites. The last with me is Feu Brilliant which blooms into May. It is a medium-sized Darwin of a pure spectrum red, that blooms year after year with the early white iris and has proved one of the best varieties for permanence. Never very large, the flowers have remained about the same in size.

There are a few varieties like this red one and the old-timer, Clara Butt, that stay with you for years and are colorful if not magnificent. Few tulips, however, come back with anything like their former glory the second year. Left in the ground they deteriorate; taken up they mold. I have come to the conclusion that the best way for the general gardener to have tulips is to spend money on them—much money if possible. If not much, the little must be spent to good advantage. Tulips are so important to the spring garden that a yearly expenditure is warranted, even on the smallest budget.

My tulip allowance is a minimum. In order to stretch it as far as possible, I have been investing in the multifloras. These are bunch-flowered tulips with several flowers to a stem. Monsieur Mottet, the most floriferous, is one of the cheapest tulips to be had; its only drawback is that it has not been developed in a wide range of colors. The others are expensive, but worth it. Monsieur Mottet is an early one. The flowers open a creamy white in early April, and turn to rose as they fade. They are described as ivory white, and the rose can spoil a scheme planned for all-white flowers, or one that includes yellows. The flowers of this tulip are not large, but they are delicately formed and appear four or five to a stem, so that even a dozen bulbs produces from fifty to sixty blooms.

Madame Mottet, also early, is more expensive and has not as many flowers to a stem. It is a bright rose pink, the shade of *Azalea amoena coccinea*, a very trying color.

Rose Mist is listed as a pink variety, but that is misleading. Like Monsieur Mottet, it comes out white and later is misted over with rose. But the flowers are large and become pink at an early stage. They are a pleasing color.

Golden Rod is one of the loveliest tulips, but it is not at all gold. It is the pale baryta yellow of Lady Bank's rose and of *Rosa Hugonis*, which bloom at the same time. It is not a yellow to combine with the alyssums and wallflowers with which I planted it under the impression that it would be a deeper color, but it is in keeping with the paleness of cowslips. This is the yellow that is so lovely with azaleas in tones of red-violet. I remember banks of azaleas mirrored in the black cypress water at Airlie, with masses of Lady Bank's rose hanging from the railings of the rustic bridges.

Wall Flower is also an unexpected color, not wallflower red but a dark maroon, and not two-toned, as described, but a self. It is a striking contrast with pale yellows and can be repeated with the pansy Alpenglow. This is the last to bloom.

There are a few other bunch-flowered tulips that I have not tried (you can get no idea of what they will be from the descriptions), but the choice is limited.

Wall Flower tones in with the rich browns and reds of the Breeder tulips. I like to plant it with Dom Pedro, Rêve d'Or, red and yellow pansies, alyssum, wallflowers and California poppies. And I like the tulip Bronze Queen with yellow and bronze pansies and the iris Nymph. In the borders where these tulips are planted the poppies and pansies bloom on with the dwarf hemerocallis.

This spring Isabel Henderson indulged herself in quantities of purple tulips in a series of tones between purple and mauve. The most intense, Sir Trevor Lawrence (and heaven knows where she got it—I have searched every catalogue) is, as near as I can make out from Ridgway (for purples are hard to check), a slightly-greyed magenta. The next, The Bishop, is bishop's purple; then comes the greyer Reverend Ewbank, and Anton Mauve which fades to a silvery lavender that is very beautiful with the other tones. Another purple sequence might be carried out in tones varying from the light lavender Valentine to the dark, raisin-purple Bacchus.

Bulbs with Tulips

Camassias are cheap and permanent, so should be planted in quantity. They bloom with tulips, their soft blue-violets supplementing the tulip colors, but they are more suited to the wild garden than to the formal borders, where their long spikes are untidy after the first few flowers have faded. In the West they grow in low moist meadows. In gardens they grow equally well in a heavy moist soil or a fairly dry one, and in sun or part shade.

The wide starry flowers of *Camassia Leichtlinii* are a pale blue-violet tinged with pink. They bloom in some shade in rich, moist woods-soil, with the pink buds and blue flowers of Virginia-bluebells, *Mertensia virginica*. Once the camassias are established, their season is a long one, extending into May and overlapping the bloom of the iris as well as that of the tulips. The flower stalks are tall, three feet or more, and the flowers are the largest of any species. There is also a white form, even lovelier than the type, which blooms the last of April.

C. Quamash blooms the middle of April, usually a week or ten days later than *C. Leichtlinii*. The flowers are smaller and of a deeper blue, and the stalks are shorter. They are dauphin's violet, a shade that is lovely with the Japanese roof-iris, *I. tectorum*. The roof-iris belongs to the crested section. It is one of the prettiest of the species and grows easily in sun or shade, in wet or dry soil. The flowers are flat, of a dull blue-violet marked with manganese violet. The leaves are broad and decorative. Mrs. Rowntree says that the deep blue of *C. Quamash* is relieved in the camass meadows by a yellow owls clover. In gardens it is brought out by the great yellow daisies of leopardsbane, *Doronicum caucasicum*. This tall daisy is difficult to establish. Nearly every spring I buy new plants that seldom live over the season. This is probably because I have been trying to make them grow in a hot dry border when they prefer a moist soil and some shade. No other perennial lends such distinction to the spring garden.

Camassia Cusickii is the handsomest species, according to Elizabeth Rawlinson. I have never been able to get a good form; in fact, it is hard to get it at all. As described and pictured, it should look like a foxtail lily with a spike to four feet. As it came to me, it is small and insignificant with watery-blue flowers. It blooms about the middle of April.

The squills are companions to the tulips, the large late-flowering types blooming along from the end of March to the end of April. They bloom well under all conditions and present no difficulties. The Spanish bluebells, *Scilla hispanica*, bloom in all degrees of shade, also in full sun, and in any kind of soil. They are in delicate tints of lilac and blue-violet, and are particularly useful in white. These are among the first of the flowers that give much and ask little. They bloom through April. The small meadow squill, *S. pratensis*, Hungarian in origin, is not so showy as the bluebell, but it is a dainty species that stays in bloom for nearly a month, and is very floriferous. It blooms about the tenth of April. The flower stalks are eight inches tall; the pale wisteria-blue flowers are like a fine mist. This is said to need a light soil that is moist in the growing period and dry in the resting period, but it does not seem to be at all particular.

The Cuban lily, *S. peruviana*, which is neither Cuban nor Peruvian but a native of the Mediterranean region, is a garden curiosity. It makes a glossy rosette of foliage in winter, and every other year in late April presents an enormous stocky scape of numerous starry blue flowers. The scape is conical at first, then gradually flattens into a disk. With me it is the last squill to flower. Grown under glass in the North, this odd and rather stylish species is perfectly hardy in North Carolina, and probably to Washington.

Iris with Tulips

The irises of the intermediate section are between the dwarf and tall bearded varieties in height and season. They add much to the borders when the tulips are in bloom, for they are good bloomers with a wide range of color. I should like to see more of them in gardens.

A favorite with me is Porcelain Blue, one that came from my grandmother's garden. It has variegated foliage, and flowers of two tones of red-violet that blend with a border of pink tulips, blue phlox (which is not blue at all, as a color chart proves, but a red-violet that is not far removed from the iris in color), Viola Blue Perfection (also red-violet), pinks, the showy bleeding-heart, and the annual centranthus. Grouped with the bleeding-heart is a white iris and the tulip Pride of Haarlem. Bluet is another of the red-violet intermediates. The small ruffled flowers are of the opalescent tint of the true pallida. It is one of the most floriferous and fragrant of the intermediates.

Nymph, a pale yellow that is slightly olive, is very satisfactory. Even better is Yellow Hammer. It is taller, and a deeper color. It is, in fact, one of the best yellows I ever had in a bearded iris.

Iris albicans is the common white variety that blooms at this time. It is much too common. The only time I ever tire of white is when this iris blooms in every garden with dogwood and *Spiraea reevesiana*. The flowers are almost always caught by frost, and the foliage, much given to disease, is unsightly for the rest of the year.

Iris Kochii is the purple iris that is so common in April, but I never tire of the intense jewel-like color, and I prize the species for its willingness to bloom at the foot of oaks and for its loveliness with the pale yellow of the common cowslip.

Purple King, another dooryard iris, is valuable for its height and because it will bloom in shade. It is planted to good effect in the copse with unspurred columbine seedlings of the same degree of vulgarity and the same shade of mulberry purple. The somberness of the iris and columbine is relieved by self-sown *Alyssum creticum* and johnny-jump-ups.

A few of the tall bearded varieties come into bloom with the tulips. It is well to keep them in mind in order to avoid undesirable color combinations. They are usually too late to be counted upon as part of the tulip scheme.

Titus, one of the earliest, is the beautiful but violent color known as Matthews' purple which is really only once removed from magenta. It is a close match to *Lunaria biennis*, and these two tall bright flowers can add much to the April border if one is skillful with colors. The flowers are large, and there are many to a stalk.

Lord Lambourne begins to open dark buds in mid-April. The dark falls and light iridescent standards of this old variety are more effective in the garden than many of the newer sorts.

Purissima, the largest and finest of the white iris, is also very early. Its one fault is a tendency to diseased foliage.

Flowering Trees and Shrubs for High Spring

When we started the Garden Center of the North Carolina Garden Club, one of the first calls was from a tourist who had driven through Raleigh in April, and wanted to know the name

of the flowering tree that looked as if a mauve veil had been spread over it. It was the garland crab-apple, *Pyrus coronaria*, of all the flowering shrubs the one that lends itself most delightfully to planting with tulips. It should be planted in open sunny gardens where there is room for the interlaced branches to sweep the ground. I should like a garden in April, in which a wild crab is planted about with the tulip Rose Mist, *Camassia Leichtlinii*, and quantities of the phlox Emerald Cushion.

Where there is room for planting shrubs and bulbs together, Sargent's crab, *Pyrus Sargentii*, would bloom with the earlier tulips. It comes out a little earlier than the native one. Sargent's crab is low and spreading (to six feet in height) with a profusion of white flowers that are pink in the bud. Even very small plants are covered with bloom, so that it is a good flowering shrub for the impatient. The flowers are followed by bunches of small bright fruits. This is one of the species immune to apple rust—which the wild crab is not, being almost certain to develop orange spots on the leaves soon after blooming.

Toward the middle of April the river plum, *Prunus americana*, is white in the margins of the woods and along fence rows, and on the Chapel Hill campus. It should find its way into gardens. It is a tree of snowy flowers, dark branches, and charming habit.

My very favorite of the woods shrubs is the red chokeberry, *Aronia arbutifolia*. The pink buds and the creamy white, strawberry-stamened flowers are as lovely as arbutus. They bloom in delicate clusters on leafless, pale grey branches. The shrub is not much in itself, being very slender and of wayward growth, but it is decorated again in the fall when the bright red berries ripen. The red chokeberry grows in evergreen shrub bogs and therefore prefers moist parts of gardens though it does well enough in dry parts.

The snow-wreath, *Neviusia alabamensis*, blooms in gardens in Chapel Hill and Raleigh late in March and early in April. The flowers are many-stamened and without petals. The delicate charm of this rare Southern shrub is lost when it is planted among more gorgeous varieties, but it is delightful in a leafy place. It is supposed to be difficult in gardens. The difficulty may be in not remembering that it comes from limestone country, and requires lime in the soil. The snow-wreath belongs to the rose family and is related to the spiraeas. It is a slight shrub, growing to not more than six feet, and seldom to that.

Some of the viburnums bloom with tulips. The doublefile viburnum, *V. tomentosum*, is a handsome shrub for moist ground but droops very quickly where moisture is scant. There is often a drought at the time it blooms. It makes a tall shrub (to ten feet) with spreading branches in the form of a cross— a white cross when the branches are covered with bloom. *V. Carlesii*, blooming at the same time, is a species much written up, but disappointing where I see it in this region. These are oriental species. The native black-haw, *V. prunifolium*, is not one of the showiest of the flowering trees, but it has value in a woodland planting, or in shade in the shrub border.

The thorny branches of the trifoliate orange, *Poncirus trifoliata*, make an impenetrable thicket when it is grown in a loose hedge. With shearing it fills out neatly. As a small tree this little orange bears white flowers in early April, and golden fruits in the fall.

Scotch broom, *Cytisus scoparius*, blooms over a very long period, beginning in late March if the spring is early. It is one of the few yellow-flowered shrubs blooming with tulips. It is not long lived but is useful in many places because of its drooping habit.

The jetbead, *Rhodotypos tetrapetala*, usually called white kerria with us though it is not a kerria, is much like a mock orange in habit and flower. The fruit is a small, shiny, black berry.

The evergreen azaleas hardy in the Middle South begin to bloom in late March. They are not difficult if planted in soil well mixed with leaf-mold and manure and mulched yearly with old leaves. Among the best shrubs for flowering in shady places, they flower even better in sun and make more compact growth.

The Kurume azaleas with their small glossy leaves, compact habit, and bright flowers are dwarf evergreens, slow growing, and usually less than three feet in height. The harsh tones of the red-violet *Azalea amoena* and its rose red variety *coccinea* are not easy to use with other colors, but either one planted in an out-of-the-way place makes a gay splash, for these are among the best shrubs for adverse conditions. No other evergreens will bloom in deeper shade, or grow in poorer, drier soil. The named varieties require care that is repaid by the multitude of delicately colored flowers.

The Kaempferi hybrids are more vigorous than the Kurume azaleas and produce larger flowers. They are the hardiest of the evergreen sorts. In color they range from red-orange to red-violet tones; the one that I am familiar with is Mary, a very floriferous azalea with large flowers of a soft begonia rose.

The large-flowered Indian azaleas are hardy with us, but are not well adapted to withstanding the fluctuations of our winter temperatures. *A. Ledifolia alba* is all right. The flowers of the colored forms are apt to be caught in cold spells. One that Billy Doar brought from Summerville more than ten years ago has bloomed once in all that time. Then it was covered with enormous, delicately colored lavender flowers.

One of the shrubs introduced into the colonies in the very early days of American gardening is the Persian lilac. It is found in every old garden in the South, but not so frequently in modern ones. The common kind is the form said to be the true Persian lilac, *Syringa persica laciniata*. It blooms at the end of March and early in April. The tiny flowers, as fine as mist, are lavender or white. The pinnately-cut leaves are a grey-green. Mrs. Lipscomb, whose passion is lilacs, and who has grown many kinds in Greensboro, recommends several other species for this climate. She says, if you have only one lilac, have the Chinese *S. Sweginzowii*; it grows like privet, and has fragrant lilac flowers. She recommends the Rouen lilac (*S. rothomagensis* in the catalogues, *S. chinensis* in *Hortus*), because it is very easily established. It is one of the earliest to flower and makes a small bush to four or five feet. She says also that the Giraldi hybrids are better in our climate than the French hybrids. The Giraldi hybrids were developed from a drought resistant form of the Chinese species, *Syringa oblata*. They flower very early, two weeks ahead of the French hybrids, and escape the heat. Of these, Lamartine, a single lilac with flowers of a lavender-pink, is the earliest and best.

Tall Bearded Iris

Beginning in April with the tulips, the bloom of the tall bearded iris lasts nearly two months. Among the very early varieties is a tall pallida with flowers of classic form and a fragrance that fills the borders and drifts into the house. It is called *I. pallida dalmatica*, and has long been in cultivation in the South. Everyone who has inherited iris claims to have the true form. To possess the true pallida is something like belonging to the Colonial Dames. This and a deeper blue called Princess Beatrice are found in gardens where the old has not been discarded for the new, and it is best to seek them there and beg a start, for the names of the pallidas are much confused, and there are many poor forms in the trade. The deep blue blooms later than the pale one. It is commonly planted with pink peonies, or with lemon lilies and Italian anchusa. Both iris are strong growers, and should be divided frequently. Otherwise the crowded rhizomes rot, and the flowers are small and few.

Isolene, one of the earliest of this section, is a beautiful and distinct bicolor with drooping falls of a deep red-violet and domed standards of a lighter tone, the whole flushed with gold. It blooms in my garden beside a common columbine, which has flowers shading from hellebore red to deep hellebore. This columbine came from Blanche Penland. I admired the parent, and was given a seedling. It is *Aquilegia vulgaris*, a form which is more vigorous, persistent, and colorful than the long-spurred hybrids. The foliage is handsomer, and in good forms the flowers are large and the stems long and many-flowered. I have been searching in gardens for choice color forms to plant with iris, for there is not much variety in plant lists. Whenever I see one that I like, I begin to wonder what I have that its owner lacks. Seedlings come true to color when the plants grow to themselves.

It is impossible to describe a number of iris without sounding like a catalogue, and it is a waste of time to designate certain varieties as the best, for no two people will agree on this. However, I have noticed several that stand out because they are superior in color and form and grow well in this part of the world. One that impresses me again and again is Baldwin. It is a very tall, manganese violet self with darker tones. Its clear, intense color and fine form set it apart in any collection. Sensation, described as cornflower blue but actually a wisteria violet, has very large, long-stemmed flowers with flaring falls. I always like the winged effect of the varieties with horizontal falls. Buto, a dark purple self, is a superior Madame Gaudichau. Black Wings is even darker, the blackest and most velvety of all purples. Venus de Milo is outstanding among the white iris for purity, size, and form. Its creamy flowers are decorated with a golden orange beard.

The so-called pinks, Frieda Mohr, Dog Rose, and Magnifica, bloom in borders of foxglove, sweet William, valerian, honesty, and pinks. In my garden the rose-flowered form of the gas plant, *Dictamnus albus*, blooms with these. Where spring comes more slowly, it blooms with the Japanese iris. It is called the gas plant because in climates where it blooms in summer the flowers give off a gas that will burn if the air is very still and the night very hot. The trick would not be possible in late

April. The plant is refreshingly lemon scented, with an odor so strong that it is apparent when you are weeding nearby. The pale lilac flowers are veined with a deep reddish purple that is the color of the buds. They are like small butterflies. This plant will grow only in deep rich soil where there is sufficient moisture. In such a place it improves every year; it should be left indefinitely in the same spot.

A small-flowered but gay and floriferous spiderwort, *Tradescantia bracteata rosea*, grows in the margin of my pink iris border. During the latter part of April, and well into May, the dwarf plants are a mat of true purple. Unlike most spiderworts this little western species is not very tolerant of shade. It is a new idea to me that spiderworts are to be cherished instead of discarded, an idea that I acquired from Violet Walker along with other garden lore. The large-flowered hybrids that are beginning to creep into the trade are very different from the common spiderwort; they are not so tall and weedy, and the flowers come in a variety of colors. After a long search through the catalogues I have at least come across the lovely Leonora (seen in Violet's garden), and it bloomed this spring for the first time. I was particularly anxious to have Leonora, because—according to Colonel Grey, who seems to be much more interested in the North American tradescantias than we are—it originated in North Carolina. The flowers are royal purple, the richest, deepest color found in the hybrids. J. C. Weguelin is chicory blue, and Blue Stone is wisteria violet. These are the colors as I checked them in Ridgway, but they are really indescribable. The crystalline flowers change in every light. These blue-flowered hybrids grow to eighteen inches; the lavender-flowered Pauline is over two feet. One of the prettiest colors of all is a form of *T. bracteata* called Appleblossom. The flowers are not the color of appleblossoms, but they are a very delicate shade of lilac. This is more dwarf than the others. Here, these hybrids do not bloom all summer—as I have read that they do elsewhere. With the exception of a few scattered flowers of Pauline and J. C. Weguelin, they bloom in May and bloom no more. These new sorts filled me with such enthusiasm that I begged from the laundress a start of the discarded *Tradescantia virginiana* (how often we go to our colored friends to replenish plants that they have kept and we have not), and planted it in a dark part of the copse where the ribbon-like leaves and three-cornered, spectrum violet flowers are delightful among ferns. The spiderworts prefer moist places. They shrivel in dry soil, and a drought finishes them for the season. Most of them prefer some shade.

The best yellow iris that I know is Happy Days. This is one of the newer large-flowered sorts that has done well in gardens in North Carolina for several seasons. The amber and wax-yellow flowers come in mid-season, early May, on well-branched, three-foot stalks. They are good with the olive yellow of the iris Jean Cayeau and with the dark-centered, wax-yellow blossoms of the verbascum Cotswold Gem. The verbascum, bought last year as a perennial "adapted to hot dry summers, and in bloom from July to frost," was delightful in the spring border, but failed to put in an appearance the second season, nor did it have time, blooming so early, to reach the catalogue height of four feet. But it made stocky, three-foot stalks that bloomed long and well.

A number of tall bearded iris begin to bloom in May, after the early ones have faded, and last into June. Sir Michael is a purple bicolor with dark falls and light standards. It is very late and very handsome. Ambassadeur is a wine and faun bicolor. A background of lemon lilies brings out the rich red of the falls and lights up the standards. These, with the primrose of the late and medium-tall iris Coronation, are a study in values.

With me Blue Jay is the last of the bearded iris. Its lateness and lovely color, a blue-violet that looks blue, are all that it has to recommend it, for the flowers are as small and short stalked as intermediates. But it is not always the finest flower that fills one's needs. A spot of color at the right time, and in the right place, is far more important than perfection of bloom. When spring flowers are fading, and summer flowers are buds, Blue Jay is that spot. It blooms for me in a stretch of blue and gold, with pale yellow California poppies, a dwarf veronica, and my favorite day-lily. The last came to me over the garden fence without a name, and is called "Miss Sally," but is, I think, one of the two varieties in the trade known as Queen of May (or May Queen). The other variety blooms later, and is altogether different in color, size, and length of stem. Miss Sally is a tall day-lily, to three and a half feet, with deep chrome flowers, that comes between the early dwarfs and the late varieties, filling what would otherwise be a lapse in the day-lily sequence. It blooms abundantly in early May, and repeats in the fall. The veronica is a treasure. It is a dwarf form of *V. spicata*, blooming before the type and after the creeping species. It blooms very profusely and, like the day-lily, fills a gap in the border.

Most of my bearded iris have suffered much from theory. Those that have done best were planted in the perennial borders where they get an autumnal application of cow manure—which is not always well rotted. Those in well-limed beds where no lush growth of neighboring plants is allowed to cover the rhizomes in summer, and where bonemeal is the fertilizer, have made poor growth and bloomed little. The rhizomes have been riddled by borers and devastated by rot, and the leaves have been disfigured with fungus. This year after they finished blooming, I dug new leaf soil, bone-meal, wood ashes, and sheep manure around all of the poor ones, and already I imagine improvement. One of the many fallacies of iris culture is the belief that they may be moved at any time. In the South, fall is the only good time to buy new ones and reset old ones.

Early Day-Lilies

In April begins the long and satisfactory bloom of that indispensable perennial, the day-lily. The early day-lilies are low growing and of three types: pale yellow, medium yellow, and deep yellow or orange. Clumps of these are charming in a border of early iris and mid-spring perennials. The pale yellow in the trade as *Hemerocallis minor* is not the true species, which is a much smaller plant, but it is a charming little day-lily. On each scape there are two or four large fragrant flowers of a clear lemon chrome. The scapes are slender and slanting, to eighteen inches long. This is a dainty, charming species. The leaves are as narrow as grass. One of the first to bloom, it appears from the fourth to the twentieth of April, and the flowers stay open more than a day. It has a tendency to repeat; one year some plants bloomed all summer. Almost always there is a good crop of flowers in the fall.

The medium yellow is a more vigorous type, blooming from mid-April to mid-May and increasing with alarming rapidity. In my garden, Sovereign and Gold Dust are very much the same: a very light cadmium yellow with reddish brown buds and many flowers crowded together on a scape. The scapes are two feet high.

The deep yellow is the cadmium yellow of Ridgway, which is almost orange. The broad dwarf day-lily, *Hemerocallis Middendorffii*, has thick short buds and wide petals. The flowers are large and bright. It is often the first to bloom, repeating at intervals in the summer and fall. The flowers of the narrow dwarf day-lily, *H. Dumortieri*, are the same color, but are smaller and not so wide open. The petals are narrow and pointed. The distinguishing character of this species is the way the scapes strike out from the ground at an oblique angle. The golden summer day-lily, *H. aurantiaca*, is similar, except that the cadmium yellow segments are faintly marked with cinnamon. Here it does not bloom in summer, but with other early sorts in April and May. Apricot, a hybrid of the broad dwarf day-lily, is the color of its parent, but the flowers are larger and the scapes taller. It blooms a little later. Two other hybrids in this class are Orange Man and Tangerine.

These day-lilies bloom in my garden in a yellow and blue border with a sprinkling of apricot poppies, and with yellow pansies, alyssum, and *Potentilla Warrensii*. The alyssum is a descendant of a plant acquired as *A. creticum* which died after blooming but left a crop of grey seedlings that bloom the first year and perpetuate themselves so freely that there is always yellow to fill in where yellow is needed. These may be crossed with another species which came to me as *A. sinuatum*. They bloom from the first of April to June, and while somewhat weedy, are pretty with the day-lilies. With me no alyssums are permanent, and *A. creticum* is the only one that ever reseeded. *Potentilla Warrensii* is a shrubby perennial that behaves (with me) as a biennial, but keeps itself going. It grows to one foot and is covered with bright yellow flowers that bloom in the morning. It begins to bloom in late April.

A tall and early gaillardia, the Sun God, blooms with early day-lilies and iris. The flowers are large, to three-and-a-half inches across. They are a beautiful golden yellow with deeper centers. They appear the last of April, and I have seen them in bloom in November, but they do not fulfill the catalogue promises of indifference to midsummer heat and drought. In acquiring beauty they have lost some of the sturdy qualities of the red and yellow blanket flower. And with me the Sun God is not persistent. The rule for keeping it is to divide the outside of the old plants in fall, resetting the divisions. It never works for me.

The blue flowers that bloom with early day-lilies are *Linum perenne*, the prostrate veronica True Blue, and two sages of low stature. The meadow sage, *Salvia pratensis*, is a short-lived perennial that is more useful than attractive. Elizabeth Rawlinson has the better *Salvia Jurisicii*. This blooms a little later and lasts nearly two months. The plants are low and spreading, with fine grey foliage and small blue flowers.

Iceland poppies are not for this climate, but there are similar species from parts of the world with a temperature more like ours. These will thrive and persist in southern gardens. They are the Spanish poppy, *Papaver rupifragum*, and its geographical varieties *P. pilosum* and *P. atlanticum*. Their salmon-orange flowers are held on wiry stems two feet above the tufts of silver foliage. *P. atlanticum* from Morocco prospers with me. It is easily raised from seed sown in the open borders, and seeds itself thereafter. Any light soil will do; the poorer the better. It prefers sun but will grow even in some shade. The flowers appear in April and May, a few through the summer. They are three inches across.

The bright colors of the horned-poppies vary the yellow and orange pattern of the early day-lilies. They are biennials or short-lived perennials said to bloom the first season if they are sown before October. Mine never get started early enough to bloom before the second year. The yellow horned poppy, *Glaucium flavum*, is the easiest to grow from seed, but it is small flowered for its size. It is three feet tall. The flowers of the variety *tricolor* are much larger; they are a flame scarlet shading to scarlet and marked with black patches. The grey leaves are decorative through the winter. The long, curved seed pods (to eight inches) are like horns. *G. leiocarpum* is a smaller plant (twelve inches or less) with a grey rosette of deeply lobed leaves and large brilliant flowers of pure scarlet. The dark red—almost black—marks on the bases of the four petals form a cross. The horned-poppies grow in light poor soil in full sun. They endure hot, dry weather very well and are not too affected by humidity.

Linaria dalmatica is a tall toadflax that makes a good early perennial. I know of no source for plants, but it comes easily from seed. The seedlings bloom the first year, but they are sprawling. After that the stalks are tall (to three feet) and stiff. In May and June they are covered with small snapdragon flowers of the coolest yellow. Cut back at the end of June, they bloom through July and into August. Early in the season the lemon-colored flowers and narrow grey leaves are very pretty against a mass of dark purple larkspur. Low-growing plants should be in front to hide the leggy base of the toadflax.

Siberian iris, *Iris sibirica*, and day-lilies are a good combination for a soil too wet for bearded iris. The red-violet of the iris Emperor is not to be allowed near day-lilies that shade into orange. This and Snow Queen are lovely with pale yellows. The blue-violet of Perry's Blue, one of the cherished blues of the garden, is delightful with both orange and yellow day-lilies. Siberian iris like a rich moist soil, but they will put up with any. Snow Queen is one of the best perennials for flowering in poor ground in dark places.

Delta Iris

Between the tall bearded and the Japanese sections, and overlapping with both, bloom the tall and slender irises from the lower Mississippi Delta and the swamps and bayous of southern Louisiana. These have long been in gardens in the deep South, and have slowly travelled to gardens in other parts of the country, but they were generally overlooked as material for the flower borders before the researches of Dr. Small in 1925. I never look at the bright flowers blooming so serenely in my garden without remembering Mrs. Peckham's tale of accompanying Dr. Small on one of his collecting trips; of being waked before daylight by his pounding on her door, of tramping through sultry, mosquito-ridden marshes not knowing what sort of reptiles were underfoot, with no thought of food until long after dark, nor bed until midnight.

Long ago, before the Delta irises were in commerce, Mrs. Dabney brought some of the wine-colored flags from her garden in Vicksburg to her garden in North Carolina. As they increased, she generously divided with her friends. I remember thinking they were the most beautiful color I had ever seen in a flower, as glowing as the wine of the red scuppernong. And I remember being very much disappointed when those that came to me failed to bloom in the dry border where I planted them. Mrs. Dabney's garden was dry too, but she had green fingers. She also had wagon loads of manure spread over her entire garden every fall. My later acquisitions found a perfect environment in the afternoon shade of the Japanese iris bed. All of the Delta group are at their best here, but they will grow in drier places and in full sun if the soil is deep and mixed with generous proportions of peat and manure.

The colors of the Delta species are tones of red-orange, red-violet, and blue-violet. There are also white forms. Beginning with the copper flag, *Iris fulva*, in late April, they bloom in succession until early June. Dr. Small describes the copper flag as varying from orange through the salmons to crimson and scarlet. The several color forms that I have had all bloomed the same dragons-blood red, an odd color that is hard to place in the borders and is impossible with other iris. After moving it about for years, I took a leaf out of Elizabeth Rawlinson's book and planted it with wild columbine, *Aquilegia canadensis*. The small flowers of this species are more suited to the wild garden than to the formal borders, and the color is charming with the picric yellow and nopal red of the columbine.

Next in order of bloom is the wine-colored flag, *Iris vinicolor*. The large dark-red flowers are lightly poised on slender stalks that reach a height of over four feet in rich damp soil. The falls are spread horizontally and marked with a yellow line that is raised in a sort of crest. The dark flowers look richer against pale pink spires of single larkspur, with the rosy annual centranthus in the foreground, or with the cool yellow of the *Thermopsis caroliniana* and lemon lilies, *Hemerocallis flava*. The thermopsis is native to mountain slopes from Georgia to North Carolina and is one of the finest spring perennials, growing to more than four feet in good soil and improving each year that it is left undisturbed. It is as lovely as the lupines that it resembles, and more satisfactory for us. The form of the lemon lily known as the variety major is superior to the type; it is almost everblooming, repeating in midsummer and again in the fall.

There are infinite variations of the dark-red iris, but with a few exceptions the differences are too slight to count in the garden. *Iris imperialis* and *I. chrysophoenicia* stand out as darker than the rest. The first looks unlighted because of the faintness of the yellow crest. The second is distinguished by an unusually broad and bright crest.

The purple hybrid, *Dorothea K. Williamson*, is the most burning color I have seen. The wide triangular flowers (measuring five inches from point to point) make a brilliant pattern against masses of the white daisy, the Swan. It is of medium height, having the low-growing *I. foliosa* for one parent and the not-so-tall copper flag as the other. This lovely hybrid is very invasive, but it is well to let it spread where there is room, in order to have plenty of flowers to cut.

The blue-violet types bloom late. The big blue flag, *Iris giganticaerulea*, is less ethereal than the wine-colored flags. The stems are thicker, the petals broader, and the flowers more imposing. It varies in color from soft blue-violet to royal purple. There is also a white form which, like all white flowers, is lovelier than the loveliest colors, and of course rarer and more expensive. But mine was given to me by Mr. Busbee, who does not care what he spends on plants. The big blue flag grows with a clump of wild indigo, *Baptisia australis*, that flourishes in the heavy moist soil of the iris border. It is a beautiful blue, much deeper than the iris.

Iris mississippiensis belongs to the short-stalked hexagona group. It is low and spreading, less than a foot in height. It will tolerate drier soil and less acidity than any others of the group. This species is one of the last of the group to bloom, beginning in late May and continuing into June. The flowers are large in proportion to the length of stem and are a deep soft blue-violet.

Iris hexagona itself is also a late bloomer. It is the most beautiful iris of this group. In the garden this species is not nearly so vigorous in growth nor so free of bloom as the others. Some years ago my cousin sent me a clump from Saint Simon's Island. It has bloomed less and less and has been almost crowded out by *I. vinicolor*. The color is the most wonderful blue I have ever seen in a flower. It is nearest to the dauphin's violet of Ridgway's chart, but very much more intense. The flowers are five inches across, on twelve inch stems.

Japanese Iris

If all originators were as fanciful as the Japanese in naming flowers, much pleasure would be added to gardening. The names given to iris by the Japanese are poems beautifully and exactly describing the flowers, as Far-flying Swallow, Snow on the Purple Robe, Blossom in the Wine Cup, Morning Mists, or Floral Display of Heavenly Appointment. Mr. Busbee says he has one that is called Grey Stork Magnificently Standing, but a fruitless search through the catalogues and the *Iris Check List*[2] leads me to believe that he made it up.

My own varieties have been in the garden so long, since

[2] *American Iris Society: Alphabetical Iris Check List*, ed. Mrs. Wheeler H. Peckham, Baltimore, 1919.

before I was careful about records and labels, that the very early and common white one called Gold Bound, and the very late and vivid purple one with the misleading name of Mahogany, are the only two I can attempt to identify. The first to bloom is a tall, single, dark purple with a bright yellow crest. A double purple is very late. There is a tall white one, veined violet (the variation of this in named varieties is infinite, and all are homely) and there is a shorter white one veined with the beautiful soft blue that is the color of old blue china. One of the loveliest is an early single lilac very delicately made, of medium height. It is veined with Chinese violet, and there are blue markings at the center. It blooms with the creamy, pink-anthered *Spiraea palmata*.

The herbaceous spiraeas as companions to the Japanese iris have been an excellent solution to one of the chief problems of the borders. Their bold leaf patterns and feathery flowers are charming with the stiff swords of the iris leaves, and they do well in moist, heavy soil. These easily-grown perennials of Europe, Asia, and our own woods and meadows are not all spiraeas, but they will be found under that name in the catalogues.

The goats-beard, *Spiraea aruncus*, of our mountain woods—called bride's feathers by the mountain people—blooms late in May with the earliest of the Japanese iris. It will grow also with perennials that require a drier situation, and will grow in deep shade. The ivory plumes and pinnate leaves equal the handsomest of the astilbes. When goats-beard is naturalized with iris along streams, or in informal plantings, the American elder is a proper background. The lacy white flowers of the elder come in May and early June and are followed in July by bunches of reddish purple berries that turn black as they mature.

The meadowsweets are filipendulas to botanists, but they are spiraeas to gardeners. Dropwort, *Spiraea Filipendula*, is a pretty, low-growing perennial to twelve inches or more, with dark fern-like leaves and sprays of white flowers and pink-tipped buds. It is the first of the meadowsweets to bloom, coming in mid-May. The double form is superior to the single.

Next to bloom is the very handsome queen-of-the-meadow, *S. Ulmaria* var. *plena*. This is one of the fine border perennials. The large panicles of double creamy-white flowers are beautiful with dark purple Japanese iris. The foliage is particularly good. This and *S. palmata* grow to between three and four feet. *S. palmata* has bright green leaves like large, deeply veined maple leaves. They are striking in the spring, but they have a tendency to turn rusty later in the season. This meadowsweet blooms with the early varieties of Japanese iris. The flowers are pink in the type and cream-colored with red stamens in the variety *elegans*. *S. venusta* is similar but is taller and later blooming. The flowers are rose color. *S. lobata* is like *S. venusta* except that the flowers are a paler rose, and *S. camtschatica* is also similar but has white flowers. These three bloom late, almost too late for the Japanese iris, but they are good with the perennials that follow the iris in late June. They grow to five feet in moist soil and are for the back of the border. The deeply-lobed leaves measure to ten inches across. *S. venusta* and *S. lobata* are native; the others of European and Asiatic origin.

The tall white phlox, Miss Lingard, blooms with purple and white Japanese iris, and with the Imperial larkspurs, Blue Spire and White King. Miss Lingard is not a very permanent variety, but I renew it from time to time because of its beauty and early bloom. It comes in late May and lasts until the time of the garden phlox.

The somber, purple varieties of the iris need yellow in the background. Most of the yellow perennials for this season, *Achillea filipendulina, Anthemis tinctoria,* and the Sun God gaillardia, require sun and soils drier than those suited to the iris. Beyond the dark clumps of the iris, in a drier and sunnier place, but where they can be seen together, I have massed giant mulleins, *Verbascum olympicum.* These are rather a nuisance to keep going for they take three years to bloom from seed. But they are spectacular at the back of wide borders where their five-foot stalks tower above the other perennials.

Japanese iris must have a rich moist soil and part shade; their failure in this climate is due to the lack of these. I read from time to time that drainage is essential, and perhaps it is where there is much freezing in winter, but the water often stands on mine after long rains, and I cannot see that it does them any harm. I have never been able to succeed with them in the perennial borders, but they grow as well as could be wished in a low bed of heavy clay, where they get a generous supply of cow manure in the fall and a generous hosing during and after bloom, and where they are in afternoon shade. They never rot and have no disease. The only drawback is that some little black bugs riddle the flowers. I never do anything about it. I suppose there is some delectable poison that the bugs would prefer to petals, but I always think they may not turn up—and sometimes they do not.

Flowering Trees and Shrubs for Late Spring

The most important shrubs for late April and May are the mock-oranges. After seeing the variation of plant and flower in Mrs. Gibbs's collection[3] of over ninety it seems to me that gardens might afford more than the old sweet syringa, *Philadelphus coronarius*, delightful as it is. I could not imagine a garden without sweet syringa to produce small single white flowers from mid-April into May, to raise up large families of seedlings that grow rapidly into shrubs to fill up gaps in the hedges, or to plant in difficult spots where everything else dies. But I should like to see some of the splendid Lemoine hybrids with their charming French names—Pavillon Blanc, Manteau d'Hermine, Gerbe de Neige, Mer de Glace—and their lovely pure white flowers, single or double, sometimes frilled, and sometimes scented. And I should like to see in gardens the fragrant wine-marked flowers of the purpureo-maculata strain. These are my favorites, especially the gardenia-scented Belle Etoile.

The white flowers of the snowbells come with the iris. The

[3] Gibbs Hill, Staunton, Virginia.

oriental species are small trees. In May they are covered with drooping racemes of campanulate flowers. *Styrax Obassia*, the fragrant snowbell, is superior to the more commonly planted Japanese snowbell, *S. japonica*. These are hardier than the shrubby species of the southern states. *S. americana* grows in southern swamps and likes a moist soil. It makes a medium sized shrub to about eight feet. *S. grandifolia* is a better species than *S. americana*, but I cannot find a source for it other than the woods.

Silver-bells are related to the snowbells. Three species are native to the South, but the one in gardens and in the trade is the snowdrop-tree, *Halesia carolina*. It grows in the mountains and in the piedmont. In cultivation the snowdrop-tree is slender and graceful in habit. In late April, white, shallowly scalloped bells are hung along the stem in clusters of two or three. A pink form is described in *Trees of the Southeastern States*.[4]

I am glad that I garden in a part of the world where jasmine grows. I take delight in having as many as are hardy above the Far South, and I have spent some vain and foolish efforts on those that are not (such as *Jasminum pubescens*). A number bloom in May. *J. floridum*, very similar to the winter jasmine except for time of bloom, is a spreading, glossy, small-leaved shrub to three or four feet. The Italian jasmine, *J. humile* (of Asiatic origin), is an erect and vigorous shrub with larger flowers and larger leaves than the other two. It blooms in May and continues into the summer, which *J. floridum* does not, although it is represented as blooming from spring to frost. The flowers of the Italian jasmine are yellow, and the leaves are the characteristic light yellow-green. This species is said to grow to twenty feet, but the largest one I know here is about six feet tall. It is said to be hardy to Maryland. Once in January I saw the primrose jasmine, *J. primulinum*, in bloom in South Georgia, and brought a root from my great-aunt's garden, thinking to add to my winter flowers. Here, it has persisted for several

[4] W. C. Coker and H. R. Totten, Chapel Hill: University of North Carolina Press, 1937.

years, but the large, butter-colored flowers (so far superior to *J. nudiflorum*) have not opened before late April. This jasmine is a scandent shrub that can be trained to climb, or left to grow naturally into a large mass of drooping branches.

The star jasmine, *J. officinale*, with tiny, white, scented flowers and pale, finely-cut foliage, was once a common vine in the South. I think we do not pay enough attention to vines. There are so many half-hardy ones which are very showy, and which will grow out of doors to Washington or Philadelphia. Of the pink jasmines, *J. stephanense* was a disappointment, but *J. Beesianum* is lovely. It is not really pink; the flowers are white with a pinkish tinge. The buds are red. The variation in color is charming when the plants are full of bloom. It is more of a vine than a shrub and will grow to a good height, with support. It grows very rapidly, covering some feet of fence in a season. This species is recommended as drought resistant and as excellent for covering banks. None of the jasmines is evergreen in the Middle South.

Deutzias bloom from early April into May. The slender deutzia, *D. gracilis*, is a dwarf shrub of less than three feet that blooms with tulips. The later, taller kinds bloom with iris. Of these the most desirable are the pink-flowered forms, especially the rose-panicle deutzia, *D. rosea*, a medium sized shrub to five feet. Deutzias are valuable for bloom in shade.

The beauty bush, *Kolkwitzia amabilis*, is another pink-flowered shrub for late spring. It comes out in mid-April with the tulips and blooms with the early iris in late April and early May. The silver-pink flowers and silver-grey leaves are a not too conspicuous background for tulips and iris. It is a large, rounded shrub to eight feet in height, and almost the same in width.

Two yellow-flowered shrubs of the rose family bloom with bearded iris. The single kerria, *K. japonica*, blooms late in April, and blooms in shade. It is an enchanting shrub with slender, arching branches, wrinkled leaves, and small flowers of light cadmium yellow. It grows to about four feet, but it is always very fragile and needs to be planted with wild flowers rather than shrubs that might crowd it out. It is as lovely as the commonly planted double kerria is vulgar, though it is not so vigorous nor ironclad. Both kerrias bloom in late April. The shrubby cinquefoil, *Potentilla fruticosa*, that blooms in New England pastures in July and August, blooms in my garden in April and May, and a little through the summer. It likes lime, and will grow in wet or dry soil, but it grows and blooms well only when it is in full sun. This is a nicely rounded, symmetrical dwarf to three or four feet high, compact, and with narrow grey leaves.

The rose acacia, *Robinia hispida*, is a shrub not to be brought into the garden, especially the small garden, without considering its rapid spread by suckers that reach out on all sides. Where there is room for a thicket, the grey-green pinnate leaves and rose colored, wisteria-like flowers are rather charming in April and early May. The clammy locust, *Robinia viscosa*, blooms later. The flowers are deep pink in the bud, and pale when fully open. These grow to ten feet or less. There are other shrubby locusts native to the mountains and sandhills of the Middle South. A number of them are in the trade, but they are more appreciated in northern gardens than at home. They are shallow rooted legumes suitable for planting in poor soil. The black locust, *Robinia Pseudoacacia*, with racemes of white pea flowers in late April, is one of the loveliest of flowering trees, but one of the most perishable.

The yellow-wood, *Cladrastis lutea*, is more beautiful than the black locust and far more satisfactory. It is native only in a small area in the southern mountains, and is very rare. All these years I have lived in North Carolina I never laid eyes on the yellow-wood until I saw it in bloom this year in late May in the Brooklyn Botanic Garden. And for this there is not the excuse that it is not available, for it is in at least one North Carolina nursery. The drooping racemes of white flowers are more delicate and graceful and more fragrant than wisteria. The pinnate leaves are of the soft, cool grey-green that is characteristic of the legumes. The bark is smooth and grey, and the tree itself has a lovely outline. One of the good points of yellow-wood is its resistance to drought. It blooms in Chapel Hill sometime in May.

Another spring-flowering tree of the legume family is the European laburnum, *L. vulgare*. The wisteria-like racemes of bright yellow flowers come in late April. The laburnum is commonly called golden-chain, but Miss Isabel refers to it as dripping sunshine. It is useful because of its shade tolerance.

The hawthorns bloom from the middle of April all through May. For us the native species are preferable to the English thorn, *Crataegus Oxyacantha*. The earliest date in my records for hawthorn blossoms is from a tree in the neighborhood. It bloomed in a forward season on March twentieth. This tree bears very large and very red berries and has very long sharp thorns. It is of a charmingly irregular growth habit, which is characteristic of the hawthorns, and to me their chief beauty. Their one drawback is the revoltingly fishy odor of the flowers of most species. For this reason I would hesitate to bring one into intimate quarters. At a safe distance, or for those who do not object to the odor, the grace of the native thorns is as apparent in gardens as in woods. The delicate pattern of the small leaves and the ethereal beauty of the white flowers will overcome most aversions to their odor. One of the very good native species for cultivation is the cockspur thorn, *C. Crusgalli*. It is delightful in flower, and the large, dull red berries persist into the winter. Dr. Totten considers the parsley haw, *C. apiifolia*, the finest of all. When I said that describing plants not in the trade would not encourage gardeners to use more natives—would, in fact, have the opposite effect—he said, "Well, if Bright Andrews hasn't got it I'll see that he gets it." A distinctly southern species, native from Virginia to Florida, it is beautiful in leaf, flower, and fruit.

Early in May the most beautiful of the woods viburnums is in bloom. This is the Southern black-haw, *V. rufidulum*, called blue-haw (from the color of its berries) to distinguish it from the other black-haw, *V. prunifolium*. It is native from Virginia to Florida, but the southern gardener will have to go to Ohio to get it from a nursery. It is said to be almost impossible to transplant from the woods. This species makes a small tree less than twenty feet tall. The maple-leaf viburnum, *V. acerifolium*, is another woodsy shrub that has a great deal of charm in an informal planting, with its lacy white flowers and the pretty pattern of its maple-like leaves.

The native azaleas, although not evergreen, are as lovely in flower as the Japanese kinds, but they are less appreciated. One of the rarest and most choice species, the pink-shell azalea, *A. Vaseyi*, blooms in Chapel Hill in Mrs. Totten's rock garden early in May. The flowers are the color of apple blossoms, and the habit is exceedingly graceful. This species occurs only in the North Carolina mountains, and it is one of the native shrubs that is available in the trade. The flame azalea, *A. calendulacea*, blooms in the mountains late in May, but in the piedmont it blooms toward the first of the month. The flowers range in color from yellow through orange to red. It is of open growth to ten feet tall.

The mountain stewartia is summer-flowering, but the beautiful *S. Malacodendron* of the coast blooms in April at Orton Plantation near Wilmington. The large white flowers, filled with purple stamens, measure four inches across. This is a small tree to twenty feet. It is not at all prepossessing when out of bloom.

I wish that some of our more interesting native shrubs were as popular as the fringe-trees, *Chionanthus virginica*, that repeat their colorless pattern of shredded petals and pale leaves in nearly every garden in April. The flowers remind me of slaw. It would be nice if a few gardeners would plant, instead, one of the slender magnolias that grow in the mountains, or the red buckeye.

The red buckeye, *Aesculus Pavia*, grows on the coastal plain from Florida to Virginia. It is a shrub or small tree with spikes of small, brick red flowers in mid-April. The common horse-chestnut, *Ae. Hippocastanum*, blooms late in April, and the red horse-chestnut, *Ae. carnea*—a cross between the two—blooms early in May. The last is a shapely tree of medium size with flowers as showy as those of the common horse-chestnut, and of an exquisite shade of salmon pink. These little-planted trees are far better than the gaunt paulownias in bloom everywhere in the late spring.

The flowers of broad-leaved evergreens are important at

all seasons, but particularly in late spring when the mountain-laurel and rose bay are in bloom. In Raleigh the mountain-laurel, *Kalmia latifolia*, blooms late in May. Although associated with the mountains, it is native all the way to the coast and does as well in gardens in the piedmont and coastal plains as in those in the western part of the state. The pretty calico flowers, the glossy, pointed leaves, and the neat form make it one of the best broad-leaved evergreens, but it is not at all common in cultivation.

The rose bay, *Rhododendron catawbiense*, is native only in the mountains and piedmont, but it grows in gardens to the coast. I have seen it in full bloom at Orton in the middle of April. A white-flowered form that grows in a dark corner behind the rectory at Saint Mary's is one of the most beautiful things I have ever seen when it is in full bloom in the middle of May. The pure white flowers are marked with old gold. The shrub is compact and shapely, about ten feet tall. It could not be in a less favorable spot. With oak trees all around, I have never seen a leaf over its roots, but it could not do better with a deep mulch to keep it cool and moist all summer. Beside our own native *Rhododendron carolinianum*, *R. catawbiense*, and *R. maximum* there are numberless hybrids ranging in color from pale pink to red and purple, and in height from dwarfs to giants. There are also splendid white forms.

On the coast the banana shrub, *Michelia fuscata*, reaches luxurious proportions. At Orton there are two perfectly matched specimens on one of the shady terraces leading down to the old rice fields. They must be fifteen feet wide and as much, or more, high. Inland they are much less grand, but in Chapel Hill and Raleigh there are long established plants that bloom yearly and fill the air with fruity fragrance. The flowers are like small magnolias with red-edged, ivory petals. They are not showy on the shrub. This is one of the evergreens difficult to transplant. Shrubs of any size should be stripped of their leaves before they are moved.

The South is rich in magnolias, though only *M. grandiflora* with its wide and shining evergreen leaves and its carved ivory blossoms is really well known. Several deciduous species grow to tree size and bear large white flowers. The first of these to bloom is the umbrella-tree, *M. tripetala*. This is a small tree very common on creek banks and in damp woods in piedmont North Carolina, where the large pale leaves—like banana leaves—seem strangely exotic. The large, floppy, cream-colored flowers appear soon after the middle of April. They are followed by red fruits. The umbrella-tree occurs as far north as Pennsylvania. The somewhat similar *M. Fraseri* is a mountain species found only in the South. The great-leaf magnolia, *M. macrophylla*, native from North Carolina to Georgia, is even more tropical in appearance. This is a big tree, and the enormous leaves and flowers are like something in a fairy tale. When a botanist wrote Dr. Coker that no magnolia flower could be as large as the one described in *Trees of the Southeastern States* as eighteen inches across, he sent the botanist a flower twenty-three inches across. And the leaves, by Dr. Coker's measurements, are to thirty-two inches long. Ordinarily the flowers are merely twelve inches across, and the shapely leaves about two feet long. The fragrant flowers are followed in the fall by rose-colored cones. This magnolia blooms in Chapel Hill in late May and June. It is hard to establish in gardens, but once established does well in cultivation. In May and June when the sweet bay, *M. virginiana*, blooms in the swamps, the small, many-petaled, tuberose-scented flowers are brought to market in the farm women's baskets. The sweet bay is evergreen in the South. All magnolias need moisture and a soil rich in humus.

In gardens along the coast there is a dwarf evergreen from the Orient that blooms from April to frost, but most profusely in late spring. It is burdened with the name of *Damnacanthus indicus*, supposedly because of fierce thorns, but it is not at all thorny. Raleigh must be about as far north as it will grow, for Caroline Long's, only a hundred miles farther north, was killed in the severe weather last winter. Mine was unhurt, which proves that it will endure to six degrees above zero. It came to me from Florida with Mr. Hayward's warning that it would probably not be hardy. It is a most amazing shrub as to bloom, seldom being without small purplish buds and white flowers as long as it is well watered and in full sun. I have not known it to fruit, which is a pity, for the coral berries are said to persist through the winter until the plants are in bloom again. The branches root very readily where they touch the ground, and the little shrubs grow rapidly. It may be a good plan to keep new plants on hand, for the old ones get leggy. They are improved by the shears and make a neat low hedge for edging borders. But they are not evergreen here.

Two small heaths from the evergreen shrub bogs will grow in gardens where there is shade and moisture. In the bogs they reach six feet, but they will be much less in cultivation. Like all heaths they require an acid soil and much humus. The bog fetter-bush, *Pieris nitida*, blooms in April in the pocosins, and in May in my garden. It is not showy but is very pretty with its small, drooping, pink flowers and thick smooth leaves. *Zenobia pulverulenta* blooms early in May. It is by far the loveliest of the heaths in flower, with long racemes of inverted urns, very pure white among the pale oval leaves. The leaves are very thin and do not persist in cultivation. These evergreens, native only to the southeastern states, are difficult to find in the trade. I know of one source only for the zenobia, and none for the fetter-bush, which was collected for me by Belva Bennette who lives where such things grow, and values them. "I heard you were making a wild garden," she wrote, "and I wanted to make a contribution, so my mother and I went nearby to the woods and found some native evergreens, and one flower. I am sending you a fetter-bush. Notice the angular stems. We have it in high and low, some with white and some with pink flowers." I think that learning to know the native plants, and bringing them into cultivation, is a more practical way of conservation than making laws to leave them untouched. I think this because so often I have left them in the woods to enjoy another season, and when the season came, and they were revisited, woods and plants were gone.

> We'll to the woods no more
> The laurels all are cut.

Annuals

Most of the common annuals are spring-planted and summer-blooming. Those that are fall-planted and spring-blooming add a great deal to Southern gardens in March and April and May. This is a list of the ones that are easily grown. Gardeners who have more skill and patience than I can add to it. I have found that fall sowing is the important point in the culture of early annuals. To be at their best they must get started while it is cool and make their bloom before the hot weather comes. Another important point is early sowing. September seeds make strong plants before frost comes, and these give the best spring bloom. But it is hard to sow seeds in beds still full of flowers, and those that must be sown in the places where they are to bloom are a problem. Those that can be sown in the seed beds in September, and set out in the borders in spring in the spaces between dormant perennials, are the most useful.

Mr. Tong always said that seeds should be sown in September or November, never in October. September seeds get a good start and can take care of themselves; November seeds stay in the ground all winter and come up in spring; but October seeds come up too late to get hardened before cold weather, and they are apt to be killed. I miss Mr. Tong's contributions to garden lore. He used to say, "You had better ask me all of these things while you can, Elizabeth; I won't be here always to tell you." And I miss his enthusiasm. He was born in England and had an Englishman's love of plants. No other love is like it. He worked in nurseries until, in his old age, he had saved up enough for a little nursery of his own. If he made anything, it went into his iris collection. Always in all weathers he could be found hovering over his plants, except on the occasions when he went, scrubbed, brushed, and polished, to talk to the garden clubs. Once I asked to take some of his lists to a club in another town. He said "I guess it is all right for you to take them, Elizabeth, but I never do it myself. I don't want folks to think when I come to talk about plants, that I come to sell them."

Johnny jump-ups, *Viola tricolor*, once planted, seed themselves thereafter. On my records the earliest date for bloom is the fourth of February. By June they begin to bloom out, and even before that they get leggy. They will tolerate considerable shade and the meanest conditions. The prune purple of the flowers is the perfect color to contrast with spring yellows, and the dark velvet petals are effective with white. They bloom for weeks on end with the white flowers of the lacy, everblooming verbena of Southern gardens. This verbena is one of the best perennials for mild climates. If part of it gets killed in a severe winter, there is more than enough left to come back in the spring, covering twice as much ground as before.

In spring when visitors say, "What is that lovely—" I murmur "nemophila," without waiting to hear "—blue flower." For it is the one plant that moves people who can admire a flower without wanting to know its name, to seek an introduction. If pressed for a common name, I have to admit "baby blue-eyes." This is one of the earliest annuals, and one of the easiest, blooming lavishly in poor soil and in sun or part shade. With me it never self sows, perhaps because I pull up the plants before the seeds mature. I always sow seed in September, and unless the season is very late, the little plants begin to bloom in February when they are only an inch or so high, the right height for early bulbs. Later, with the tulips, they spread into tangled masses. Usually by May they are shabby and must be discarded. Because of their prostrate habit, nemophilas are most effective at the edge of a raised border, or on top of a wall. The flowers are the gentian blue of *Hyacinthus azureus*. They close after noon.

Following the advice of some arm-chair gardener, I first planted meadow-foam, *Limnanthes Douglasii*, as a "drought-proof annual for poor, dry places in the rockery." Planted in such a place in February, it bloomed in May and dried up almost before it bloomed. Later, when I learned that it grows in the West in marshes and wet meadows, I sowed it again (this time in the fall) in a damp place. Its culture should be obvious to anyone with a garden dictionary at hand, for the name means marsh flower. With moisture and an early start it bloomed in April, making a charming edging with the Ata-masco-lily from our own meadows. The Atamasco-lily, *Zephyranthes Atamasco*, will grow in drier places as well. It improves with cultivation. In rich, moist soil the stems sometimes reach a foot in height, and the flowers three inches in length. The bulbs multiply rapidly, and the clumps are exceedingly floriferous. This species often repeats in late summer and fall. The meadow-foam is low and prostrate, with crisp, yellow-green foliage and myriads of yellow and white flowers. The bloom lasts for several weeks. My first sowing has perpetuated itself. This is an annual to sow in place, but the small seedlings can be transplanted.

Another of the earliest annuals is the California-poppy, *Eschscholzia californica*. When it is sown early, the grey foliage of the seedlings is a pleasure through the winter, and the plants are in bloom before April. In checking my records I noticed that only those from September sowings bloom early and well. California-poppies reseed indefinitely, but they should not be allowed to do so for the plants become straggling and the flowers small. Seldom seen in other than the common yellow and orange forms, they come in scarlet, nopal red, Brazil red, rose, and cream, and in all sorts of fancy single, semi-double, and double flowers. These bloom later than the type. The flowers of Geisha are four-petalled, the petals curiously plaited in the center. They are cadmium orange with a scarlet reverse. The effect is orange in the forenoon, and scarlet in the afternoon when the flowers are closed. Enchantress is advertised as pink, and it is pink—a real rose that is repeated in larkspur. The flowers are large and semi-double.

Several spring annuals provide the blues that are rare in flowers. One is a species of vipers bugloss, *Echium plantagineum*, from southern Europe.[5] The flowers are a deep gentian blue with the characteristic pink tinge of the borage family when they are newly opened. This species makes a bulky plant to about two feet. It is much more floriferous than the vipers-

[5] This blue must be a selected form. The seeds came from California. Seeds from an eastern seedsman produced very poor red-violet flowers.

bugloss of fields and roadside, and less coarse. Another member of the borage family, the Chinese forget-me-not, *Cynoglossum amabile*, produces in May a mass of amparo blue that lasts through June. Seedlings spring up as soon as the bloom is past, and the new plants bloom through the summer.

Collomia biflora (*C. coccinea* in catalogues) is a pretty and easily raised annual from South America. It is the uncommon and intense pink that is a tint of pure red untinged by violet. Plants from fall-sown seed bloom from mid-April to June. They will grow in any soil, but they are taller in good soil where they reach a height of two feet. This is a sun-loving annual, but plants in part shade do well enough. It can be transplanted or sown where it is to grow.

There are a number of good spring annuals in the tints of red-violet. Among them are two catchflies. *Silene pendula*, the Mediterranean catchfly, has flowers in tints from Hermosa pink to rose pink. The only strain that I can lay my hands on has double flowers with fringed petals. This makes low compact plants with velvet foliage. September sowing produces bloom early in April; my later sowings have been unsuccessful. The seedlings transplant readily, even when they have reached a good size. This is a trait that pleases me well, for annuals are always coming up on top of other plants, or where their colors clash with those of their neighbors. It is such a satisfaction to be able to move them off to some other spot where there is an unfortunate gap in the border, and where they are in harmony with the prevailing colors. I had hoped this catchfly would perpetuate itself after the first sowing without my further effort, but that did not prove to be the case. The sweet William catchfly, *Silene Armeria*, is an old-fashioned annual that comes back year after year, and is one of the most useful annuals that one can have in a garden. It has this fault, that the flower-tipped branches are too heavy for the slender stalk, and the plant must be lightly staked or else planted where it will have the support of stronger plants. This spring I had bloom from mid-May to late June from seeds sown in October. In the borders the small flowers were a mist of the most delicate shell pink, shading to Tyrian pink and Tyrian rose. With the catchfly bloomed the slender, small-flowered gladiolus that grows in country gardens. This gladiolus is another of the lovely things that elude catalogues and circulate from neighbor to neighbor. You will find it in gardens whose roots are in the past, or sometimes in the farm market. It is probably a parent of modern forms. The flowers are of the tone politely called "rosy purple," but it has a definite garden value in spite of the color, and it is pleasing with the rose-colored catchfly. It blooms in May.

Centranthus macrosiphon is one of the easiest annuals to grow from seed. A five-cent package produced plants to fill all of the gaps in my borders, and to pass on to neighbors. They are fall sown for April bloom. The colors range from shell pink to Tyrian pink. The flowers are much like those of the perennial *Centranthus ruber*, but the foliage is different. The plants grow to a height of two feet, but they begin to bloom at a few inches, so they must not be set back too far in the border. They are easily transplanted. This is an annual to fall back on when seeds are not in the ground by the end of September, for late sowings are successful.

Pink hawks-beard, *Crepis rubra*, is a slender flower like a pale pink dandelion. It is worth having if planted as early as February, or better still in the fall. It blooms from mid-April to mid-June but will not tolerate heat. It is recommended for full sun and a dry soil, but it does not tolerate drought either. It must be sown where it is to bloom. This is a frail plant, to eighteen inches in height.

In late spring the annuals, particularly larkspur, are more important than perennials. Single larkspur blooms with the tall bearded iris, usually from the last of April. In good soil the plants reach a height of five feet and reseed indefinitely without deterioration. The magnificent stock-flowering forms are later. They come with the Japanese iris. These, too, grow to five feet when the soil is rich and moist. All larkspur must be sown in the fall; spring sowings are not at all successful.

Salvia Horminum var. Blue Beard is a showy annual sage that blooms all summer in more favorable climates, but must be grown here for late spring, from the middle of May to the end of June. It is the bright purple of the floral leaves that makes the display. This sage is best sown in the seed beds, then set out in the borders in early spring. It grows to three feet.

The large, delicately-colored flowers of the opium poppies, *Papaver somniferum*, are much to be desired where the heat is too great for the oriental varieties. They seed themselves very freely, and the bright flowers and grey leaves can be very effective if they are allowed to come up where they will and are weeded out where they are not wanted. I like the wide single flowers better than the shaggy, peony-like doubles. They come in many colors, but they can be acquired (as far as I know) only in mixture. I have gradually encouraged the shell pink and begonia that I like by rogueing the others. These are in a border with the rosy milfoil, *Achillea Millefolium rosea* (which I could not garden without), and the slender lavender spires of that weed, *Campanula rapunculoides*, and the grey-leaved artemisia Silver King. The campanula is too invasive to allow in good soil, but it is very useful for the shady end of a bed that terminates in an oak tree. The poppies are tall, three or four feet, and are to be kept to the back of the border. They do best when sown in the fall.

Fall-planted Shirley poppies bloom with tall bearded iris. The apricot tones are desirable, and one year I had some very large and tall single white ones that seeded themselves as readily as larkspur and bloomed a second season. The unconsidered use of scarlet field poppies has ruined the color effect of more gardens than any other flower except perhaps the orange forms of the oriental poppies, or tiger lilies.

Love-in-a-mist, *Nigella damascena*, is a late spring blue that seeds itself as readily as larkspurs do and blooms at the same time. It grows in sun, in any soil, and should be sown where it is to grow. Miss Jekyll, the best form, is a lovely pale blue, to eighteen inches in height.

Spring-Flowering Vines

Flowering vines that are native to us, and those borrowed from other places, add to the profusion of scent and color in spring.

The Cherokee rose, *Rosa laevigata*, is naturalized in the Far South, and it is hardy in the Middle South though the buds are sometimes caught when the springs are early, as are the buds of the lovely pink Cherokee, *R. anemonoides*. The enormous single flowers of this hybrid are the color of a wild rose. In favorable seasons both bloom in April with the tulips. The white Cherokee often blooms again in the fall. I have seen it very full of bloom in December. *R. bracteata*, the Macartney rose, blooms later—at the end of May—and escapes the cold. It blooms some through the summer, and I have seen flowers in November on the hedges in Chapel Hill. The large, white, single flowers are like the Cherokees. This is more of a shrub than a climber, but it will climb with support. Mermaid, a hybrid of Macartney's rose, has the long-blooming habit of the parent. After heavy bloom in May and June there are flowers at intervals throughout the summer and fall. This is the most beautiful rose in my garden. The single, creamy yellow, golden-stamened flowers are four inches across, and the foliage is the best of any climbing rose I know. The glossy leaves are resistant to disease. All of these roses are rampant. Do not put them in cramped quarters.

Rosa Banksiae has been in the South since 1860, when it was brought to Macon, Georgia. The fine pale leaves, and bunches of small, sweet, double, yellow flowers are on smooth, thornless canes. The flowers are sweetest early in the morning before the dew is off, or just at evening. In my garden the Banksia is twined on the summerhouse with *Akebia quinata*. When March is nearly over, and April is beginning, the pale yellow roses and the curious little mauve and maroon flowers of the vine bloom together. It is a combination to be recommended. The Banksias should not be much pruned because they bloom on old wood. Any pruning that is done should be undertaken immediately after the bloom is over.

The Climbing Pink Daily is one of the old-fashioned roses that is as much a part of the South as the Cherokees and Banksias. It blooms in profusion in the spring, sometimes as early as March, a little through the summer, and again in the fall. One year I picked a frosty bunch for Christmas. In the fall the flow-

ers are particularly charming. Their color is deeper than in the spring, and they do not open fully.

In April, woods and gardens are bright with the flowers of Carolina jessamine, *Gelsemium sempervirens*, and sweet with their fragrance. This is a vine hard to transplant, but once established in woods soil it will spread into a thick evergreen screen, all the more valuable because it will tolerate shade. Another evergreen vine from the woods blooms at high spring. This is the cross-vine, *Bignonia capreolata*. It is one of the limited number of climbers with persistent foliage that will cling to masonry without support. The large yellow trumpets open early in April; they are a tawny yellow. Two native honeysuckles bloom in April. One is the well known coral honeysuckle, *Lonicera sempervirens*, and the other is the beautiful and rare *L. flava*, a distinctly southern species that grows in Dr. Coker's garden.

Clematis crispa is a small-flowered southern species that is often found in old gardens, and is called "blue bell" by those who have long known and cherished the delicate tracery of the leaves and the charming shape of the nodding, dull-blue flowers. The flowers come into bloom very early—by mid-April—and continue into the summer. This clematis grows in swampy places along rivers, but it will grow in very dry soil. It is not easy to transplant from the wild, and the only one I have been able to get started is a seedling raised for me by Miss Janet Badger. Sometimes seedlings come up about the mother plant. The blue bell is a slight vine that can be used where other climbers would be too heavy.

Actinidia chinensis is a tender Chinese vine, hardy to Washington, with big, round, fuzzy leaves and creamy-white single flowers. It should be planted to grow overhead, otherwise the flowers are hidden by the leaves. The growth is rapid, ten feet in a season. It blooms early in May and is in bloom for two or three weeks. Full sun and a rich soil are recommended, but it will grow and flower anywhere, even in shade. The fruit is edible, but in order to produce it vines of both sexes must be planted.

The Chinese wisteria, *W. sinensis*, blooms in the South at high spring, when the dogwood, tulips, and purple and white iris are in flower. The exquisite white form is earlier than the purple; in some seasons the first flowers are killed by the cold. There is always some bloom later, but it is only in early seasons, when the fragile white flowers bloom before the leaves come out, that they are so very beautiful.

The little native *Wisteria frutescens* is not as showy as the oriental sorts. It is a slender vine blooming in May. The flowers are small and rather colorless, and in short racemes. It might find a place where heavier vines would not do.

Roses for the South

There was a time when gardens in the South were filled with charming old-fashioned roses with pleasant names and delightful perfume. Unchecked by the pruning shears, they grew to ample proportions and bloomed generously from spring to fall, without benefit of a relentless program of dusting, spraying, and mulching. Now that they have so nearly disappeared, rosarians are eagerly seeking to bring them back into favor. A great wail is going up for the lost Tea roses, the Moss roses, the Chinas, and the Bourbons. Many that have been pushed aside and forgotten are being brought out again and petted. The growers, as usual, are being blamed for having given them up when they were no longer in demand, but I think a little catalogue searching would bring to light as many as most of us have room for. They can still be picked up, one here and one there, in the southern nurseries, and a search in old gardens would probably reveal most of those that are missing. Almost any plant can be found in time if gardeners are eager enough to possess it. More often it is lack of appreciation rather than lack of available plant material that makes our borders so all-alike and devoid of charm. The reason for bringing back these early roses is that, in addition to their peculiar grace and wonderful fragrance, they are particularly well suited to our climate, more so than many of the modern roses.

In the old days, before they were discarded for the modern race of Hybrid Teas (which are far from being well adapted to growing conditions in the South), the Tea roses were great favorites. The Tea rose, or tea-scented rose, is so called because its odor is considered like the aroma of a very fine China tea. The loveliest of its varieties, and to me the loveliest of the roses in my garden, is the old-fashioned Duchesse de Brabant, a delicately scented and delicately tinted flower usually called "the Duchess" in these parts—though it needs to be distinguished by its full title for duchesses are common among roses. The small, cupped, pink flowers appear almost without interval from April to winter. When we first came to live in our house there was a rose that we called the "White Duchess" among those that we found in the garden. The creamy flowers, faintly flushed with pink, were particularly lovely in the fall. I cherished this rose above all things until suddenly, and for no reason except that it was so well liked, it died. Mrs. Lay says it was the variety Mrs. Joseph Schwartz, a name that I cannot find in the catalogues, but someday I shall see it again in a garden, and perhaps I shall be given a slip. Another delightful old Tea rose is Safrano, with its semi-double saffron-tinted flowers that smell of spice. In Georgia one grew at my grandmother's under the window where she sat with her sewing. It was a great favorite with her generation. Other yellow Teas are the citron-colored Alexander Hill Gray, the pale Isabella Sprunt, Lady Hillingdon, and the deep yellow Perle des Jardins. Among the pinks are Maman Cochet, Mme. Lombard, and Mrs. R. B. Cant. This last is not outstanding in spring when the modern roses are at their best, but in the fall the color deepens and the form improves. There is also a white Maman Cochet, and in the South the best loved white Tea rose is the creamy flowered Devoniensis, called with us the Magnolia Rose. Lady Hillingdon and Marie Van Houtte are especially endowed with the tea fragrance. Marie Van Houtte is a two-toned rose, the yellow petals tipped with pink. The merits of Tea roses are an endless profusion of bloom, resistance to disease, and a preference for a warm climate. Their great fault, a habit of hanging their heads, was one of the problems overcome by the delightful Elizabeth in her experiences in her German garden.[6] In order not to be obliged to go down on her knees to admire them (for Tea roses grow to a small size only, if they grow at all in cold climates), she ordered a hundred standards. "Not but what I entirely approve of kneeling before such perfect beauty," she explains, "only it dirties one's clothes. So I am going to put standards down each side of the wall under the south windows, and shall have the flowers on a convenient level for worship."

My favorites among the China roses are the Dailys. They have bloomed in the Longview garden for several generations, and I find their names in that delightful manual, *Parsons on the Rose*,[7] but they do not seem to be in the trade. Parsons classes them as China roses and describes the Daily Blush as the oldest of this type. The Daily Blush is a stiff, shrubby rose with glossy leaves and red buds that pale as they open. The Daily White is similar in form. These are tall roses. At Longview

[6] M. Arnim (Elizabeth), *Elizabeth and Her German Garden*, Philadelphia: Henry Altemus Co., 1899.
[7] By Samuel B. Parsons, New York: Orange Judd and Co., n.d.

the adorable dwarf *R. sanguinea* is called the Daily Red. This one is not uncommon in Southern gardens that have not discarded the old for the new. Mine came to me from the dooryard of a very old house in Eastern Carolina. The bunches of small, cupped flowers and dark buds are pretty with the fine dark-green leaves when they take on a reddish tint in the fall. Louis Philippe is another red rose of the China or Bengal type. It is still in most southern nursery collections and in most gardens in the Far South, where it is so common that it is referred to as the "cracker" rose—which is rather a comedown for a rose that has been named for a monarch. This is a strong grower, with large, double, globe-shaped flowers of a dark color.

The Moss rose, *Rosa centifolia* var. *muscosa*, or the chinquapin rose as we call it, came to me from a cousin's garden in Virginia. The funny little purplish pink flowers open from fuzzy buds that are supposed to look like moss. It makes a good-sized bush. There are numerous French hybrids of the Moss rose, some of them still in culture. One that particularly appeals to me on account of its name is called (in French) the hat of Napoleon.

Of course no amount of enthusiasm for old roses is going to lessen the popularity of the far more resplendent modern varieties. Although many of the Hybrid Teas are difficult to grow even under the most favorable circumstances, there are plenty that will flourish anywhere, even in our part of the country where circumstances are not at all favorable to the group in general. Among those that you will find over and over in gardens everywhere are the Pink Radiance, Mrs. Charles Bell, the lovely two-toned Betty Uprichard, Editor McFarland, Symphony, Killarney, Killarney Queen, and Pink Pearl. These are pink flowered. The Radiance roses are scorned by rose fanciers but no roses in my garden give more reward for less effort. The Pink and Red Radiance are not very choice perhaps, but Mrs. Charles Bell is exquisite. Killarney and Killarney Queen I have had for many years, and shall have always because of the slender buds. The Hybrid Teas are weak in yellows, but those who want yellow roses should try the Duchess of Wellington, Mrs. E. P. Thom, and Mrs. Pierre du Pont. Joanna Hill is good as to flower but poor as to foliage. The good reliable reds are that perennial favorite, Etoile de Hollande, Ami Quinard, Red Radiance (but this is not so very red), and National Flower Guild. The best whites are Caledonia, Kaiserin Auguste Viktoria, Nuntius Pacelli, and White Killarney.

Stratford is a recent Hybrid Tea that has been bred for the South by crossing the tender Maréchal Niel with La France. It makes a very large bush that should be allowed space for growth and should not be cut back to fit cramped quarters. It is free of disease and has the fragrance of the old roses.

The easily grown Polyantha type is even better in the South than in the North. Except for Cecile Brunner, the sweetheart rose, I always disliked the original Baby Ramblers with bunches of horrid little flowers in harsh colors—particularly that dreadful orange one that fades so badly. But I like the new Floribundas. They are something entirely different and very delightful. In the Test Garden of the Garden Club of Virginia a number of varieties are being tried and are doing very well. For the most part they are taller than the old varieties, but Dagmar Späth, one of the most charming of all, grows only a foot high and makes a splendid edging plant. The flowers are large for Polyanthas, very white, and semi-double. They bloom steadily over a long period. Mrs. R. M. Finch, a semi-double pink of a delicate color, is one of a number of roses of Australian origin that Mr. McFarland thinks would be especially good for our section. Another charming Floribunda is the pink Gruss an Aachen, with large flowers of a wonderful color. The name of Snowbank is misleading; the flowers are pink-tinged at first, and afterward pale to a cream color. Donald Prior and Betty Prior are enchanting single-flowered Floribundas. The first is a bright red, and the second is in two tones of pink, the reverse of the petals a shade deeper than the inside.

An Introduction to Summer

ost Southerners
need an introduc-
tion to their gardens
in summer. I think they would be pleased with them if they
could once break with the tradition of abandoning the borders
to weeds when the flare of spring has passed. To me summer
is a season for taking delight in a garden, for there is no time
when it is more inviting than in the early freshness that pre-
cedes the heat of the day, or the cool twilight and fragrant
darkness that follow it. We can have bloom in summer if we
want it, but we must plan for it and work for it. Some of the
loveliest shrubs bloom then, some of the rare bulbs, and some
of the gayest annuals and perennials. But we must discover
the summer flowers that flourish through heat, drought, and
humidity.

Drought is a problem that must be faced sooner or later, for
weeks when there is too much rain are sure to be followed by
weeks when there is none. There are two ways to face the rainless weeks. One way is to water, and the other is merely not to.
I have decided upon both. Certain borders are devoted to perennials that need moisture. Here are mallows, crinums, bergamot, garden phlox, helenium. These are given an occasional
soaking with the hose in dry weather. Other borders are kept
for bulbs that need a summer baking. These are planted with
drought resistant annuals for summer display and left unwatered no matter how long we are without rain. At least it is my
intention to leave them unwatered. Sometimes, when they get

very parched, I cannot resist seeing them revive under the nozzle.

In July or August when the sun is very hot, the weeds very tall, and the ground very hard, I may wish that my garden were smaller—in which case I should begin in the fall to enlarge it. And I often wish that I had not inherited my garden as it is, in the English tradition of perennial borders and turf (so-called) and forest trees. I think if I were beginning anew I would like to lay it out in the manner of gardens in Southern France, in a formal pattern of shrubs and flowers and pebbled squares enclosed by walls and shaded by lindens: the sort of garden that is made for hot weather by wise people who adapt themselves to their surroundings; the sort of garden that Professor Saint Peter made for himself in a prairie town, in which he could comfortably spend long summers when, released from earning his daily bread, he turned to his work on the Spanish Adventurers.

Day-Lilies

In early summer southern gardens come into a glory that has come to them only in recent years with the development of the day-lily. It is seldom that the perennial of the day proves the perennial of all others for the South, but this is one that thrives in all climates. We are particularly fortunate in a long season that allows for a second, and even a third crop of flowers from some of the persistent bloomers. These tall hybrids begin to bloom late in May. By the middle of July they are on the wane. In my garden they are gone by the first of August. The flowers range in color from the palest canary, through peach and apricot, deep yellow and orange, to rich reds.

Always when a flower becomes the favorite, the market is flooded with innumerable varieties, comparatively few of which are either distinct or superior. Among the really fine day-lilies it is difficult to make a choice, but most of us will want a variety in form, color, and height.

There are any number of good varieties with flowers of the

medium yellow that is the light cadmium of Ridgway. Ophir is the most generous with bloom. This summer I counted thirty-two stalks on a four-year clump. The bloom lasts from early June well into July. The flowers are large and well formed, the stalks four feet high and well branched. The flowers of Golden West are even larger, and are of a fine form and substance. They are a little more lemon in tone. This variety has a very long period of bloom. Amaryllis is earlier than these, and not so tall. With me it is one of the best bloomers; beginning late in May, and continuing for two months, it outlasts some of the later varieties. The large frilly flowers are very fragrant, and there are many of them. Florham, an old variety that is a great bloomer and increases rapidly, is the best day-lily to plant in quantity. It is like Amaryllis with its frilled petals and delightful fragrance, but it is not so good in form and substance, nor so large in size.

Hyperion still holds its own among the pale day-lilies, in spite of the seasons that have passed since its introduction in 1925 and the numbers of varieties that have been brought out more recently. It is one of the late varieties; usually it is not in bloom before the middle or last of June. It blooms long and well, established clumps having over twenty stalks. The flowers are large and wide open and slightly irregular. The fluted crystalline petals are an even strontian yellow, becoming greenish at the base. Sunny West is superior in size and substance—and also much more expensive. It is late in bloom. The pale yellow Queen of May (van Veen) is low in stature and large in flower. The flowers, five inches long, are of a soft color that is between lemon chrome and light cadmium, with tones of both. The stalks are two-and-a-half feet long. The bloom is for the first two weeks of June. This variety is neither vigorous nor profuse, but the flowers are distinct and lovely.

Many of the pale yellows are night blooming. Night bloomers are, I think, particularly desirable for the South. Fading is the great drawback to all day-lilies with us. Except on grey days the fresh morning colors are soon streaked by the sun. Those that open in the later afternoon, when the garden is cool and fresh, are still lovely the next morning. When they open in the half light the pale, luminous flowers of Calypso are like the color of street lights before nightfall. Lemona is another name used for more than one plant. As I have it, the flowers are funnel-shaped. They are of a heavy substance that withstands strong sunlight better than any variety I know. They open at dusk and do not fade until the following evening. All night-bloomers are said to do this, but Lemona is the only one in my garden that does. In spite of the heavy substance the flowers are of a fine texture; they are of medium size, and the stems are of medium height.

Chrome Orange and Ajax are forerunners of the other orange day-lilies in season. The distinct and starry flowers are a pleasing variation from the usual form. The segments are narrow and wide apart. Chrome Orange is of southern origin, coming from Florida where it blooms in February with Mr. Hayward. In Virginia, in Elizabeth Rawlinson's garden, it blooms in early June, and Ajax is in bloom at the same time. Both are a deep yellow that is almost orange. Pure orange is a rare color in day-lilies, even among the newer hybrids. Most of the so-called oranges are really cadmium yellow. In fact, the only flower that I have ever found which checks with the orange of Ridgway is a tall, unnamed seedling that was in bloom early in August in Mrs. Nesmith's trial garden. Goldeni, an early bloomer of medium height, is almost pure orange, but there is a hint of ochre in the recurved petals of the half open flowers. The flowers of J. R. Mann are of the soft rich tint called capucine orange. They are small, funnel shaped, and of medium height. They appear early, usually the last of May. Golden Dream and Radiant are cadmium yellow, though they are described as orange, and seem orange among less intense yellows. Golden Dream is four feet tall with flowers of medium size, good substance, and rich perfume. Radiant is shorter, with slender flowers that are never wide open. Golden Scepter is the same color as these, but the flowers are larger and there are more to a stalk. Midas is cadmium orange, one of the most brilliant of the orange tones. The flowers are large, of good form and substance, and bloom rather early in the season. Another unnamed seedling that caught my eye in Mrs. Nesmith's trial beds is Ridgway's Mars orange, a dark bright shade with some red in it.

The first fulvous day-lilies, and those with fulvous markings, Cinnabar, Gypsy, Cressida, and the like, were very disappointing with their dirty orange tones and smudges of cinnamon. More recent introductions in nasturtium, burnt sienna, and Brazil red—patterned gaily in orange, madder, and maroon—are the most resplendent colors in the garden. These rich dark shades of red and brown provide contrast in value with the pale tones. Mikado is the best of the early fulvous hybrids, and still stands out in any collection. The shallow flowers of glistening cadmium yellow are marked with a mahogany half-halo. They last more than six weeks, from the first of June past the middle of July, and often repeat later in the season. A good clump produces more than twenty stalks. Mikado is of medium height and is not vigorous enough to crowd out other perennials—one of the faults of day-lilies. The more recently introduced Linda is marked with a brighter, more reddish zone on the petals. It is taller and more erect than Mikado and is later in bloom. Mrs. Nesmith's little Moonray has the same dark zones on a pale background. This is a charming, small-flowered day-lily with many flowers on short, slight stems. In delicacy and grade it is quite apart from all others. Bagdad is brilliantly colored, with wide-open flowers of a dark red-orange marked with a reddish brown that is in sharp contrast to the orange throat. It blooms in June. Chengtu is one of the bright fulvous day-lilies that stands out in the collection at the New York Botanical Garden. This is a Chinese species that is late in bloom; unfortunately, it is expensive. The flowers are a pale orange with a bright yellow throat and zones of Brazil red. Theron is a dark mahogany red. It is the darkest flower I have seen.

To me the pinks are most disappointing. Everybody agrees that the original fulva rosea is very fine, but I have yet to see a pink hybrid worth a second glance. Perhaps I would think better of them if I grew them myself. I have often noticed that a flower in my own border is more pleasing than the same flower in some one else's border.

In my garden, day-lily bloom ends with Mrs. W. H. Wyman,

Bay State, and Margaret Perry. Bay State is rather dwarf, with funnel-shaped flowers the color of tritonias. This blooms from early July to the end of the month, and may repeat in August and September. Margaret Perry is like *Hemerocallis fulva*, but neither so coarse nor so vigorous, and the flowers are smaller and paler. It is very acceptable in the borders as other varieties fade, and it has a long period from the end of June to the first of August. Every year, later blooming day-lilies are added to the growers' lists, extending a season already long. One of the most recent late bloomers is Chandra, an improved Mrs. W. H. Wyman. In Mrs. Nesmith's garden the much-branched and many-flowered stalks are nearly five feet high. The flowers are pale yellow. Chandra is effective and expensive. High Boy, another tall and late pale yellow with stalks five feet high, is within the price range of the general gardener. I thought when I saw the large pale flowers in the New York Botanical Garden in early August that they would be interesting in contrast with the dark tones of Theron and Chengtu. These last were still in bloom at that time.

Hemerocallis multiflora is the latest of the species. This delightful dwarf, much used in hybridizing because of its late and numerous flowers, is somewhat like the early flowering day-lilies, low in stature, and its stiff stalks crowded with a multitude of small yellow flowers. This is the only day-lily I know that blooms in North Carolina in August, with the exception of the repeaters.

Hemerocallis bloom best in full sun, but they tolerate shade. Shade is recommended for some of the varieties that fade badly. Hemerocallis will grow anywhere, and will endure any amount of drought, but they need a deep, rich, moisture-holding soil for full bloom and large flowers. A good hosing before and during the blooming season helps. Even when there is rain, the ground beneath the heavy foliage is apt to be as dry as dust. A mulch of cow manure in the fall and a commercial fertilizer after blooming are the best fertilizers. Dividing the clumps every third year seems to be the rule, but I find that they continue to improve if left undisturbed.

The Garden Club of North Carolina has recognized the importance of day-lilies to our section by establishing a Hemerocallis test garden in Winston-Salem with Mrs. F. F. Bahnson as chairman. Mrs. Bahnson has already one hundred and twelve varieties, of which she is checking the date of bloom and learning the habits. She has also three hundred seedlings of her own. Some of the seedlings have already bloomed and have shown interesting variations from the established types.

For several years Miss Nannie Holding has been taking notes on some of Mr. Betcher's hybrids in her garden in Wake Forest. When I went to see them near the middle of July, the best bloom was over, but I was impressed anew by the size and beauty of Hyperion, much finer in her garden than in mine. The variety in Miss Nannie's collection that appealed to me most was a rather low growing and late blooming one called Golden Eye. The flowers are small, but they are of a graceful shape and altogether charming. At the end of the day they had held their color better than any of the others; they were very near Ridgway's orange. This is an abundant bloomer, which in mass gives as gay an effect as any day-lily of that color that I have ever seen.

To Bloom with Day-Lilies

The day-lilies Ophir, Amaryllis, Golden Dream, Hyperion, Bay State, J. R. Mann, and Mrs. Wyman bloom in June and July in my garden, in a border of spurge and white phlox mixed with the deep blue of veronica and the orange of the butterfly-weed and tritonia. These with other yellow and white perennials, and the cosmos Orange Flare, are a bright and cool scheme for early summer, and one easy to effect and maintain. Early in June there are masses of calliopsis which are discarded as the phlox comes on. Gaillardia Sun God repeats the golden yellow of Ophir and Amaryllis. This summer there is a tall mullein at the back of the border. It is a seedling of last year's *Verbascum densiflorum* which must not have been *V. densiflorum*, as that species is said to be sterile. This is the contrary way of garden plants. When you get a good thing there is always some mystery as to its identity. And a good thing this mullein is, blooming the first year from seed, and having a long season from early June to late July. It is as tall as the Olympic mullein (to seven feet), well branched, and has the same charming, lemon yellow flowers.

Lepachys pinnata is a Western coneflower that comes into bloom between the twentieth and twenty-fourth of June. It is interesting in checking the garden records to see how punctual some plants are, while others may vary six weeks in the date of the first bloom. In four years this coneflower has varied four days, and for four years it has bloomed steadily through July, becoming more decorative each season. The large flowers, with narrow, lemon yellow rays drooping from dark brown cones, have a grace that is lacking in the coarser rudbeckias to which they are related. The tall stalks, scantily furnished with pinnately-cut grey leaves, come up between the day-lily foliage and take up almost no room. After the bloom is over, the stalks can be cut back, leaving places for late summer and fall flowers. To be out of the way when out of bloom is one of the most desirable traits a perennial can have.

The various forms of *Chrysanthemum maximum* bloom with the day-lilies. Alaska daisies come first, early in June, two weeks ahead of the old-time Shasta daisies. The glistening white flowers are large, the stems short and stocky. With me, these last only for the season. The very dwarf Arctic daisy, *C. arcticum*, is more permanent, but the flowers are small, no bigger than those of field daisies. This fall-flowering species blooms late in June in North Carolina. In spite of its provenance, it does well here if it can be agreeably settled in a spot not too hot and dry.

For us the best border veronica is Blue Spires. It blooms from mid-May through July, then repeats later in the season. A cross between *V. spicata* and *V. longifolia subsessilis*, it has the good points of both parents and the faults of neither. It is an erect plant to two feet, with six-inch spikes of the deep blue-violet of the balloon-flower. *Platycodon grandiflorus*, the balloon-flower, is one of the standard perennials that will not do well for me. I see fine tall clumps in other gardens, but mine are always spindling. Once entrenched, it improves with time and should be one of the most permanent plants in the borders. It is certainly one of the most beautiful when well grown.

The fernleaf yarrow, *Achillea filipendulina*, one of the dependables for early summer, is a coarse four-foot plant that has a place in wide borders if it is kept with the lemon yellows and away from the orange yellows that make its old-gold flowers look dull. The golden Marguerite, *Anthemis tinctoria*, is another coarse perennial of this season. It is best in full sun and poor soil. The flowers are lemon chrome in the type, and lemon yellow in the variety Moonlight.

For moist soil the Japanese loosestrife, *Lysimachia clethroides*, and day-lilies are a good combination for June and July. In dry soils the long white spikes of the loosestrife are stunted. Where there is moisture, the very white flowers and the fresh, dark, oval leaves stand up well under hot sun. It is amazing that such a good flower is so little known. I had never seen it until I came across it in an exhibit at the Virginia lily show, and I immediately introduced it into my garden.

Another handsome early-summer perennial that is seen seldom in catalogues, and almost never in gardens, is sidalcea. The lavender tones of the garden forms of *Sidalcea malvaeflora* are pretty when planted with pale day-lilies, or with the great lavender-tinged trumpets of regal lilies. It is in England that these natives of America have been appreciated as border plants. Rose Queen towers to four-and-a-half feet. The slender stalks are crowded at the tops with small flowers mallow-like in form and mallow purple in color. The prodigal bloom lasts but a short time, perhaps two weeks. After that the stalks can be cut back to the base to give place to later perennials. Rosy Gem is half as tall, with flowers of eupatorium purple. Sidalceas grow in sun or light shade. They need a rich moist soil, and a thorough drenching with the hose, if it is dry when they are in bloom.

The day-lily Calypso might be planted where the pale citron flowers show against the chartreuse foam of *Thalictrum glaucum*. This magnificent meadow-rue, with its almost five-foot flower stalks and its excellent foliage that is decorative nearly the year around, is the only one—with the exception of the natives—that I have been able to do anything with. It likes good soil, drainage, and part shade.

Day-lilies and torch-lilies are stylish together. I can think of no more brilliant colors for June than masses of a golden day-lily such as Amaryllis or Florham with the glowing red-orange of *Kniphofia Pfitzeri* and the deeper red of *Lilium elegans*. *Kniphofia Pfitzeri* is almost everblooming with us, sending up bright stalks at intervals after its main bloom in June, and repeating in the fall. Towers of Gold blooms the first of July. This magnificent torch-lily sends up four-foot stalks of flowers that come out a pale greenish color, warming to picric yellow, and shading to cinnamon pink at the tip of the spike. An established clump sends up ten or more stalks in July, and as many in the fall. Dwarf hybrids of the same color but less than two feet in height bloom from May to October.

And there are lilies to bloom with hemerocallis. The tiger lilies, *Lilium tigrinum*, grow like weeds and increase so enormously that there are quantities to bloom in the borders with the rufous orange of the hemerocallis Margaret Perry and the spotted yellow ochre of the ephemeral blackberry-lily, *Belamcanda chinensis*, with enough left over to fill all dark corners with grenadine red. But Violet Walker has ordered this mosaic spreading species out of the garden, and, such is my respect for Violet, mine are already gone. In their places are species more delicate in form and color, but not so robust in constitution. *L. Hansonii* blooms early in June, with thin leaves in whorls along the slender stems and pale, nodding flowers of the turks-cap type. It is one of the easier species; it grows in shade in any well drained soil, and being of the stem-rooting group should be planted at a depth of ten inches. *L. Willmottiae*, blooming in mid-June, follows Hanson's lily, and is followed in the middle of July by *L. Henryi*. These three pinky orange species make a nice succession through the day-lily period. Willmott's lily did not persist with me beyond the first season, but once established—it is not one of the difficult sorts—it spreads by stolons to make a wide clump. The dark-spotted bittersweet orange of the flowers is a charming color. The slender stems must be staked to keep them from bending with the weight of the bloom. This species needs some shade and a leafy, moisture-holding soil. The bulbs should be set six inches deep. Dr. Henry's lily is one of the good and permanent species for all gardens. It will grow in sun or shade, prefers a heavy soil, likes lime but is not dependent upon it, and is stem rooting. The salmon orange flowers are on slender, four-foot stalks that require staking. The bright grenadine tints of these three species are off color with orange and golden yellow day-lilies, but they are delightful with some of the fulvous varieties.

In Mrs. Lybrook's rock garden in Winston-Salem I came upon the Roan lily, *Lilium Grayi*, just coming into bloom on the seventh of June, in a very flourishing condition. I asked her how she grew it, and she said that it had looked sick in the spring so she gave it some cow manure and a five-seven-five fertilizer and cotton-seed meal. The Roan lily is a southern species growing in mountain meadows in North Carolina, Virginia, and Tennessee. The bell-like flowers shade from yellow at the throat to coral red and dragons-blood red; they are spotted with maroon.

Phlox and Bergamot

Garden phlox is the foundation of perennial borders in June and July, and its scent is the scent of summer. The plan for summer borders begins with the choice of phlox and proceeds with the choice of perennials to plant with it. What to plant with the rosy red tones (usually described as salmon), the gayest of all garden colors and the most difficult to use skillfully, is an old problem. For me it has been solved by the introduction of *Monarda didyma*, the old-fashioned wild bergamot, in its original spectrum red, and in the pink garden forms. The pink varieties are in the trade with names such as Salmonea and Salmon Queen, but they are not salmon. Like the so-called salmon phlox they are tints of almost pure red, with the vaguest hint of purple. Salmon Queen, wild bergamot, and a color form acquired as Sunset and described as mahogany, but almost as red as the type, are striking in combination with phlox such as R. P. Struthers, Rheinlander, Thor, and Lilian. The first are good old kinds that prevail. Lilian is the best pink phlox that I know, far better than Columbia which has proved anything but a success with me. Columbia lacks vigor; the bloom is poor, and it is far from disease proof. Lilian is much more thrifty. It has large trusses of a tint of pure red that is a little paler than begonia rose. In my garden, phlox and bergamot and a pretty pink balsam in the foreground are frosted with the spreading branches of the silver-leaved artemisia. In a wide border, mallow marvels can be planted behind the bergamots, to bloom with them in early July and to replace them later in the month. The very tall bergamot, between four and five feet in good soil, must be massed at the back of the border with the phlox Rheinlander. It does not need staking. The bergamot Salmon Queen is one of the most exquisite garden colors. And unlike other delicately colored perennials it is not delicate in constitution, but increases almost as rapidly as the type. The red of the type is beautiful in mass with the tall white phlox Von Lassburg, or planted to itself with a green background. It lasts longer in shade; it has been in bloom for six weeks in the copse with ferns and shrubs. One of the most delightful qualities of bergamot is its refreshing odor. Picking the flowers, or merely brushing against the leaves, is as reviving in hot weather as a whiff of *eau-de-cologne*.

The red-violet bergamots are equally lovely with red-violet phlox. I have been making a collection of these by begging in gardens and buying in market. The market stalls are a fruitful source of plant material and information. I have collected color forms of phlox purple, rosolane purple, aster purple, amaranth, and daphne pink. These are pretty with the pale lavender and bright magenta seedlings that spring up in gardens where phlox is planted, and with the almost true purple flowers of the phlox Caroline Vandenburg. The last is not a vigorous nor a permanent variety, but it is a very handsome one. It blooms late in the season. The light mallow purple of the everblooming aster, Barr's Pink, is good with phlox and bergamot in these colors.

There is also a white form of *Monarda didyma*, with flowers smaller than those of the type but very numerous. They are tinged with lavender, and they tone in with lavender flowers but look dirty with pure white ones. This white bergamot blooms earlier than the color forms.

Bergamot, phlox, and mallows need a deep, moist soil and a weekly hosing in the blooming season. Without water they are not worth having, but with it they bloom long and well. Monarda must be kept from crowding out the other plants, but this is easy to do because the shallow roots are easily pulled up. It should be divided frequently, and the time to do this is in the spring. If phlox is allowed to go to seed, strong-growing magenta seedlings will soon crowd out the good forms.

Long-Blooming Perennials

Certain perennials are almost everblooming in these parts, but they are not the ones usually described in the catalogues as "covered with flowers from spring to frost." Many plants that bloom continuously where there is more rain and less heat have only a short season with us. Others have a short season in colder climates, but bloom on and on where the summers are long and hot. Planted among less lasting, and perhaps more striking flowers, they are there to fall back on in the inevitable periods when there is little else.

Several salvias are long in bloom. The autumn sage, *S. Greggii*, native to southern Texas and northern Mexico, and offered by Texas growers, flowers from April to November. It is a shrubby perennial, to three feet or more, with flowers of the bright shade of rosy purple admired by the Victorians but not much in favor now. The color varies however, and I have seen flowers of a striking shade of rose red. The variety *alba* is very fine, with pure white flowers larger than those of the type. The autumn sage grows best in good soil and in full sun, but it shows a willingness to flower in the shade and under adverse conditions. This sage is hardy to northern Virginia.

The gentian sage, *Salvia patens*, is a tender perennial from the mountains of Mexico. It is as much bluer than other blue sages as mountain skies are bluer than other skies. This species can be grown as an annual where it is not hardy. With me it is perennial but not long lived. Not one of the drought-resistant sages, it requires a rich, moisture-holding soil. It is a small plant with me, to a foot and a half, and not very spreading. The large flowers are a brilliant smalt blue, with darker spurs. They last but a day, and appear at intervals from June to mid-November. The flowers are more beautiful than those of any other species, but I have not found them very abundant.

The salvia most commonly planted is the mealycup sage, *S. farinacea*, another Texas species. It does well only in sun and where it has room to spread over several feet, and it thrives in poor soil. The silvered blue spires make a good showing over a very long period, from early June to November. I know of no better perennial where continuous bloom without much effort is required. It grows to four feet high. The far more beautiful *Salvia azurea* is a native of the lower South that blooms from early July to fall and grows in dry soil. It is an erect perennial, to four feet, with large flowers of a pale, corn-flower blue.

Some years ago I found a dainty white flower, much like a double feverfew, in Catherine Taylor's garden in Greensboro. She had it from Dreer as a Double Japanese Aster. Dreer, upon being questioned, replied that they had it from Japan, and were not able to identify it positively. They said they had dropped it from their plant list because they sold so few. So it is up to me to keep it in gardens. The plant I brought home from Catherine's increased rapidly, and I press divisions upon every one who shows a slight interest. This nice little aster, or whatever it is, comes into bloom about the first of June, and from then on it is starred with small pure white flowers. The foliage is very fine; the compact, finely-branched plants grow about two feet high. If the spent stalks are cut back to the roots, new ones will replace them very quickly. This is better than shearing to keep the plant in bloom. It likes full sun and prefers some moisture.

In my garden I am glad to have a plant that blooms so faithfully from June through August as *Achillea nitida*, and one that keeps such good foliage in trying seasons. It is similar to *A. Ptarmica* and its garden forms but is more satisfactory for this part of the country. I suppose *nitida* refers to the shining leaves. They are very narrow and finely toothed, dark green and glossy. The flowers are white rayed with bisque centers; they are set in loose corymbs. The somewhat sprawling plant reaches a height of more than three feet. It is something of a spreader and might be too much so in a rich spot. It will tolerate any amount of drought.

Here, the New England aster, *A. novae-angliae*, does not wait for September to bloom, but begins early in June and goes on steadily till very late fall. The large, intense violet-purple flowers of the type, and the light mallow purple flowers of Barr's Pink (which is not at all pink) supply continuous color if the plants are sheared occasionally. These grow to between three and four feet, and they may spread out over more space than they deserve. Keep this in mind in borders where there are less vigorous perennials.

The cornflower aster, *Stokesia laevis*, is one of the most satisfactory perennials for the South, but with me it does not bloom all summer as reported. It blooms profusely in June and repeats a little in the fall. In the wild it grows in moist places from South Carolina to Florida. In the garden I find it does best in a light dry soil that is not too rich. The wisteria-colored flowers, more like cornflowers than asters, are two-and-a-half inches across. The plants are low growing with somewhat procumbent stems and long, smooth, grey leaves in basal rosettes.

Much has been written about bringing the butterfly-weed, *Asclepias tuberosa*, from roadsides to gardens, but it is seldom seen in the borders. I think this is due to the difficulty of transplanting the long tuberous roots. Plants will not live if the roots are cut. Once established, they are permanent and entirely satisfactory. One of the best points in favor of the butterfly-weed as a garden plant is that it blooms early in June with the day-lilies (long before it is in bloom in the fields), and repeats in August when the departure of the day-lilies has left the borders much in need of a fresh gay color. The flowers are mikado orange. They seem to me much redder in the fields than in cultivation. The plants do not take up much room, and the clean foliage makes a good appearance between the blooming periods. Flowering spurge, *Euphorbia corollata*, is another long-blooming native (June to August) that we do not use properly. This is also hard to establish, but once settled is there for a life-time. The white flower-like involucres last almost indefinitely, leaning over lower plants in a cool white spray.

A mist of sea-lavender, *Limonium latifolium*, in the market stall in July reminded me that I had had none for years. And reminded me of the flower markets in Barcelona where it was sold with belladonna-lilies, *Amaryllis Belladonna*.[1] The pale pink lilies bloomed once in my garden in mid-August, but only once. The foliage reappears year after year, but there are no flowers after the first season.

The native bleeding-heart, *Dicentra eximia*, is subject to one of the dreadful bacterial wilts that are prevalent in the South, and in my garden in particular. There seems to be nothing to do about it. I was in despair at one time, but a number of wilt-resistant individuals seem to survive their weaker companions. Once healthy plants of the bleeding-heart become established, they are dependable and almost everblooming. They improve yearly and become fine ferny clumps. They bloom first toward the end of March, and from then until winter there are sprays of drooping, opalescent flowers.

Three verbenas have taken a very important place in the dry sunny part of my garden where the soil is somewhat poor, kept so for plants averse to manure. *Verbena bonariensis*, native to Buenos Aires, is an escape in the Lower South, where it has become a conspicuous roadside weed. It came to me from Violet Walker. Plants are very easily raised from seed, and seeds are available. This is a tender perennial that can be raised as

[1] Now *Callicore rosea*. See *Herbertia*, ed. Hamilton P. Traub, Vol. IV (1938), p. 109.

an annual, but only second-year plants make an adequate display. It self-sows abundantly. The plants are coarse but colorful in mass, and to be relied upon in time of drought. The long slender stalks are scantily furnished with the wrinkled leaves, and topped by the small heads of hortense violet flowers. They are to four feet. *Verbena venosa*, also native to Argentina, is another tender perennial recommended as an annual, but blooming little the first season. Established plants bloom from early May to late fall. They are perfectly hardy in piedmont North Carolina—sometimes a little too much so, for they are strong growers, and the prostrate plants spread rapidly. The flowers are larger than those of *V. bonariensis*, and of a deep lasting petunia violet that does much for sun-faded beds. The trailing moss verbena, *V. erinoides*, is perennial with me. It blooms well as an annual, and reseeds. The light green, finely cut foliage is cool to look at, and the white or intense violet flowers bloom from May into winter.

These two low-growing verbenas, the trailing heliotrope, leadwort, and the poppy-mallow are splendid edging plants for trying summers; they are good to fall back upon wherever bare ground needs to be covered. From April to November the trailing heliotrope, *Heliotropium amplexicaule*, found in southern gardens, produces scentless lavender flowers, freely in full sun, not so freely in shade. A nuisance if allowed above its humble station as a filler in difficult places, it is one of the flowers always available to make up a small bouquet. I cannot remember ever having seen this species in nursery lists, but it goes from garden to garden. The lively smalt blue of leadwort, *Ceratostigma plumbaginoides*, is the perfect contrast for the lemon and orange of *Zinnia linearis*. It blooms a little in June, more in July and August, and a little in September. With cool weather the leaves turn a pretty reddish color. The foliage is excellent in shady places, but the flowers are few. The poppy-mallow, *Callirhoë involucrata*, of the prairies and mesas of the middle western states is a trailing plant with mallow-like flowers to two-and-a-half inches across, and with grey veined, deeply cleft leaves. It blooms in spring and summer. In bright sunlight the red-violet of the flowers—brilliant in contrast with the white centers—is a strident color. In shade it acquires a translucent quality that is very lovely. The plants are not long lived, but there are always new seedlings coming along.

Gardens that are not watered can still be gay in dry summers if one is satisfied with coarse perennials such as the false sunflower of the eastern states and some of the gaillardias. No other flowers bloom so long or so well under all conditions. The false sunflower, *Heliopsis helianthoides* var. *Pitcheriana*, is a rather sprawling plant, to about three feet in height. From early summer into the fall it is covered with wide, cadmium yellow daisies. The toughest and most floriferous of the gaillardias is the dwarf form called the Goblin. Plants from seed in no way resemble the neat little mounds pictured in Thompson and Morgan's catalogue as desirable for rock gardens, but they are more compact and presentable than the common blanket flower. Spring sowings produce bloom late in the summer. Second-year plants begin to bloom in May and are never without flowers from then until frost.

Annuals for Summer

The failure of certain plants in my garden is put down to the climate, and not to any fault of my own. And then I am undeceived. For years I struggled with hunnemannias. I planted seeds in fall and spring, both early and late. I scarified them. I tried different sources. I got Mr. Tong to start plants in the greenhouse. (These did not survive transplanting.) After that I gave up. Then one summer morning I came upon hunnemannias in a flower stall outside the market. They were fresh with dew, pale and delicately frilled, wreathed with fine green leaves, and altogether lovely. The colored woman who kept the stall said she had grown them. I asked when the seeds were planted, and she said she couldn't remember rightly, but she thought it was at the end of March or the beginning of April. She had been cutting flowers for market since early June. "They won't grow for me," I said, "I reckon colored people just grow flowers better than white people." "And I was saying to a lady yesterday," she countered, "that you all grow things better than we can . . . you have more to do with."

The summer adonis, *A. aestivalis*, is another enchanting annual that I have tried for years to get beyond the seedling stage. I found it in bloom in July in Dr. Burlage's garden in Chapel Hill, grown for its medicinal value. The plants were spindling and the flowers small, but he said I should have seen them last season. The garden value of this low growing, fine leaved annual is in the lovely burnt orange color of the anemone-like flowers. There is also an autumn adonis, *A. annua*, with which I have been equally unsuccessful. I must get Dr. Burlage to try that.

Fortunately all annuals are not so adverse to my borders, for those that thrive are essential to summer bloom. A long season requires continual cutting back, pulling up, and setting out. Annuals fill the gaps where other plants have bloomed and departed. Many of them are of value because of their indifference to heat and drought. Those that I depend upon are the ones that seed themselves and come back year after year as faithfully as perennials, and those that come so easily from seed that even the laziest summer gardener cannot object to the slight effort of sowing them.

The prickly-poppies, along with cosmos Orange Flare, marigolds, and white cleome are the main dependence. The poppies flourish under the blazing sun and also on overcast days when heat is spread like a wet blanket. The crinkled petals and the marbled leaves are unwilted at noon. Their season is from early May to late fall. Sometimes the flowers escape the first touch of frost and bloom into November. Prickly-poppies come in white and two colors, a pale yellow and a dark dull red. The white, *Argemone grandiflora*, is the best. The flowers are very large, to four inches and a half across, and the plants are between three and four feet wide. If the first stalks are cut back in midsummer, new growth will come up to bloom in the fall. The yellow form listed as *Argemone grandiflora* Isabel is a smaller plant with flowers to three inches across. The color is the pale lemon that goes with everything. The special charm of the white and yellow poppies is the dark red stigma. The red

A. platyceras rosea is a still smaller plant, and its foliage is finer. The color is a difficult one to make use of, but it can be used to good effect at times. The white-veined leaves of these poppies are very decorative, but their sharp spines are exceedingly painful to conscientious weeders. The species requires a light soil, full sun, and plenty of room. Like most annuals they will not tolerate crowding. If the first flowers are allowed to seed, a second and even a third crop will keep the succession of bloom. Spring is the time to sow seeds for the first time. After that there will always be seedlings enough to spare. They cannot be successfully transplanted.

Cosmos Orange Flare, an early dwarf form of the Klondyke cosmos, is long in bloom. The chrome orange flowers are bright spots in the borders from the middle of June until frost. This is listed as a half-hardy annual, but it is hardy with us, and once started reseeds indefinitely. The seedlings can be transplanted. The stocky plants are from three to four feet high. The summer forms of the common fall cosmos are very useful for cutting. Sensation blooms in July. Not as tall as the fall cosmos, it grows only to four feet. The flowers are large, to four inches or more across, in white, red, and the usual shade of cosmos pink. The Early Express types are even more dwarf. They come in the same colors and also bloom in July.

Marigolds of all kinds make gay borders for hot weather. Planted in succession and in variety they bloom all summer and fall. I am very much pleased with Limelight, one new to me this year. The flowers are of the pompon type; their color is a clear pale yellow that is delightfully cool. The plants, described as dwarf, are trim, compact bushes between two and three feet tall and covered with bloom all through July. They will bloom in August, but the foliage turns brown if the season has been dry; marigolds do not like drought. The spreading, dwarf habit and fine, clean, aromatic foliage of the French marigolds ranks them high among common annuals. Harmony is the best of these. It blooms early and late, and the gold and maroon flowers are equally good for garden effect and for cutting. *Tagetes signata pumila* is an edging plant, symmetrical in form, with fine cypress foliage and tiny yellow-orange flowers. Sown in early May, it blooms from late July to frost, never getting taller than nine inches.

The magenta flowers of the coarse spider-flower, *Cleome spinosa*, are common in country gardens, but they are allowed in sophisticated borders only as a last resort. The pure white cleome is another matter. It is one of the most beautiful of the heat-tolerant annuals. This has not been in commerce, but Violet Walker generously spreads the seed wherever she goes— and she goes everywhere. She hands them over only on condition that the magenta be excluded, for otherwise the white soon runs out. When only the white is planted, it perpetuates itself. This very coarse annual, with its bold leaf pattern and domes of delicate, long-stamened flowers, grows to three or four feet in height, and spreads as much. The self-sown seedlings come into bloom the last of June, continuing until hard frost. On not too dark nights the enormous domes are dimly white.

When days are hot, and nights are cool, night flowers are to be considered. The showiest of these are the great white trumpets of the datura, *D. meteloides*. They are lavender tinted and exotically perfumed. The lavender stems and grey leaves are presentable in the daytime when the plaited flowers are limp. Plants from April sowings bloom in June.

Once nicotine, *Nicotiana affinis*, is seen in New England gardens, it can never be looked upon with the same pleasure in ours. But I still plant it, for no other flower is the raspberry color of Crimson Bedder, and no other white is as pure as white nicotine. Besides, I like the way that it comes out in the cool of the evening and makes the night fragrant. Sometimes the plants live over the winter, but they are apt to be sprawling the second season. I prefer new ones in the spring—especially since Lucy Dortch raises the seedlings and divides with me.

I have been going through the catalogues searching out evening-primroses for summer nights. All come easily from seed, and most of them bloom the first year. I think the Texas *Oenothera Drummondii* the best of the yellow-flowered annuals, and once it has bloomed there will be a yearly crop of seedlings. The variety *nana* is better than the type, though both are somewhat weedy. The sprawling plants are lavish with pale, luminous flowers that open while we are at dinner and stay open the following day, if it is the least bit cool or cloudy. They bloom in May, and on and on. The white-flowered, dandelion-leaved sundrop, *Oe. acaulis*, from Chile, is the loveliest of the species, with stemless flowers to four inches across, and leaves so like dandelions that it is very likely to fall into the hands of the weeder. This biennial, or short-lived perennial, bloomed late in May from a November sowing. The perennial *Oe. missouriensis*, said to bloom the first year from seed, is the best species as to daytime appearance. In fact it is the only one at all presentable. The lemon-colored flowers are four inches across. They are open only at night. The long, pointed leaves are a beautiful wax green, veined with grey. The stems are bright red. The plant is compact and procumbent.

Certain annuals are good only for cutting, but they are very important for that. Zinnias (all but the dwarfs) and African marigolds belong in the cutting garden only. Also useful in this respect are the annual coneflowers and sunflowers. *Rudbeckia bicolor* is a low annual to eighteen inches with bright yellow rays zoned brown, and dark centers. The variety Kelvedon Star is twice as tall, with semi-double flowers. Planted the last of April, these begin to bloom early in July. The sunflowers Primrose and Stella are forms of the cucumber-leaf sunflower, *Helianthus cucumerifolius*, native from Texas to Florida. The flowers are from three to four inches across, with twisted rays and brown centers. Stella is a golden yellow, and Primrose is a very pale yellow, the ray flowers in sharp contrast with the dark disk flowers. Primrose is very tall, to eight feet, and Stella to four or five. Early spring sowings produce cut flowers for June.

Dwarf summer annuals fill the places left in the margins of the borders when hot weather dries up pansies and English daisies and the little pink and blue annual forget-me-nots. There is always ageratum, of course, no matter how well it is weeded out, and the weedy kind does much better in rainless periods than the compact, named varieties. There are also quantities of *Zinnia linearis* and *Torenia Fournieri*. The zinnia seeds itself abundantly in dry places, and the torenia in wet places. Both are easily moved in any state of development, and there are always extra ones to use in emergencies. The zinnia is one of the many good annuals from Mexico that come to our aid when drought is prolonged. The profusion of bright single flowers of lemon and orange never flags through the summer and fall. The spreading, bushy plants are about a foot high.

Torenias are charming annuals from the Orient. They grow in sun or shade and in dry or moist soil—but much better in moist. They will go a long while without water, but not without looking the worse for it. A little water revives them at once, if they are not too far gone. Self-sown seeds wait for warm weather to germinate and do not flower before the first or middle of July. Seeds must be sown indoors for bloom in June. *T. Fournieri* is blue with a pansy purple lip and a yellow throat. There is a white form called the Bride. It is not a pure white, but of a lavender cast. The smaller flowers of *T. Baillonii* are yellow and brown. This is very difficult to get above ground. Mine has never reseeded, and I have not been able to get seeds to germinate in the open. Sometimes even those Mr. Fowler sows for me in the greenhouse fail to come up. I guess this is why this most delightful annual is not more popular. It is very trailing—too much so for edging. But there is no better annual for late bloom in the rock garden; it does not bloom until August.

Balsam, *Impatiens Balsamina*, is another oriental annual with thirsty, succulent stems. I never liked garden balsams, but last year I changed my mind because of some pink ones that Isabelle Henderson gave to Miss Toose, and Miss Toose gave to me. They are the pure pink that has no hint of either orange or violet, a rare and lovely color that makes a garden fresh and dainty on hot days. The little rosettes, like tiny camellias, are clustered thickly along the main stem. They grow under the protecting leaves, untouched by sun. This year I sowed seed on May the tenth, and the first flower bloomed on the twenty-first of June. The seeds came from Park as Camellia Flowered Balsam, Salmon Rose. There are a few seedlings from last year's plants.

Cupheas are hot-weather plants from Mexico that can be grown as summer annuals. They are wonderfully drought resistant, and are easily raised from seed, blooming in about two months from the time of sowing. The multicolored Avalon hybrids range from pink to purple, in bright colors that glare back at the sun. Cuphea Firefly, a brilliant red tinged with purple, is low and spreading. It makes a bright edging with alyssum. *C. purpurea* is an erect plant about a foot tall. The rose red flowers are like crape-myrtle, which is not to be wondered at since both belong to the loosestrife family. Cupheas transplant easily—always a good quality in annuals, for young plants coming on in seed beds are essential to continuous bloom.

Browallias are an easily grown annual for summer and fall, long suffering and undemanding. The slender plants of *B. elata* are less than a foot high. The small flowers do not count for much individually, but their color is pleasing in mass, and they will bloom in dry soil in sun or shade. Self-sown seedlings come into bloom early in June. The more showy *B. speciosa* is a greenhouse plant.

Calliopsis, *Coreopsis tinctoria*, follows larkspur, filling the interval between spring and summer. The tall forms mist over the borders with myriads of small, gayly zoned flowers, and fine pale leaves. They are soon gone. Some of the dwarf forms are excellent for the front of the beds, particularly Golden Crown, a form of *C. Drummondii* with flowers two inches across. These are a light cadmium yellow with a small central zone of maroon. The plants are slight, with scant foliage. They must be planted close together for effect. They grow to less than two feet, and bloom longer than the other forms of calliopsis, withstanding much in the way of drought and unfavorable growing conditions.

All hot gardens should have gazanias. They are the sturdiest of South African daisies, and in my experience, the only ones adapted to our growing conditions. Ursinias, dimorphothecas, venidiums, and felicias dry up as soon as the summer gets to be really unbearable. But the crisp gazanias never lose their freshness. As annuals the hybrids of *Gazania splendens* have done well. Seeds sown under glass in early spring produced bloom by the first of June. Plants from those sown in the open the last of April bloomed late in July. So far they have not proved perennial, but new plants set out in the fall lived through the winter. The hybrids are said to run to all sorts of bright tones of orange, red, and yellow, but mine are invariably the same lemon chrome decorated with a central ring of grey dots. The nine-inch scapes spring from a basal rosette of charming, lance-shaped leaves, bright green on top and curled at the edge to show the silver-white underside. These very satisfactory daisies bloom until November. They will grow in any sunny spot, but they are best in a moisture-holding soil.

The Amaryllis Family

In my garden a month seldom goes by without bloom from some member of the amaryllis family, but it is in summer and fall that they become the center of interest. Many of these are among the less hardy species that have been in general culture in gardens only in Florida and southern California, but are hardy enough to grow out of doors in the Middle South. We can form some idea of the ones likely to winter with us from records of gardens in the milder parts of England. I have been interested in comparing the hardiness of those in my garden with the bulbs in Colonel Grey's Hocker Edge Gardens in Kent. Last winter's temperature of six degrees above zero was a test of some crinum, zephyranthes, and hymenocallis species that had become established in the borders during a series of mild winters. Several failed to reappear this spring. A few made the usual foliage but did not bloom. Most of them came through unharmed.

Interest in the amaryllids has been increased in this country by the advent of the American Amaryllis Society, whose year book, *Herbertia*, now in six volumes, offers information, encouragement, and cultural direction to those who are interested in growing the bulbs of this brilliant family.

Allium [2]

Mrs. Rowntree asked, "What is all of this excitement about alliums? . . . Mrs. Walker . . . then Elizabeth Rawlinson . . . now you. . . ."

I do not know that alliums are so exciting, but I am finding them a great dependence during hot weather. There is one with grey leaves and lavender flowers that blooms well, if not brilliantly, from late May through August. This is the most common species in gardens. It is in the trade under a number of names, such as *A. tibeticum* and *A. karataviense* which it most certainly is not, as *A. montanum*, and as *A. senescens*. I shall refer to it as *A. senescens* until I am corrected. This species and other lavender-flowered alliums are dull only if they are planted with too bright colors. With grey-leaved foliage plants and the subdued red-violets of the common roadside penstemon, *P. hirsutus*, the native *Sedum pulchellum*, and the cornflower aster they are almost gay.

In July and August the pale pinkish *Allium tanguticum* blooms. This is a charming and dainty species, very floriferous. Last of all are two other small alliums, also pale and very full of bloom, that come late in August. They were the first in my collection. Years ago Violet Walker (who never comes empty handed) arrived with one in each hand. She had forgotten their names—if she ever knew them. Probably someone arrived in her garden with one in each hand. I accepted them rather unenthusiastically and put them where nothing else will grow. But I have come to value the delicate opal coloring of the flowers in the trying days of late summer. All of these lavender-flowered alliums have stiff, flattened stems less than a foot tall, and glaucous, strap-shaped leaves that are about as long as the stems. The umbels are many flowered.

[2] I am following the Amaryllis Society in classing the Alliums with the Amaryllidaceae. *Herbertia*, Vol. IV (1938), p. 112.

All alliums are not lavender, although the beginner gets that impression. Two very similar red ones come in the middle of June. The dark purplish red flowers of *A. sphaerocephalum* are in compact balls, about an inch in diameter, on fragile scapes to thirty inches. *A. globosum* is similar, but the flowers are a little smaller and the slightly redder color is near Ridgway's Bordeaux. The foliage of both species is so like that of wild onions that it takes great restraint to resist pulling them up when the beds are being weeded. A quantity of either is effective with a background of pansy purple hollyhocks, and a foreground of wine-colored prickly-poppies, *Argemone platyceras rosea*. Mr. Clement has a dark red allium that blooms in the mountains in August. It has no name, being designated by the number 9538. This is not as handsome as the earlier species, but it might be very useful for later bloom, especially in the rock garden. These dark reds are very important garden colors.

A yellow species, *Allium flavum*, also blooms in June, but it is not showy in the borders. In the rock garden the slight stalks and loose sprays of nodding lemon colored flowers can be very charming. The stems are eight to ten inches high. The foliage is cylindrical and rather sparse.

All of these alliums grow very easily in poor, light soil in full sun.

Cooperia

The prairie-lily, *Cooperia pedunculata*, a native of Texas and Mexico, is closely related to the zephyranthes and is very like them. This, too, is called a rain-lily and has the same habit of popping up after summer rains. The reddish buds open in mid-afternoon, or as soon as the sun is off them, and the flowers remain turned up to the sky in their characteristic pose until the next evening. They are dead white, crystalline, and very thick petaled, and they fill the night with a strange, disturbing sweetness. To me, one of the chief delights of gardening in the South is the perfumed darkness of midsummer nights. I try to have all manner of evening-blooming and evening-scented flowers, and of these the most fragrant and the most charming is the prairie-lily. The first buds push out of the ground at the very end of April, and there is bloom at intervals through May, June, and July. The bulbs are cheap; a lot of them should be planted in the margins of the borders or in the rock garden. They multiply slowly, but they are very permanent; once in the ground, they come up faithfully year after year. Prairie-lilies need to be planted among dwarf annuals and perennials, for their foliage is scant and not attractive. The lax grey leaves lie on the ground and look untidy.

The prairie-lily is found growing in both well-drained and moist soils, and usually in part shade. In the garden the bulbs in deep shade never bloom. Those bloom well that are in poor, light, well-drained soil in full sun, but perhaps they would bloom more freely with moisture. The zephyranthes do. The small, round, long-necked bulbs must be planted four inches deep.

Another species, *C. Drummondii*, called evening star, is said to be of no garden value. I should like to decide this point for myself, but it has never bloomed for me. I think the bulbs have finally disappeared, though they put up tufts of threadlike foliage for several seasons.

Crinum

Of the seventeen crinums that I have grown in the open, ten have proved hardy. The tropical splendor of their lush foliage and large flowers is unbelievable in a garden where the temperature sometimes approaches zero. The bulbs of some of them are six or seven inches in diameter. The basal tapering leaves, in ranks like corn leaves, are to five feet long. There are from six to nineteen flowers in an umbel, opening in succession, two or more a day. The stout scapes are from three to four feet tall. Most species are night-blooming; the flowers droop at noon, but freshen in the evening. All crinums bloom more freely when they are well watered and generously mulched with manure. The clumps bloom better every year that they are left alone, but they can be dug and divided when increase is preferable to bloom.

Crinum Powellii album, a white form of one of the oldest

and best hybrids, is said to be hardy to Philadelphia. It makes a better showing than other sorts, because the bloom comes at one time instead of at intervals. An old clump sends up as many as twelve scapes a season, and five of these may be in bloom at once. It blooms through June, sometimes into July, and occasionally repeats in late summer. The fragrant flowers are pure white.

Mr. Houdyshel's hybrid of the *Powellii* type, Cecil Houdyshel, is one of the best garden crinums, being hardy and a constant bloomer, and producing as many as seven scapes a season. It blooms almost continuously through June, July, and August. The flowers open in pairs. Although all of an umbel of from eleven to sixteen may not mature, a single scape is in bloom for over two weeks, and before it has bloomed out another has pushed up through the foliage. The pointed segments are white at the base and flushed at the tips with Persian lilac, a paler color than the deep lilac buds. The heavy perfume is not pleasing to me.

Crinum Moorei is a distinctively charming South African species long cultivated in Great Britain. It is said to have been sent to Glasnevin Gardens in 1863 by a friend of Dr. Moore's, to have grown there in the open, and to have flowered "sometimes in the autumn, sometimes in spring." With me it comes in July or August. In my garden—perhaps because it is in a very dry border under a scarlet oak—this species is a very shy bloomer, producing only one or two scapes in a season. The scapes are less than two feet tall, tapering and slender, topped by an umbel of six or more hooded flowers, vanilla-scented, and of a soft, cameo pink. The comparatively short leaves are tapered at both ends. *C. Moorei* needs shade; otherwise the pretty foliage will burn. It is sometimes called the long-neck crinum, an ugly name that describes the shape of the bulb. Most crinums take up such enormous amounts of space that it is well to give them a place to themselves, but this one is on a different scale, and does very well in the border.

For many years I longed for *Amarcrinum Howardii*, a hybrid between *Crinum Moorei* and *Amaryllis Belladonna*. This spring I found it listed for much less than its original price

of five dollars, and this summer it bloomed in my garden. The flower scapes appeared at the end of August and at the end of September. The flowers are more like their crinum parent than their amaryllis parent. There are sixteen or seventeen to a scape, several open at one time. The color is a clear rose. Like the amaryllis the flowers are white-throated, with a hint of green. They are of an exquisite and indescribable fragrance that is something like vanilla but much more subtle. The leaves are like the leaves of crinums and, unlike those of the amaryllis, appear in early summer and last until frost. The scapes are twenty-four inches high, and the leaves are not much longer. This rare amaryllid is interesting not only for its beauty, but also because bi-generic hybrids are unusual. I cannot recommend it yet for gardens, as it has not been through a winter, but I feel very encouraged by the two blooms, for few rare bulbs bloom their first season in a new climate. My bulb came from southern California where the hybrid originated. It is grown out of doors there. The fact that its crinum parent does so well here makes me hopeful.

C. Kirkii and *C. Kunthianum* are species of the milk-and-wine type, with milk-white segments keeled with wine color. They bloom at intervals from the end of May to October. These are the best crinums for cutting. The flowers stay fresh longer in the house than in the garden, and as many as twelve to an umbel may be open at once. In the garden several open in the late afternoon, just before dark, and eight may be open at once. The fall bloom is lovelier than the spring bloom because the flowers stay fresh in the middle of the day. *C. Kirkii* comes from tropical Africa. There are from eight to nineteen unpleasantly scented flowers, faintly wine streaked. *C. Kunthianum* comes from tropical America. The tubes of the large, open flowers are very long and gracefully curved. The keels of the pointed and recurved segments (to four or five inches long) are a dark wine color that shows through on the inside. The fragrance is delightful, not like the cloying odor of many species.

This summer, late in August, the southern swamp lily, *Crinum americanum*, bloomed in my garden for the first time, though the bulb has been growing there for five years. This species is of particular interest because it is the only one native to the United States. Its flower is very different from that of most crinums, being more like a giant hymenocallis. The white, linear segments are narrow and drooping. There are from three to six (usually four) fragrant blooms to a scape. The scape is twenty-four inches long, or less. The narrow, tapered leaves, a sleek, dark green, are not much longer than the scapes. Now that the swamp lily has bloomed, I mean to try it in other places, for it has increased fivefold in five years, and I have enough now to experiment with. I put the original bulb in a wet place because it grows naturally in swamps; but I have read that it will endure much drier situations. It grows in sun or shade in its native swamps and meadows. I am delighted to find that I was mistaken in thinking that this crinum would not be hardy in North Carolina. The bulbs have been through a winter when the temperature dropped to six degrees above zero, and they will not often be subjected to weather colder than that.

Hymenocallis

The white spider-lilies (I call them white to distinguish them from the red spider-lilies that bloom in the fall), are curious and delicate flowers with linear segments, and stamens which are united to form a cup. They bloom in the summer at intervals, the basal strap-like leaves appearing before the flowers. With the exception of one from Africa, the species are native to the Americas.

The Peruvian daffodil, *Hymenocallis calathina*, is the showiest of the white spider-lilies. This is not a bulb to leave in the ground over the winter, but I always do; sometimes it blooms, and sometimes it does not. When it does, the white flowers scent the whole garden with their strange, disturbing perfume, and when it does not, there are still the handsome broad leaves to make an interesting foliage accent in the summer border. To be sure of bloom, the bulbs must be stored over the winter. When they are planted in the spring they bloom in June; left in the ground they bloom in July. The flowers are white with green throats. The segments are only a little longer than the deep, wide cups. The cups are fringed. The buds open one or two at a time, and an umbel lasts nearly two weeks. The leaves are to two feet long, the scapes about the same. The hybrid, Sulphur Queen, is not as vigorous as the type, but it seems to be as hardy or hardier. The flowers are not sulfur but the pale creamy color called naphthalene yellow. The foliage is pale green.

One of the best of the hymenocallis that I have ever had is Mr. Houdyshel's "species number 2." Unfortunately it is not as hardy as the Peruvian daffodil, although it is more certain to bloom if it survives. A bulb that had come through the three previous winters succumbed to the last. Established clumps bloom in June and July. There are from seven to twelve flowers to an umbel. The stout, flattened scapes are nearly two feet tall. The bright-green style and filaments make the large white flowers look even whiter. The very narrow, drooping segments are almost four inches long, and the cup is very shallow. The leaves are narrowed at both ends, and are as wide and dark and shining as those of the Peruvian daffodil.

The hardiest hymenocallis that I have had has braved all winters so far to bloom in June. This year it bloomed again in July. It is an unidentified species with narrow leaves and narrow segments that are over four inches long. It is planted in the copse with ferns and the common little white oxalis which blooms charmingly all summer in a damp shady place. All of the white spider-lilies like a rich moist soil.

H. caribaea from the West Indies and *H. galvestonensis* from Texas are counted among the hardier species, but neither has proved hardy in my garden. A delightful native spider-lily came to me from the North Carolina mountains as *H. occidentalis*. This blooms in August. The deeply grooved, strap-like leaves die down before the appearance of the ethereal flowers. There are from four to six flowers to a scape.

Lycoris

Hall's amaryllis, *Lycoris squamigera*, is a hardy bulb from Japan. The naked scapes come up in summer, and the wide, grey, narcissus-like leaves do not follow until January. The spot where the bulbs are planted should be marked so that they will not be disturbed when nothing shows above ground. The clumps should be left alone until they cease to bloom, and then lifted and divided after the foliage dies away in late spring. They bloom indefinitely in poor soil, increasing very slowly in the borders. From four to seven fragrant, opalescent flowers are borne in umbels on tapering, thirty-inch scapes. The first fades as the last opens so that as many as six may be out at a time. The petals are like a changeable silk in Persian lilac with tints of violet, tints that are repeated in the drooping flowers of the wild bleeding-heart. The lacy foliage of the bleeding-heart softens the effect of the bare scapes. The scapes appear about the middle of July and last into August.

Lycoris incarnata comes from central China. It blooms a little later than Hall's amaryllis, the first scapes usually making their appearance late in July, but sometimes not until August. The flowers are smaller, the scapes shorter (to two feet) than those of the Japanese species, and the bulbs multiply faster and bloom more freely. There are from six to eight (mostly eight) flowers to an umbel. The segments are very narrow, very pale (almost white), keeled with tourmaline pink and tipped with blue. The edges are crisped. The filaments and style are daphne red. The striped buds open in succession, the first flower lasting until all are out. An umbel in full bloom is very lovely.

With both of these bulbs, shallow planting is essential to bloom. They flourish in humid weather, and bloom equally well in a sunny border or in shady places under trees. They like a light, well-drained soil mixed with leaf mold.

Mr. Jacques Busbee has a dwarf form of *Lycoris radiata* which he says blooms in August. The bulbs came from Virginia.

Pancratium

The sea daffodil, *Pancratium maritimum*, bloomed in my garden this summer for the first time. The bulbs were put out in March; the leafless scapes appeared at the end of July. The scapes are flat and very short, only six inches high. There are from six to nine flowers to an umbel. Two long buds striped with pale green open each evening and last until the next evening. The flowers closely resemble pure white daffodils. They are so delicate as to be almost transparent. The fragrance is of vanilla and something more sophisticated. The staminal cup is toothed, and the recurved segments are very long and narrow. I almost missed them when they came up under a spreading salvia. All of these fragile amaryllids that make no sign of their presence until the scapes appear suddenly, and as suddenly bloom, are apt to bloom unnoticed under the leaves of other plants. It is well to plant them to themselves with a low, loose ground cover. The fine foliage and violet flowers of the moss verbena is the perfect cover for the sea daffodil.

I have tried this pancratium twice before. The bulbs were planted in the fall and came through the winter but did not persist. I think this was because I put them in moist soil under the impression that, being related to hymenocallis, they would like the same conditions. On the contrary, the pancratiums like a very light dry soil in a very sunny place. This species comes from the shores of the Mediterranean.

Sprekelia

The Jacobean-Lily, *Sprekelia formosissima*, is well named formosissima—most beautiful—for of all flowers that grow in a garden it is the most distinctively beautiful in design and color. Clusius called it the Jacobean- or Saint-James-lily because of a fancied resemblance to the emblem of the fiery sword worn by the Spanish knights of Saint James. This Mexican amaryllid is a half-hardy bulb said to winter with safety as far north as Washington. Like many bulbs of this temperamental family, it blooms most surely when lifted and dried off, but it has been grown in the open in English gardens since the days of Mrs. Loudon, and I have been told that established plantings bloomed in old gardens in Petersburg, Virginia. I felt certain that I could bloom it in mine without lifting the bulbs, and at last, after five years, I have done so. It remains to be seen whether the performance will be repeated; even if it is not, it will have been worth the trouble.

In England, the Jacobean-lily is noted for flowering in its own good time, regardless of season. With me the long, red bud appeared early in June and opened on the eighth. As to location, Mrs. Loudon (in *The Ladies Flower Garden of Ornamental Bulbous Plants*)[3] recommends a very warm, dry one, in full sun. With this in mind I tried a bulb at the top of a retaining wall, and this was the bulb that bloomed. It bloomed in front of a santolina, and I could not have found a more beautiful background for the rich nopal red of the flower. The Jacobean-lily is like no other flower that grows. When the long red bud opens the flower looks very big in proportion to the eight-inch stem. It measures six inches across, if the narrow segments are uncurled and stretched out. The slender, ensiform leaves are shiny and are a pleasing dark green. Mrs. Loudon advises deep planting—with the bulb at least four inches in the ground—in a rich soil.

Zephyranthes

The zephyr-lilies are small, solitary flowers that appear and disappear as suddenly as spring snow. Because they often follow summer rain, they are sometimes called rain-lilies. There are two types: those with comparatively large, lily-like flowers and comparatively wide leaves; and those with smaller, goblet-shaped flowers and very narrow leaves. The latter is like a bright, long-stemmed crocus. With the zephyr-lilies I have included two species formerly classed as *Zephyranthes*, but now referred to the genus *Habranthus*.

Zephyranthes grandiflora (Z. carinata) is a lily-flowered species. In spite of coming from the tropics (Mexico to the West Indies) it is one of the hardiest species, and is said to winter safely in Philadelphia. As a child I thought of the little rose-colored lilies as the sign and seal of summer. My grandmother in Georgia grew them in her garden, and my grandmother in West Virginia grew them in little pots on the front porch. Those in my garden came from Georgia. They have been with me so long and have increased so much that their bloom

[3] London: William Smith, 1841.

makes a sea of pink. The season is in June, but there is scattered bloom in the late summer and even to the end of September. The flowers are large, to over three inches long, on ten-inch stems. They open out flat at midday and close in the afternoon; this is a characteristic of the genus. The shimmering leaves are grass green.

Z. robusta (Habranthus robustus), also lily-flowered, comes from Argentina, near Buenos Aires. It is said to be tender, but it has been in my garden for five years and bloomed every summer except one. With me it seems to be perfectly hardy, but it has not bloomed after the cold of last January. The flowers are white, tinged with a delicate pink, and green throated. They are as large and long stemmed as those of *Z. grandiflora*, and like them are scentless. The leaves are broader than those of any other species, and very glaucous. *Z. robusta* is capricious as to bloom. The flowers usually appear once a month from June to September, but they may bloom twice a month, or not at all.

The crocus-flowered species are more fragile and less showy than the lily-flowered type. They are at their best in the rock garden, or with the wild flowers. Three of the yellow-flowered species that I have had have persisted. Several others failed to become established. *Z. citrina* is a great bloomer. There are flushes once or twice a month from late June to October, the bright flowers on long slender stems appearing two or three at a time. In color they are between lemon chrome and light cadmium, with decorative, light cadmium anthers and green throats. The color is said to vary, but I have not had enough bulbs to show a difference. The flowers are very sweet. The leaves are long (to sixteen inches), narrow, and somewhat lax. They are a light green flecked with red. This species occurs in Yucatan. *Ajax* is a pale hybrid of *Z. citrina*. The flowers open into flat, citron yellow stars. It has proved a shy bloomer with me, and capricious, making its appearance in August, or in September, or not until October, or not at all.

The copper lily of Texas, *Z. texana (Habranthus texanus)*, is a small and charming flower, primuline yellow within, and brick red without. It is an inch and a half long. The leaves are very narrow and shiny; the stems are to five inches tall. When the clumps are established there are frequent flushes of several blooms from June to September. Seeds of this species, and those of *Z. citrina* and *Ajax*, should be allowed to ripen, as these plants seed freely but increase slowly from offsets.

Z. rosea, in the trade sometimes confused with *Z. grandiflora*, is a tiny, rose-colored species from the mountains of Cuba. The flowers are the size of those of the copper lily, the stems half as long. This blooms shyly in August and September. So far, I have found it winter hardy, but not persistent.

The zephyr-lilies vary in their requirements, but these, with the exception of *Z. rosea* which needs light soil and drainage, bloom best in a rich, moist, acid soil.

Trees and Shrubs for Summer Bloom

Shrubs that bloom in summer are not so widely known nor so well appreciated as those that bloom in spring, but they are as lovely and as varied, and there are more of them than you would think. To those who do not like to make an effort in hot weather, a well-considered collection—with the addition of a flowering tree or so—would bring an abundance of bloom, and grateful shade, too, during these trying months. Planted with summer bulbs, these would make a very fascinating garden that would almost take care of itself.

June is almost as flowery as April when the early summer trees are blooming. Mimosas, catalpas, vitex, and koelreuterias are all out at once. If the mysterious blight, against which there seems to be no control, continues to attack the mimosas, *Albizzia Julibrissin*, they may disappear as the chestnuts disappeared. Of course you always think yours will escape. I cannot bear to think that a time will come when there is no mimosa blooming outside my window in June.

Koelreuteria paniculata has made its way in spite of its name. I am always surprised, when June comes, to see so many. They are planted among other trees and shrubs where their straggling growth is lost from sight until a film of pale yellow spreads over it in early summer. The flowers are followed by inflated, pale green fruits that are supposed to be attractive but are rather unsightly to me. The incised leaflets of the compound leaves make a delicate pattern. This is a good tree for our part of the country, because of its indifference to heat and drought. In the open it makes a light, graceful specimen, twenty or thirty feet tall. The common names for koelreuteria are not very satisfactory, as golden rain-tree and varnish-tree are shared with laburnum and sterculia. The latter, *S. platanifolia*, is another June-flowering tree, but the greenish flower panicles are not so decorative as the broad, tropical-looking leaves and the bright green trunk. It is hardy here, but cannot be safely planted much farther north. It is said to be hardy to Washington, but it gets cut back in northern Virginia.

Every year in early June, I go by a little house with two bird-of-paradise shrubs, *Poinciana Gilliesii*, at the front door. This year, after the coldest January on record, they are not there. And yet, in the Ohio valley, I have known them to come up from the roots after much lower temperatures than we have here. After less severe winters than the last, the gay plumage of this tropical American shrub is one of our summer pleasures, and when the cold proves too much for them new plants can readily be raised from seed. From June to September the red and yellow flowers with long, tail-feather stamens appear against the fine grey leaves. The straggling habit is best concealed by planting in clumps. A good, well-drained soil, a quantity of cow manure, a little lime, and a warm, sunny situation fill its needs.

Flowering pomegranates, *Punica Granatum*, are hardy in most parts of the Middle South, and are reported at Baltimore. One survived many cold winters near Staunton, Virginia, climbing to Elizabeth Rawlinson's second-story window before it was finally killed by a colder winter. Most of the bloom is in early summer, but there are splashes of scarlet against the dark, highly polished leaves from April to frost. The pear-shaped buds are like wax ornaments. They are as decorative as the ruffled double flowers. Pomegranates should be pruned in winter to encourage flower buds on the new wood. They prefer deep soil, and are best in the open, but they will grow wherever they are planted.

Brought to England in the eighteenth century, and from there to America, the Cape-jasmine, *Gardenia jasminoides*, has become almost as much a part of our South as of the Cape of Good Hope. I have even found it growing along the roadside in South Carolina. Cape-jasmines are hardy along the coast as far north as Norfolk. At Norfolk they are occasionally frozen back to the ground. In the piedmont, Raleigh must be about their northern limit. Here the waxy leaves and creamy flowers are worth the efforts of those who can bear to be disappointed after an "unusual" winter like the last one. This summer there are no flowers on the gardenias in Raleigh gardens (most of the shrubs are the season's growth), but there were bucketsful in the market stalls in June. The market flowers came from a short distance to the east, but from the coastal plain, which shows what a difference a few miles, and a change of soil, can make in plant hardiness. The flowers of the variety *Fortunei* are larger than those of the type, and they repeat in summer and fall. But this form is not quite so hardy. The dwarf form, *G. radicans* (of catalogues), is hardier than the type, but not entirely evergreen. The small, pointed leaves, and miniature gardenias are delightful in the rock garden in June.

The European hybrids of *Ceanothus americanus* are available in southern nurseries. The French blues, and tints of rose are very lovely, but the strain has proved disappointing in the garden in two ways, in time of bloom and in hardiness. Instead of blooming in midsummer, they bloom in late spring or early summer. Even Gloire de Versailles, the latest of these, blooms with me at the end of May. And this, said to be the hardiest of the hybrids, was killed last winter. I cannot think why it should not be able to stand a temperature of six above, since it came from Asheville. But it is long since we have had such a winter, and I hope it will be long before we have another. Of the two other hybrids in town, one was killed, and one cut back to the roots. Gloire de Versailles is not disappointing as to bloom. The abundant flower panicles are like a fine blue mist. Perle Rose is like the inside of a shell. The others are variations of blue and rose. All are shrubs of from four to five feet. They need a light soil that is well drained but not dry, and plenty of sun.

The yellow flowers of the various shrubby St. Johns-Worts are sprinkled through the early summer in sun or shade. All that I have bloom about the same time, from early to late June, but, up to this time, they have not bloomed far into the summer. I see them in bloom in the mountains at the Nik-Nar nursery in August and in September. They are very easy and dependable shrubs on the whole, and some of them are very showy. The exotic species have larger flowers than the natives. The best known of these are *Hypericum calycinum*, and its hybrid *H. Moserianum*. *H. calycinum* is a ground cover to one foot, grows in poor soil, and travels rapidly by suckers. It is not entirely evergreen. The leaves turn brown in very cold weather and are unsightly in spring unless the branches are cut back to the ground. New growth does not start until late in the season. The horizontal branches are tipped in June with large, solitary, lemon-colored flowers with a tuft of pink-anthered stamens. The flowers are to three inches across. *H. Moseranum* is similar but the leaves and flowers are smaller and the plant is twice as tall. The tips of the branches are drooping. *H. calycinum* grows well in sun or shade, but it does not bloom in shade. *H. Moserianum* requires sun. Probably the best of the large-flowered exotic species is *H. Hookerianum* from the Himalayas. It is said to bloom from July to September and should be tried in the South. But I have not seen it, and the plant that I bought under that name turned out to be the common native, *H. densiflorum*, of which I already had too many.

The native hypericums are comparatively small-flowered, but some of them are very useful. Two low-growing southern species (to three feet) are particularly attractive. *H. aureum*, the golden St. Johns-Wort, begins to bloom in my garden early in June. The pale lemon petals are somewhat reflexed, making the very large puff of amber-colored stamens all the more prominent. The oval leaves are a light blue-green. *H. aureum* prefers moist soil and shade. *H. glomeratum* comes from the North Carolina mountains. According to Small it is found on Grandfather Mountain and at Table Rock. It is later in bloom than *H. aureum*, coming in late June in my garden, and in August in the mountains. The flowers of both of these hypericums are clustered at the tips of the branches. *H. densiflorum* is common in the South, and native as far north as New Jersey. It comes from swamps and marshes but it will thrive and bloom in the poorest, driest soil, and under trees. This is one of the least choice and most useful species. It grows to six feet. The flowers are small and wax yellow in dense clusters. The leaves are long and narrow. *H. densiflorum* and *H. prolificum* are much alike in appearance, but the first prefers an acid soil, and the second a limy soil.

In June there are two late azaleas. *A. macrantha* is an evergreen Japanese species beginning to flower late in May. The flowers are large, and of a soft rose color, and the habit is dwarf and spreading. The sweet azalea, *A. arborescens*, blooms late in June in the piedmont and in July in the mountains. It is a tall (to ten feet) lank shrub with dark deciduous foliage. The white flowers and shiny leaves smell of heliotrope. In June also *Rhododendron maximum* is in flower. The flowers are white to pink, the evergreen leaves large and very glossy.

The oakleaf hydrangea, *H. quercifolia*, blooms in June in shady places where the soil is not too dry, and in the fall the leaves are the color of wine. The wide flower panicles are a greenish white with warm tints. The flowers turn pink before they fade. The leaves are very large, and of a striking pattern. The shrub is spreading in habit, and to six feet tall. This is a native of Georgia and Florida, but it is surprisingly inured to cold and is winter hardy even to southern New England.

The bottlebrush bush, *Aesculus parviflora*, of the Georgia and South Carolina woods, blooms in Dr. Coker's garden in early June and past the middle of the month. The green and white pattern of the tall, erect flower spikes and the large digitate leaves is delightful. This shrubby horse-chestnut is a broad shrub to six feet or more in height, spreading by suckers to make a thicket. It grows in the sun or some shade, and prefers a rich, moist soil.

Abelias are of interest because they bloom all summer long, and there are more varieties than the too common *A. grandi-*

flora. Already these are beginning to appear in nursery lists, and I hope they will soon be in gardens. *A. grandiflora* var. *Sherwoodii* is a compact, flattened form of *A. grandiflora* that does not grow above two feet. The horizontal branches are widespreading; they soon cover an area of five or six feet. With its pretty shining leaves, the red stems of the new growth, and the small, pure white, sweet-scented flowers (not smudged with dirty lavender), it is a happy addition to the much too short list of small evergreens. So far the foliage has stayed a fresh green all winter. The branches are very close to the ground but the tips do not seem to take root. This abelia begins to bloom by the middle of June and continues through the summer. *A. Schumannii* is said to be tardily deciduous, but mine kept its green leaves all through the severe weather of last winter when normally evergreen foliage was discolored. This is a Chinese species noted for its long season of bloom, from June through the fall. The tubular, lavender blossoms are much larger than those of the common abelia. Shrubs only a few inches high are covered with bloom, so that the little plants are delightful in the rock garden. They eventually grow to five or six feet.

The false-spireas are called sorbaria, from sorbus, the mountain-ash, because of their ash-like foliage. Their first tender green appears very early in the spring while other shrubs are still bare, and the intricate pattern of their pinnate leaves is charming in summer with the fine sprays of tiny white flowers. *S. arborea*, the one commonly grown, blooms with me at the end of June. The variety *glabrata* is better than the type. It makes a large shrub to fifteen feet in height. This is a Chinese species. I have also *S. Aitchisonii* from the Himalayas—similar to *S. arborea* but not so tall—and *S. sorbifolia*, a smaller species (from three to five feet tall) from northern Asia. These are slow to become established; they have not flowered yet for me. The false-spireas grow and bloom in some shade, but they bloom better in full sun. However they are not tolerant of drought, and they must have a deep soil to reach perfection. They grow rapidly and spread quickly. In fact they spread a little too quickly for the good of nearby shrubs, and

An Introduction to Summer   129

should be planted where the suckers will not interfere with their neighbors.

In mid-summer, flowering shrubs to supplement the bloom of the border flowers are even more necessary than earlier in the season. And there are very beautiful shrubs for this time of the year. The loblolly bay, *Gordonia Lasianthus*, of the southern swamp margins and evergreen shrub bogs is not in cultivation because of the difficulty of transplanting even nursery grown stock. I cannot believe that any native is impossible to grow in the proper place, and I mean to continue to try it. I think spring is the time to set it out. To me this is one of the most beautiful of our flowering evergreens. The cupped, magnolia-like blossoms and the round buds are as perfect as if they were carved of ivory, and they have the peculiar beauty that is common to the gordonias, the stewartias, and the tea plant.

The mountain stewartia, *S. pentagyna*, of the southern Appalachians is another member of the tea family with white summer blossoms. The fluted petals form shallow cups like the flowers of the tea plant but much larger. In the type the stamens are yellowish, but there is also a form with purple stamens.[4] This native species makes a small tree. The Japanese stewartia, *S. Pseudo-Camellia*, called summer camellia, is an enormous tree in the Nikko forests, but in cultivation it is a slow-growing shrub. The flowers (to two-and-a-half inches across) are smaller than the flowers of our native plant, with the characteristic crimped petals. The pale stamens are tipped with yellow. In my garden this blooms in late June; very small plants bloom freely. The stewartias have a name for being difficult in cultivation. They require an acid soil and a summer mulch to keep their shallow roots from drying out. The native species will grow in sun or shade, but the Japanese stewartia needs sun.

Our native sour-wood, *Oxydendrum arboreum*, has the heath family's aversion to being moved to a new place, but once started, it is a tree that is ornamental in two seasons— in June and July when the branches are hung with strings

[4] Coker and Totten, *Trees of the Southeastern States*.

of small lily-of-the-valley flowers, and in fall when the long pointed leaves turn to scarlet.

For summer bloom in a situation that is very dry and sunny, the wild senna, *Cassia marilandica*, is useful. In the July heat the grey, acacia-like leaves, and the pale yellow, chocolate-tipped flowers are as fresh as spring. The herbaceous stalks make a growth of five or six feet in a season, providing a pleasing background for the late day-lilies.

Crape-myrtles, *Lagerstroemia indica*, are so much a part of the South that we are apt to forget that they are equally familiar in other places. They originated in China and are described as "indica" because they are so generally planted in India. They are grown in the south of England, though they are not hardy near London, and there are trees to twenty-five feet in the botanic garden in Padua—the oldest botanic garden in the world. The parts of the world in which crape-myrtles grow are very good parts for us to turn to for plant material. In this country crape-myrtles will probably not stand beyond Virginia, for they cannot endure temperatures much below zero. Many were killed to the ground in Winston-Salem last winter when the thermometer dropped to fifteen below. Crape-myrtles flower on the current year's growth, and the flowers are much improved by pruning in early spring before new growth starts. They need a yearly mulch of manure, which they seldom get because people seem to think that common plants need no care. They bloom a little in June, are at their best in July, and continue through August. The popular color in crape-myrtles is the flashy "watermelon pink." To me the most pleasing tones are the greyed lavenders found in old plantings. These subdued colors are charming with the grey of the branches. The white form and the pale pink are good too. The ones to be avoided are the magentas.

On hot July afternoons my copse is both aromatic and sweet—aromatic with the scent of sun on the pinestraw path, and sweet with the fragrance of the Japanese glory-bower, *Clerodendrum trichotomum*. In August the starry white flowers fall, leaving the pink calyx clusters. These are a dull pink against the bright rose of the crape-myrtle beyond them. In

September the pink deepens to pomegranate purple and forms a frame for the turquoise berries that change to dark blue as they mature. The berries last until the end of September, or sometimes—if they are not eaten by the thrushes—until the end of October. In shade the glory-bower grows rapidly into a small or medium-sized tree of open habit and charmingly irregular outline. In the sun it is densely symmetrical. The variety *Fargesii*, often counted as a species, is smaller than the type, with smaller, pointed leaves, and is later in bloom. It is to be planted to itself because of the suckers. It is recommended for hot, sandy soil. This variety comes from China.

In midsummer I always watched for the bright flowers of the coral-tree, *Erythrina Crista-galli*, in the Briggs' front yard. One summer there were none. Later, in another part of town, I came upon two enormous specimens, more resplendent than ever, in full bloom. The Briggs had moved, taking the coral-tree with them. It had come with them, years before, from Wilmington to Raleigh, and a deep rooted coral-tree is something to move. Now, after the unprecedented cold of last winter, both bushes are dead. But mine is still alive, and so is the one that Mrs. Briggs gave to a neighbor; these were probably in more

protected places. The coral-tree is said to survive out of doors to Charlottesville and Washington. In Brazil, where it originates, it is a real tree. Here it is killed back to the ground in winter, but the strong shoots that come up very late in the spring grow rapidly into a wide, spreading bush six or eight feet in height and as much through. Even as a shrub it is a very gorgeous affair, with smooth, oval leaflets of a cool grey-green, and long terminal racemes of enormous, pea-shaped flowers of nopal red. Mine has not bloomed, perhaps because of the shade of the white oaks, perhaps because of the setback of moving it from Georgia. As far as I know, the coral-tree is in the trade only in California.

In June, at the Brookgreen Gardens, near Georgetown, S.C., Mr. Tarbox pointed out *Elliottia racemosa* in bloom. This is one of the rare shrubs of the world; it is endemic to restricted areas in South Carolina and Georgia and is practically unknown in cultivation. Many of the wild stands have been destroyed since its discovery, nearly a hundred years ago, by Stephen Elliott. Mr. Berckmans sent plants to Kew, and these, Mr. Bean says, are the only specimens in Europe. It is a deciduous shrub of medium size, or sometimes a small tree. The oval

An Introduction to Summer   133

leaves are rather coarse. The white flowers are in terminal racemes. The culture, should you ever acquire one, is the same
as for other heaths. It is hardy only in the South.

Late Summer

Toward the middle of July, phlox and day-lilies are forlorn, and
other summer flowers have practically bloomed out. There are
still alliums, and annuals surge in continuous waves of color,
but there is need for something spectacular, a need that is met
by the goldband lily of Japan, *Lilium auratum*. The culture of
the goldband lily calls for coal ashes and poor soil. Small bulbs
grown in this country are the proper ones to buy, but results
from these will probably be less dazzling than from the mon-
ster Japanese bulbs that are prey to disease. Results from the
latter sound like a seed-catalogue testimonial. Three bulbs
planted in a heap of ashes (as a substitute for the volcanic ash
on Mount Fuji) produced five stalks (three to one bulb) that
shot up to four and a half feet, and produced lilies twelve
inches across, ten of them to a stalk. The bulbs did become
diseased; the next season told a different story. The showy
Japanese lilies, *Lilium speciosum rubrum*, bloom the last
week in July and all through August; they are very pretty with
the second bloom of the shade of pink phlox that just matches
their red spots.

A late wild bergamot, *Monarda fistulosa*, blooms in July and
August with false dragonhead, the late tall phlox, Mrs. Milly van
Hoboken, lily-turf, and the last, scattered flowers of purple
loosestrife. This bergamot is a very tall one, with long bare
stalks of silver and lavender, tipped with silver and lavender
tassels. The stalks bend forward, spreading the flowery tops
over monotonously vertical leaves of Japanese and Delta iris.
This species grows in drier places than *Monarda didyma* and
should be in a drier place in the garden. Normally growing to
about four feet, it gets much too rank in damp soil.

False dragonhead, *Physostegia virginiana*, is one garden
flower seldom called by a garden name, physostegia being the

sole botanical term to appeal to the laity. I frequently hear my sister, who takes pride, as a rule, in her ignorance of such matters, confiding to visitors that the tall purple spike is physostegia. I should like to abandon both of these names, in conversation, and take up "obedient plant." It is said to be so called because the flowers can be turned at any angle on the spike and will remain as they are turned. The first of the false dragonheads is the white form. It blooms in June and is one of the loveliest of the early summer flowers. The type follows a little later, and the other varieties come in August. Last year Mrs. McColl sent me two new garden forms. Summer Glow is a tall variety to four feet. It is more than generous with blooms. Rosy Spire is not so tall and comes into bloom later. Both are a decided tone of red-violet that is an improvement over the original garden form. The old variety, Vivid, blooms last of all. It is a still deeper color and grows to about three feet. These last three varieties will bloom on until frost if the spent flower spikes are nipped off so the new ones can develop.

Mrs. Milly van Hoboken, one of the most permanent and satisfactory varieties of phlox, is tall and free-flowering. It is at its best during the last half of July when the other varieties are beginning to wane. The color is a soft greyed pink called liseran purple. It is very distinct.

Lily-turfs, *Liriope Muscari*, are all-season plants with berries in winter, flowers in summer, and always with wide grassy leaves. The big blue lily-turf grows as slowly as a shrub, increasing in size until the clumps are two feet or more across and two feet high. The stiff, lavender flower stalks are about the height of the arching leaves. This is often listed as *Ophiopogon Jaburan*. For bloom in difficult places under trees, and in dry soil, there is nothing so dependable. It will bloom even in complete shade.

Plants blooming in shade are a necessity in summer gardens. Where spring bulbs are planted under trees, I like to plant August lilies, *Hosta plantaginea*, so that the wide pale leaves will come up through the dark periwinkle that covers the ground. The fragrant white flowers in August are only a part of the ornamental value of this most amenable of plantain-

lilies. Leaves deserve especial consideration in hot weather because of the coolness of green. A variety of tones in foliage is
as important as bloom, and there is much variation in the leaf
pattern of the plantain-lilies. In moist, leafy soil there are bold
clumps of the grey leaves of *H. Sieboldiana*. For the margins
of shady beds the narrow-leaved plantain-lily, *H. lancifolia*,
makes a trim edging with a late-summer offering of drooping,
lavender flowers.

Gypsophila paniculata is not entirely satisfactory in the
South, but there are other species. The flowers of the rather
sprawling *G. pacifica* are as fine and as cool as mist. They are
white, tinged pink, or very rarely a beautiful deep pink. The
leaves are narrow and grey. This blooms in late July and August. A similar species, *G. acutifolia*, blooms in June. Both must
be planted only where they are to be allowed to sprawl, for staking is not successful, and the procumbent stems spread over
several feet. They need a very dry, alkaline soil and full sun.

The cool boltonias, with sparse, grey-green leaves and clouds
of aster-like flowers, freshen the borders in late summer.
B. asteroides comes late in July, followed in August by the
daintier, lilac-flowered *B. latisquama*. Both are tall, the first
to five or six feet, the second to about four feet. Both need
staking; every year you think they will not need to be staked,
and every year a heavy rain flops them on the ground when
they are in full bloom. Then they must be picked up out of the
mud and tied up. It is better to do it in the beginning. The pink
is not a strong grower. It never spreads, and sometimes it disappears altogether. The white is rapacious; it must be divided
every year or so to keep it from running out.

Our most spectacular native, the gorgeous rose-mallow, *Hibiscus coccineus*, from the swamps of Georgia and Florida,
comes into bloom late in July. The flowers are not the typical
bowls of the hibiscus. They open in a flat design as simple and
as complicated as designs in primitive art, with the pale green
star-points of the calyx showing in the interstices of the separate, rose red petals. They come out at the top of a single silver
stalk, one each day (without missing a day), as if more than
one of anything so resplendent would be too much, and stay

open until tea time. They are eight inches across. The leaves are compound, with tapering, coarsely-toothed divisions, and reddish veins and petioles. This rose-mallow is for Southern gardens only, unless the roots are wintered indoors. Dr. White reports that some plants are hardy at the Blandy Experimental Farm in northern Virginia, and others not, depending on their source. I have never lost any here through winter killing. Where they are hardy, they are long lived. This is a semi-aquatic species, standing any amount of moisture but becoming stunted in dry soil. It will grow in any soil, with the attention of the hose. It has no preference as to sun or shade. In the marginal shade of a Spanish oak, the pointed leaves of the rose-mallow, with the round, pale leaves of the plume-poppy, the yard-long lances of the crinum Cecil Houdyshel, and the fine greenery of a senna seedling are as arresting in color and pattern as a spring border in full bloom. The leafage of the plume-poppy, *Macleaya cordata*, is the coolest green in the garden. It wilts quickly, and as quickly revives, but it is to be planted in moist soil only in gardens where the hose is not put to conscientious use.

Hibiscus Golden Bowl is another striking rose-mallow for late summer. It is the same height as the red rose-mallow, to seven feet or a little more, but it is more spreading. The leaves are more coarsely lobed. The petals are round and overlapping; they are a pale yellow that is in sharp contrast to the dark red of the center. The flowers are eight inches across. This does exceedingly well in dry soil. It is perfectly winter hardy with me but not long lived. I have not been able to discover its origin.

On sultry mornings, flowers of Hibiscus Manihot Sunset look as cool as lemon ice. They are similar to those of the Golden Bowl but are only six inches across. The petals are a pale, chalcedony yellow with a small eye of Brazil red. The blunt-lobed leaves are to twelve inches across. The sight of the delicate flowers set at intervals from the base to the tip of the tapering stalk would be reward enough for the effort of making a summer garden. The plants should be placed where their entire length is visible. In not too dry ground the pale cups of the mallows are charming against the dark leaves and milky sprays of *Artemisia lactiflora*. The artemisia smells like water-lilies. Manihot Sunset is a half-hardy perennial reaching to six feet in height. It is probably hardy in the Middle South,[5] but in any case it is perfectly satisfactory as an annual. Plants from seeds sown the last day of April bloomed the twenty-sixth of July at a height of four feet. Mature plants are very drought resistant, but the seedlings must be kept moist enough to grow quickly. The seedlings are wonderful for filling in for late bloom, because even big plants are readily moved. All of the rose-mallows are easily raised from seed planted in the spring. *H. coccineus* blooms the first year, but only enough to encourage the gardener sowing it for the first time.

There are all sorts and sizes of heleniums. I have tried a number but I have never been able to acquire an intimacy with any but the standard Riverton Gem and Riverton Beauty, varieties of *H. autumnale*. Both are tall and vigorous. Riverton Gem is Brazil red with an edging of cadmium yellow. Riverton Beauty is light cadmium. They are planted at the back of the day-lilies to carry their colors into another season. In front of them is the low-growing golden aster, *Chrysopsis mariana*, a weedy composite, but gay for the time of year. With it is the dwarf helenium, Crimson Beauty. Above the yellowing leaves of the day-lilies the wands of the blackberry-lilies, *Belamcanda chinensis*, hold ephemeral flowers of ochre spotted with carmine. The heleniums must have moisture and must be divided every other year. They need deep soil and full sun.

When heleniums bloom in late August, the summer is already over. The heat is not ended, for we have some of our hottest days in September—or even in October. But the summer aspect of the borders is gone. Already there is a litter of dead leaves no matter how often the grass is raked. There is a blue haze in the trees, and there is a smell of fall.

---

[5] Of several plants blooming last summer from seed, one has lived through the winter.

The Climax of Fall

*T*hink we have more beautiful weather in the fall than at any other time of the year. In the garden this season should be the climax of bloom, rich in a new beauty of its own, and not just a period when there is some color left over from summer. After the intense heat diminishes, flowers revive. The grass is green again, colors are deeper, and the air is fresher. And there are unknown plant treasures for bloom before frost. In the South, where frost comes late, we should make more of this season than we do.

Bloom at the end of the year, more than at any other season, depends upon work done beforehand. All through the hot weather fading flowers must be clipped from long-blooming annuals and perennials so that they will continue to bloom. In midsummer the soil must be enriched to give new growth something to feed upon. A mixture of wood ashes, sheep manure, and fine leaf mold is a good summer tonic. When there is no rain the borders must be watered. Daily sprinkling is not necessary; a weekly soaking is enough, if the ground is really soaked. No amount of fresh plant material can bring to life a garden that has once been allowed to dry up entirely.

And fall is the season when there is most work to be done. Fall, not spring, is the time in this region to clear away dead leaves and branches, to renovate the borders, to start new gardens, to plant seeds of hardy annuals, to set out new perennials and shrubs. The laziest gardener should be able to get all of the chores done where there is no excuse of ground that

141

freezes early and stays frozen all winter. And even if something is left undone, everyone must take time to sit still and watch the leaves turn.

The Amaryllis Family

Toward the middle of September every garden in the South is filled with the flame-like flowers of red spider-lilies, *Lycoris radiata*. On the first days of the month, when the bloom of phlox is done and chrysanthemums are not even showing color, the season for flowers seems to have passed. Then the naked scapes of the red lilies spring up from bare ground and flower almost overnight, lighting all of the dark corners and even the waste places. In any garden where there are a few, there will soon be many, for the bulbs require shallow planting if they are to bloom, and with shallow planting they multiply rapidly. In my garden they have increased until they are everywhere—everywhere except in the borders, because there are few flowers of a color that is agreeable with the brilliant nopal red of the stiff long-stamened lilies. They are most beautiful planted to themselves, and there cannot be too many of them. The quick color that flares up as suddenly as a flame burns out almost as soon. After scarcely more than two weeks they are gone.

Until recently, when it was discovered that these red spider-lilies are identical with the Japanese *Lycoris radiata*, they were known in the South as *Nerine sarniensis*, the Guernsey-lily. In *Herbertia*, Vol. IV, Mr. Wyndham Hayward gives an account of how the mistake was at last cleared up. In North Carolina we might have wondered before, if we thought at all about the flowers that grow in our gardens, about the name nerine. For the nerine is a South African genus, and the first red spider-lilies in North Carolina (and probably in this country) came directly from Japan to a garden in New Bern. They were brought to that garden nearly a hundred years ago by Captain William Roberts who was with Commodore Perry when he opened the port of Japan. The Captain brought three bulbs which were, his niece Mrs. Simmons says, in such a dry condition that they did not show signs of life until the War between the States. The original bulbs have increased and been passed on until they have spread across the state. They grow as far west as Morganton but do not survive at Asheville. Maryland is the northern limit of their hardiness; near Baltimore they sometimes survive and bloom in sheltered places. The best time to divide the bulbs is after the foliage dies down in spring.

The golden spider-lily, *L. aurea*, is very hardy but not so dependable for the Middle South as the red one. In Mrs. Bahnson's garden in Winston-Salem it survived ten degrees below, blooming the following September. Billy Hunt blooms them in Chapel Hill, but Mr. Busbee's experience has been that they do not bloom after the first season, and mine that they do not bloom at all. For years the strap-like leaves have come up in the late fall as regularly as those of *L. radiata*, but never a bud. This is the hurricane lily of Florida that blooms at the time of the tropical storms.

The true *Nerine sarniensis* is rare in this country, and would probably not be hardy with us. *N. curvifolia* in the variety *Fothergillii* has not proved so, nor *N. Bowdenii*. So far the tiny, thread-leaved *N. filifolia* is the only species that has survived more than one winter in my garden, and it has never bloomed. This year two other species have been planted, but not very hopefully, for, in my experience, the bulbs from South Africa that do well with us are the exception rather than the rule.

Red spider-lilies are better known than most of the fall-blooming amaryllids, but there are others of importance to gardeners in the South. Their beauty and variety turn the last season of the year into a second and more brilliant spring. It may be that they are really no lovelier than spring bulbs, but only less taken for granted.

The ox-blood lily came into my garden some years ago as *Habranthus*, and spent some time there as *Hippeastrum advenum* before becoming *Amaryllis advena*.[1] Whatever the difficulty with the names, there is none in procuring the bulbs under one or another of them, or of getting the bulbs to grow. In any part of the garden they grow, increase, and bloom unfailingly. A well-established clump sends up a number of scapes between the first and last of September. A handful of bulbs will make a showing in a few years, or they may be had by the hundred (as *Habranthus*) from Texas at a very reasonable price.

The drooping, crystalline flowers of a lovely clear red, between the ox-blood and carmine of Ridgway, are all the more brilliant for a touch of green in the throat and the pale jade of the scapes. The leaves appear with or following the flowers, remain green and shimmering all winter, and disappear in the spring. This delightful amaryllid from Chile is perfectly hardy in North Carolina where it has been generously and enthusiastically distributed by Billy Hunt. How much farther north it will grow I am not certain, but it is said to be hardy to New York. The long-necked bulbs should be planted six inches deep; early summer, as soon as they are dormant, is the best time for dividing, but those moved after the flowers fade will bloom the next season. Mr. Houdyshel says that bulbs put out as late as the first of October will bloom at once.

The dark color of ox-blood lilies shows to best advantage against small white flowers. I have planted them along the top of a low retaining wall, with the lacy white verbena and the double Japanese aster. I try to remind myself to cut back the verbena and the aster in mid-August so that there will be a fresh and dainty flowering for September.

This morning I have been going about the garden in search of a new place for the rarer (and more expensive) pink form of the ox-blood lily. I found two ways of using the daphne red flowers—in bloom at present with the copper lilies, a ghastly combination. One way is to include them in the margin of a long border that features the showy sedum and physostegia Vivid at this time of the year. A second bloom of the phlox Mrs.

[1] *Herbertia*, Vol. V (1938), 122.

Milly van Hoboken adds to the series of greyed red-violets and blends with the tourmaline pink of the Japanese anemone, Queen Charlotte, where Japanese anemones can be established. With me they are not at all permanent. I see them blooming regularly for Mrs. Brimly along a shady stream, but they are doubtful in this climate in the average garden.

Another way to use the pink ox-blood lily is with clumps of rosy oxalis beneath clerodendrum. The clerodendrum berries are turning to turquoise just now, against their pomegranate sepals, and the oxalis is blooming out again after a rest period during the dry weather.

If my conception of color seems monotonous (and well it may), those with a flair for such things can very easily transform simple basic schemes into something more stirring. Unless one has a talent in this direction, an unambitious grouping of related or contrasting tones is the safest foundation for garden color. It will be pleasing if not exciting. I would not dare splash colors about my garden as boldly as Isabelle Henderson splashes them on either side of the brick path that winds through her generous borders to the door of her studio. But few gardeners are artists.

Sternbergias, *S. lutea*, once plentiful in the South, were so long neglected that they disappeared from all but a few Virginia gardens. From these they have begun to be redistributed. They are called fall daffodils because of the bright yellow of the petals, but the cupped flower is more like a daffodil-colored crocus. Like all short-stemmed flowers they are effective only in quantity, especially since every bulb will not bloom every year. In September (or even late in August) the eager buds push out of the ground just ahead of the strap-shaped leaves. In favorable places they last into October. Sternbergias are so partial to shallow planting that one which landed on top of the compost pile bloomed more freely, and made more divisions, than those in the ground. A light covering and full sun are necessary for the summer baking that ripens the bulbs. They grow on the shores of the Mediterranean Sea, and they are said to be the lilies of the field. In spite of their provenance they are among the hardier amaryllids, wintering anywhere in the South, and even—it is said—to Boston.

Tuberoses, *Polianthes tuberosa*, winter in my garden, but bulbs left in the ground cannot be counted upon for bloom the following summer. They may bloom, and they may not. The buds may be killed by a degree of cold that will not hurt the bulbs. This is what probably happens to other members of the family that winter in my garden but do not bloom. Tuberoses bloom, when they do so, in August and September. I have had flowers as early as July and as late as the twenty-seventh of October. I like to plant them at the back of the bed so that the perennials in front will soften the effect of the tall bare stalks topped by small clusters of sweet, waxen flowers.

The summer crocus, *Zephyranthes candida*, comes to us from South America where it silvers the marshes of the La Plata, giving to it the name of silver river. This species blooms more profusely, and increases more rapidly, than any of the zephyr-lilies that I have had; it also blooms more continuously than any of the others. It is characteristic of the genus to produce flowers in flushes, with intervals of rest. The original handful of these bulbs that I had from Mrs. Lay have so multiplied that they have spread out over my garden, and into many others. With moisture they bloom fairly steadily from July to late fall, but most freely in September. In dry places they bloom in the fall after rain, or when they are watered. The flowers are crystalline goblets that bring a welcome freshness to heat-ridden gardens. The evergreen leaves are rushlike and shining. This is the hardiest of the species. It is said to winter at Philadelphia.

There are sometimes fall flowers from other zephyr-lilies. Occasionally *Z. grandiflora* repeats in September, and *Z. Ajax* often blooms then. And there are flushes of *Z. texana* and *Z. citrina* in September and again in October.

The fall-flowering, red-and-white-striped crinum of old gardens in East Carolina is called, as are all those of this type, the milk-and-wine lily. It is sold in North Carolina as *C. fimbriatulum*, and in Texas as the Angel Lily. Botanically it is unaccounted for. Whatever it is, it is one of the most beautiful crinums and one of the most satisfactory garden plants to be had, not particular as to soil or situation, and requiring no attention. But there will be more flower scapes if it is watered in the dry periods of late summer and fall. Like other crinums it blooms better every year that it is left undisturbed. I have had as many as eighteen scapes at one time from a group of established clumps.

The earliest date that I have recorded for the milk-and-wine lily is the third of August; the latest is the ninth of November. The late blooms are somewhat stunted, but even so they seem very fragile and lovely in that frosty season. Usually the last scapes are frozen. Always, from early August to the first hard freeze, established clumps send up scape after scape. The long, striped buds open suddenly in the late afternoon into wide, starry flowers. The narrow, milk-white, wine-stained petals are separate and pointed. There are from four to six flowers to an umbel, and by the second evening all are out at once. The foliage, of a very distinct tone of yellow-green, is particularly luxuriant.

As to its hardiness north of us, I cannot say. A bulb sent to Mrs. Bahnson in Winston-Salem lived through one winter and bloomed, but was killed by last winter's ten-below weather. Bulbs sent to Elizabeth Rawlinson were winter-killed, as were others sent at various times to a garden near York, Pennsylvania.

Late Annuals

Early in September I saw in Mr. Clement's rock garden a prostrate marigold that is one of the most charming dwarf annuals that I have ever come across. He said that it was called Pigmy Gold, and that the seeds had come from California. He gave me a handful of ripe ones. The deep yellow buttons and the clean foliage of the shapely little plants would be as desirable for edging as for growing among rocks. The list of low-growing annuals for fall is none too long. In fact it is nearly completed with torenias, alyssum, and *Zinnia linearis*. Torenias are as fresh in fall as in summer if the old plants are pulled up and late seedlings allowed to take their places. Summer-sown sweet alyssum lasts until Christmas, but spring plants bloom out in the heat. A second sowing is better than old plants that have been cut back.

Marigolds do not last through two seasons. They can be sown a second time to provide fall flowers, or late-blooming forms can be planted. Mr. Tong used to have one that he called the October marigold. No matter when the seeds were sown the plants would not bloom until October. Then they would be a mass of yellow and maroon. This was a very hardy type that escaped all but the heaviest frosts, blooming until very late in the year. But one year the crop was killed before seeds were ripe, so then there were no more October marigolds. Mr. Fowler, Mr. Tong's successor, says he thinks he has found it again. I hope so, for no plant so rejuvenates the late garden as this sturdy annual with its bright flowers and dark, pungent leaves.

Sometimes good annuals are grown for awhile and then forgotten. Now no one plants the tall Klondyke cosmos that was once so popular for fall. The six-foot stalks clothed to the ground in dark leaves and deep yellow flowers make a thick screen, and they provide cut flowers until the end of the season. Paula Patrick bordered the boys' playground with this tall cosmos, and when it bloomed, making a wall of gold, people from all around came to see. Unlike the dwarf Orange Flare, it waits for cool weather to bloom. Orange Flare blooms freely in the fall if it is continually cut back, or, if the first flowers are allowed to go to seed, the seedlings bloom in September.

The modern forms of the old scarlet sage, *Salvia splendens*, are from one to three feet tall, and bloom in soft tones of rose, lilac, and violet. Early-blooming varieties have also been developed. These are not an advantage where the falls are long and warm, and frost comes late, and where the need is for late bloom.

Bringing crotalarias from fields to gardens has done much for southern borders. The giant *C. spectabilis* is the forage crop that is so beautiful in the autumn countryside. In a good form, the golden spikes can be very showy in the garden, but I have only once hit upon a good form. Often the plants are coarse and leggy, with more leaves than flowers. Plants started early grow to five feet or more. *C. retusa* is smaller, never more than three feet high and sometimes less. The very large, lemon-colored peas are touched with brick red. The blunt leaves are a cool grey-green. These species reseed sparingly, if at all, and must be sown each spring. They are listed in most southern seed catalogues as *C. spectabilis* with the farm and field crops, and *C. retusa* with garden flowers. Usually scarified seeds are offered, otherwise they should be rubbed between two bricks, or dipped in boiling water before they are planted. Sown by mid-April they produce flowers early in August.

The success of these crotalarias made me wonder if there were not other ornamental species. An inquiry brought seeds of several sorts from the Forage Crops division of the Bureau of Plant Industry. Among these *C. usaramoensis* proved to be the only one of merit in the flower garden. Mr. Mckee, who sent them to me, said that he knew of no other source for the seed. I save some every season and try to pass them on to as many gardeners as possible, for I know of no more satisfactory annual for fall. Fortunately, this species is self perpetuating. Also, the seedlings are readily transplanted. This is a great advantage in filling in gaps in the border, and it is not true of the other two kinds. The slender grey leaves of *C. usaramoensis* are in threes. The plants are more than four feet tall and are very spreading, with branches to the ground. The long (to fifteen inches), narrow racemes are crowded with small lemon chrome flowers inconspicuously marked with maroon. The flowers at the tip open before those at the base are faded, so that the slender raceme reaches perfection before the delicate yellow turns to terra cotta, as it does when the flowers fade.

Crotalarias, being legumes, need no fertilizer. They grow in the poorest, driest soil, but they require full sun. They are called rattle-boxes because the dry seeds rattle in the pods, but in this case the scientific name is better known than the common one. I am sure that there are more good garden species in the world if I could only lay my hands on them. One that I read about in *Gardening Illustrated* is *C. laburnifolia*, known to English gardeners as the birdflower because the lime-colored flowers are like birds in flight. As yet I have found no source for this species, but it blooms in the garden of my imagination, where the flowers are rare and unobtainable.

In the spring I pull up the annual ageratum that is as determined a seeder as any weed, but no matter how carefully it is eradicated, it comes up as thickly as ever and by fall it is all through the borders, overlaying with blue the gold of crotalaria and *Zinnia linearis*. The weedy type, *A. mexicanum*, is more satisfactory than the compact, named hybrids that turn brown in dry weather.

The first year that I planted Mexican sunflowers, *Tithonia speciosa*, the plants branched to the ground, and every branch was tipped with a lacquer red flower thrust through a tangle of yellow crotalaria and a blue haze of ageratum. That was a long, golden fall. The borders have never been so beautiful since. And the Mexican sunflowers have been snatched away as too coarse for the garden. Now they are kept for cutting only, and the enormously tall plants are left on the ground when they are blown over in the August storms. They bloom as well with half their roots in the air and they are much easier to pick, for the flowers can be reached only with a step ladder when the plants are upright. Last year I had the variety Fireball, advertised as "extra early blooming, extra large flowers and extra gorgeous color." I could not see that it differed materially from the type, except that the leaves were much more hairy. Mexican sunflowers seldom seed themselves. They must be sown early in May to bloom in September.

Two annual vines may be useful for late flowers. The Alamo vine, *Ipomoea alamo*, is a pretty, fall-flowering morning-glory. I planted seeds at the end of April, and the first buds opened today, the sixteenth of September. The catalogue description (my only source of information) does not indicate the origin of the species or state whether it can be expected to become a pest. I do not think, however, that blooming so late it can set enough seeds to be troublesome. The rather small, white flowers reverse the morning-glory habit by opening late and remaining open in the afternoon. The white of the corolla is set off by the dark wine color of the throat, and creamy anthers add to delicacy of the flower pattern. The leaves are not at all like morning-glory leaves. They are a beautiful dark green, deeply lobed and intricately cut. They grow thickly and make a neat flat screen. The descriptive synonym, mile-a-minute vine, sounds rather alarming, but the growth is not so fast; in fact, not so fast as could be desired if the vine is to be used as a screen. One of the chief virtues of the Alamo vine is drought resistance.

I always try to remember to buy a pot of *Thunbergia alata* from the florist in spring to put in the garden for fall, picking out from those already in bloom the creamy ones in preference to the bright yellow. This tender perennial from tropical Africa can be grown out of doors as an annual. Seeds are offered by Park in separate colors: cream, yellow, and white. The bright, dark-centered flowers trail over the rock garden, or cover the foliage of plants that have bloomed earlier.

Late Perennials

In a climate where many standard fall flowers bloom before fall comes, or not at all, there must be a search for others that will adapt themselves to existing conditions. After repeated failure I have given up *Chrysanthemum uliginosum, Cimicifuga simplex*, and the deep blue aconites. In the fall I think of aconite in a New England garden by the sea, but I no longer try to have it in mine.

The list of perennials for September is limited. One of the best for this difficult month is the showy sedum, *S. spectabile*, which has gone out of fashion but should certainly come back in. The pale, succulent leaves are of interest before the plant comes into bloom, and in September the flat, wide flowerheads color the border with patches of subdued rose, or with a redder tint in the variety Brilliant. The color is in keeping with the bright red-violets of physostegia Vivid and New England asters, or with the softer blue violets of ageratum, blue spiraea, and the mealycup sage. No perennial is more useful for difficult places. For it is unaffected by drought or shade or lack of nourishment. I do not think there is a place where it will refuse to grow.

Small pink zinnias planted in early summer, bloom in September with the showy sedum and pale blue asters. Queen Mary, a medium-tall aster (to three and a half feet, but usually less) with smooth leaves, and comparatively large lavender flowers, is an improved form of the aster Climax. It does well with us, blooming all through September and lasting into October. A similar but better aster of unknown origin blooms in my garden at the same time as Queen Mary. The flowers of this are more numerous and of a more decided color, the habit is less sprawling. I think this is a good type for us.

The dwarf asters have not been a success in the South. I think the difficulty is with the late, dry weather. After the August rains, there are usually many weeks of drought. Victor, the least attractive of the dwarf sorts, is the only one that persists. The colorless mauve flowers appear in September. It is very dwarf, only eight inches in height, compact, and free flowering.

The second bloom of day-lilies and torch-lilies is like a return of summer. *Hemerocallis* May Queen (the tall orange one) is one of the most faithful repeaters. In cool weather the flowers last more than a day and seem to be handsomer than in spring. Fall flowers from the broad dwarf day-lily are certain, and there are buds on *Hemerocallis flava major* from the end of summer to Thanksgiving. Other sorts flower a second time in some seasons. And there are more torch-lilies. *Kniphofia Pfitzeri* blooms at intervals before frost, and in October there is a reflowering of Towers of Gold. This year I had nine scapes from the clump that bloomed so well in July.

In September the mealycup sage, *Salvia farinacea*, blooms with new vigor, and the pale spires become more intense. And at this time also, *Salvia Pitcheri* brings one of the most vivid blues to the borders. The flowers top the tall, stiff stalks. The most spectacular autumn sage is the last one to bloom. This is the Mexican brush sage, *S. leucantha*, a species that has been proved hardy only as far as South Carolina. With me the last two winters were too cold for plants sent from Mrs. McColl's garden in Bennettsville, but in milder seasons, or with some protection, established plants might live through the winter. In Virginia or in the mountains the species is definitely tender. Even in gardens where it does not persist, it is a perennial worth planting for a season's bloom, and after searching for years, I have found it listed (for the first time) in Fruitland's catalogue. This lovely salvia grows to four feet in a season, and spreads as much. The tapering leaves are a dull yellow-green. In October and November the branches end in velvet racemes of hyacinth violet. The racemes are eighteen inches long. It is the brilliantly colored calyx that makes the show. The small white flower does not count in the general effect. This sage is delightful with the clear yellow of *Crotalaria usaramoensis*, the purple of New England asters, and the violets of the verbenas *erinoides*, *venosa*, and *bonariensis*. All three salvias to be well grown must be uncrowded. They prefer full sun and a light soil that is not too well fertilized.

The ginger-lily, *Hedychium coronarium*, is a tender, tuberous-rooted perennial related to commercial ginger, and like it in appearance. It has the other pretty common names of butterfly-lily and garland-flower. Native to tropical Asia, it is very generally planted in Florida, and two other species are in the trade. Mine came with Mrs. Dabney from Mississippi. It is not common with us, although it is hardy in Virginia. Violet Walker reports (*Gardeners' Chronical*, February, 1940) that it came through the severe weather of last winter in her garden at Woodberry Forest where it has grown for five or six years protected only by a mulch of manure.

In Raleigh the ginger-lily blooms throughout September and October. It is a robust plant over four feet tall, with canna-like leaves and sprays of delightfully fragrant white flowers. The fragrance becomes more penetrating in the evening. The generic name means sweet snow. It grows in a heavy, rich soil in sun or part shade. Plenty of moisture in the growing season is essential. Mrs. Royster's great clumps, of long standing, are planted conveniently at the foot of the garden spigot.

H. Gardnerianum is a yellow-flowered species from tropical India, where it grows at high elevations. It is considered hardier than *H. coronarium*; I have kept it through two winters, but it has not bloomed.

Chrysanthemum coreanum, a pretty white daisy of uncertain origin, is the humble parent of the multicolored Korean hybrids. Inclined to be an aggressor, it may not be allowed a choice place in the borders, but few gardeners will be unable to find use for a perennial requiring no attention and blooming generously at the end of September and into October. This one also comes through summer drought better than most plants, blooms in any soil, and even tolerates a small amount of shade. The stocky plants grow to two or three feet, with dark leaves that are thin and prettily cut.

Once I made up my mind to get rid of all the blue mistflower, *Eupatorium coelestinum*, because of its spreading tendencies, and because it is attacked by a wilt when in full bloom. However, it outgrows the disease in time; the shallow roots are easily held within bounds, and the abundance of lavender violet is very desirable at the end of September, especially with a late crop of rose-colored zinnias. Its other advantages are that it will grow in poor soil and in part shade.

The perennial sunflowers, blooming in succession from late summer to late autumn, are coarse plants, but not too coarse to be very welcome when bloom is scarce. Some of them, such as the tuberous-rooted Jerusalem artichoke, *Helianthus tuberosus*, are too invasive to plant with other perennials, but there are others that keep to their places. *H. rigidus* var. Miss Mellish, a tall garden form of the stiff sunflower, blooms early in the season, and is followed in September by the linear-leaved sunflower, *H. orgyalis*. The latter is a long-legged plant (to eight feet) topped by a bunch of coreopsis-like daisies. It is not prepossessing when left to its own devices, but Miss Jekyll contrived a way of pinning the stalks down over the foliage of earlier blooming perennials to encourage the growth of extra flowers all along the stem.

The best and latest of the perennial sunflowers is autumn glory, *H. angustifolius*. This dazzling species does not begin to bloom before early October, and then it blooms furiously until the end of the month. From the ground up, the straight stalks are covered with bright yellow, dark centered daisies. It grows to five or six feet. The linear leaves are very highly polished. This very much to be desired perennial is hard to find in the trade. Mine came from Mr. Tong who had it from Mrs. Mitchener who had it from some other gardener. I know of no source for plants, and so far as I know only the invaluable Park offers seed. In the wild this species grows in swamps, but moisture is not necessary to its well being. It grows and flowers cheerfully in the driest places. All of the above species grow in dry soil and full sun. They require frequent division.

Another tall autumn flower is the Tartarian aster, *A. tataricus*, a native of Siberia, with coarse basal leaves that are sometimes two feet long. Planted at the back of a damp border the slender seven foot stalks bend over the spent perennials in front, covering iris, loosestrife, and bergamot with great panicles of pale mauve daisies from the middle of September to late October. This aster is a spreader that must be watched, but it is not hard to keep in bounds. It will bloom in sun or part shade and will do fairly well in dry places, though it will not be so vigorous as in moist ones—which may not be a drawback.

For late bloom in the wild garden I have a shrubby member of the mint family, *Clinopodium carolinianum*. This small evergreen, with narrow aromatic leaves and dull lavender flowers, is native from North Carolina to Georgia. It blooms from August through the fall.

Anemone hupehensis, a dwarf form of the Japanese anemone, is better suited to our conditions than the type. Here, it requires full shade and a leafy soil, and fits in with the wild flowers rather than the perennials. The small, rose-colored blossoms continue until frost.

In the copse a bright patch of bottle gentian, *Gentiana Andrewsii*, blooms under a strawberry-bush all through November. The crimson fruits of the strawberry-bush, *Euonymus americana*, dripping scarlet seeds, color late in September and fall before the gentian is out. This gentian is one of the

easiest of the woods flowers to establish in the wild garden, and for its lateness and blueness it is unique. It is the last flower of the year.

Garden Chrysanthemums

In the South, where frost comes late, early flowering is not one of the traits desirable in chrysanthemums for the garden. Early varieties, such as Barbara Cumming or Aladdin, open in the hot, dry weather and seldom flourish.

The Korean hybrids come soon enough. They begin to bloom before the middle of October and they last to about the middle of November. The first one to bloom is Mercury, which opens while the buds of the others are showing color. Mercury was also the first of these hybrids to appear in gardens. The flowers are single, to three inches across, and of a warm dark red touched with copper, becoming more coppery with age. Mars is pomegranate purple with an old gold center. Orion, the last to bloom, is a clear lemon yellow, one of the most dazzling of autumn colors. Saturn is orange-rufous with a narrow central zone of lemon chrome and a cadmium yellow center. The flowers are slightly smaller than the usual three inches. I love these starry daisy types, and I wish the originators had made it a rule to name them all for planets and constellations—Mercury, Mars, Orion, Saturn, and the rosy Venus are as lovely to name as to look upon. Daphne, the loveliest of the pinks, is deep vinaceous, which means a pale wine color. The flowers are single but have a few extra petals. Diana is the only dull color in the group; the flowers are a muddy rose. The rather small flowers of Ceres come out the color of ripe grain and turn pink with age. This is one of the first to bloom.

The flowers of the semi-double and double Koreans repeat the colors of the single varieties. The semi-doubles are rather smaller in size, with an extra row or so of petals. Apollo is redder than Saturn, between dragons-blood red and Brazil red, with the same cadmium center and narrow ring of lemon chrome at the base of the petals. This marking distinguishes these two, and gives them an added brilliance. Venus is a paler vinaceous than Daphne, a little toward lavender. Louise Schling—not actually a Korean hybrid, but similar in appearance and coloring—is a smoldering orange with a touch of Pompeian red, a color that carries a long distance.

The double Koreans are like the aster-flowered chrysanthemums. To me the charm of the Koreans is in the daisy-like flowers, and when they are diverted from that form they have no advantage over the ordinary varieties. There are, however, some very good flowers and some very striking colors among the doubles. Indian Summer is dragons-blood red. Caliph is a velvet flower of dark glowing red that checks with Ridgway's garnet brown (but is not at all brown). It is good in combination with the clear yellow of Midas. The Moor checks as the same color as Mars, but they are very different in garden effect; the Moor is dull, and Mars is brilliant.

When the Korean hybrids are used in the borders, their rich warm tones are dulled if they are allowed to bloom with the clear, strong colors of autumn perennials. Apollo is brilliant enough to hold its own with the fresh yellow of crotalarias, but not with the orange of marigolds, or the scarlet of the dwarf pomegranate. Only the pure yellow of Orion or the deep red velvet of Caliph, can do that. For the most part the Koreans are more effective when planted to themselves in related tones, or with other chrysanthemums, than with mixed perennials. The terra cotta of the early aster-flowered variety Granny Scoville blends with tones of dragons-blood red and maroon; Garnet Gem blends with the slightly redder shade of Louise Schling. The greyed pink and purple of Daphne and Mars, as intense and restrained as sun-faded silks, mingle as perfectly as inter-woven colors in changeable taffeta.

Most of the Korean hybrids are of average height, but there is one very tall one, and there are some dwarfs. Country Girl is a tall variety to four or five feet, with an equal spread. Innocence and Sappho are delightful, early-flowering dwarfs to about eighteen inches. The first is a pure white daisy that turns pink as it fades. This is a spreading plant, and it is very free of bloom. Sappho is a pale yellow and is semi-double; the flowers are rather small. Pygmy Gold is another yellow. It is not at all like a Korean, being a large-flowered pompon. It is not so good as some of the other dwarfs in flowering habit or in foliage, but the flowers are of a clear lemon yellow. This, too, is early.

The Korean hybrids are not very persistent. But this is not serious, for they can be raised easily from seed, and some will bloom the first year. Orion, Country Girl, Saturn, and Indian Summer are those most likely to stay on.

There are other lovely single chrysanthemums both new and old. Gretchen Piper is a large, single yellow that blooms early in the season. The yellow and white Mensas both bloom late; they are very handsome and very distinct in form, but are not often seen in gardens. The old Bronze Buckingham, a sport of Mrs. Buckingham, blooms at mid-season. And the late, floppy, pink flowers of Mrs. Buckingham I never want to be without, no matter what there is that is new and better. Ella Guilford is another good single pink, similar to Mrs. Buckingham. And at the end of the season there is the old single white that always flops over into the path and always comes after the first frost, showering fresh white daisies over flowers that have been touched.

There seems to be no strict line drawn between the pompons and the buttons. Minong, classed as a button, but really more of a pompon, is one of the best early whites. It is not very tall. Jewell is a large early pompon advertised as bright pink. It is bright but not pink. The flowers are a garish tone of mallow purple. But it is vigorous, free-blooming, and showy. These two are in full bloom by mid-October. The lovely pink Lillian Doty and White Doty come later. Irene is an early white button with small flowers like a glorified feverfew; it blooms early in October. Ethel is bright English red, and blooms rather late. It is of good habit and bushy foliage. The curiously-colored, button flowers of Judith Anderson are lemon chrome on the outside, with an orange flush at the center. This is twenty-eight inches tall; it blooms after the middle of October. The buttons are hardy, free-flowering, and adaptable to arrangement.

The early dwarfs are the familiar Pink Cushion and the ugly, bronzed King Cushion. The best of this group is Red Cushion, one of the latest chrysanthemums in bloom. It comes along with Christmas Gold at the end of November, after frost has carried off all of the others. It is about twelve inches tall. The garnet flowers are small and bright and very resistant to cold. Clara Curtis is another of the low, bushy chrysanthemums; it has lately come into prominence. This is a garden form of *C. erubescens*, a fall-flowering species. The flowers are single pink daisies. Astrid is a garden form of *C. arcticum*. The flowers come out white and turn pink. They are like single Koreans on eighteen inch stems. Astrid is very early; it has passed its best bloom by mid-October.

Chrysanthemums should be divided every year, and in this part of the country it is best to divide them early, so that the plants will get a good start before hot weather. April is the time to divide one's own, and new plants should be set out early in May. If old manure is spaded into the ground when this is done, summer fertilizing will not be necessary for garden effect. Chrysanthemums need good drainage, full sun, and plenty of moisture. A long soaking with the hose in dry weather is essential. I find that a mulch of coal ashes helps to keep them over the winter.

Vines for Fall Bloom

A number of vines flower in the fall. There are hardy kinds such as the silver lacevine, *Polygonum Aubertii*, and the Japanese clematis, *Clematis paniculata*, and there are tender climbers grown as annuals such as *Cobaea scandens*. In the South, cobea will grow to ten or twenty feet in a season from seeds planted in the open after the ground warms up. It prefers sun, but tolerates shade, and it must have moisture. Last year in November a vine planted on Mrs. Von Glahn's terrace was hung with purple bells, and the leaves were fresh and green.

One of the colorful late-flowering climbers of the Lower South is root hardy in sheltered places in the Middle South. This is the coral-vine, *Antigonon leptopus*, native to Mexico. In Raleigh one of these covers the south-facing chimney of a charming old house on Jones street. Yesterday, in mid-October, I saw in passing that there were delicate sprays of dusty rose massed against the old-rose colored brick; this had happened after one of our worst winters. The vine grows to fifteen feet in a season (it is killed back to the roots in winter) and begins to bloom in September. I have heard rumors of a coral-vine in Danville, Virginia, but I have never been able to substantiate them.

Fall-Flowering Shrubs

In any season the flowering shrubs make the garden, but they are particularly important at the end of the year when they are most necessary and least familiar. Early in September I went to see Mr. Clement and found the Franklinia, *Gordonia alatamaha*, in full bloom. I had never before seen one so covered with flowers. A flower lover who had arrived ahead of me was in ecstasies. "Why," she demanded turning on Mr. Clement, "have I not been told about this?" Mr. Clement and I exchanged glances. Garden literature in recent years has devoted much space to the picturesque history of the Franklinia. And still the rows of little trees on the North Carolina mountainside must go to England to be appreciated, for few people are moved by a written description to go out and buy a plant and put it in their gardens. So the Franklinias wait in the nurseries until someone happens along in September to be charmed by the five-petaled, scentless, white flowers, cup-shaped and filled with straw-colored stamens. But I must say that the tree, with its branches bare except for the narrow drooping leaves at the tips, is not pretty when it is out of bloom. The plants are slow growing and do not bloom until they are five or six years old. They grow in time to be small shrub-like trees. According to the taste of the tea family, they prefer a moist, acid soil, well supplied with humus.

The Argentine senna, *Cassia corymbosa*, is much more spectacular than the hardier native species, and in the South it grows out of doors. In a short time the bushes grow eight or ten feet tall, with an ample spread. At the end of August and early in September, the cool grey leaves and the corymbs of bright yellow flowers are unbelievably gay and fresh after a dry summer. Old plants should be pruned severely in spring, to force new wood for the season's bloom. But the trunks should not be cut to the ground as one is tempted to do because the branches leaf so late in the year and look like dead sticks in spring. One of the gardener's problems is where to put this senna so that it will be prominent in September and unnoticed in April. This species is easily grown from seed, and the seedlings reach blooming size in three or four years. A few of those that are self sown should be left to replace the large shrubs, for an unduly cold winter occasionally takes them off.

There are other lovely cassias, and I have tried to grow them here—for they are all very easy from seed—but *C. corymbosa* is the only exotic species that I have found to be hardy. One from Africa, *C. nairobensis*, is usable as an annual. Seeds I sowed in mid-April produced shrubs that reached ten feet by fall. I can think of nothing more decorative for a summer screen than the grey-green, broadly pinnate leaves; but the flowers came at the end of October, too late to be of much value, for they were touched by early frost. The plants were not killed until the middle of November. The cassias need full sun and a light, dry soil.

As you drive through the country in September there is a bush-clover, *Lespedeza formosa*, in every yard, but it is always the same purple one with its dull magenta flowers. In only two southern gardens have I seen the white-flowered variety *albiflora* that blooms from early September until the end of the month. The dainty flowers in erect racemes are smaller than those of the type. Their spring-like appearance is delightful in the fall of the year. Bush-clovers come up from roots in spring, sending up arching shoots to four feet with an even wider spread. They are best in sun and are not particular as to soil.

Through the month of September, the soft haze of blue spiraea, *Caryopteris incana*, is the most delicate color in the border. There are pink and white forms, but it is the grey blue-violet of the type that is so pleasing with the grey, aromatic leaves. This somewhat tender member of the verbena family is hardy only in southern gardens. It needs an uncrowded place in light soil and in full sun. It is not improved by drought. As a shrub it is of a size to fit in with perennials, growing to a little over three feet, and spreading as much. A correspondent in *Garden Gossip* (March, 1937) suggests planting blue spiraea as an annual, sowing the seeds in April. "The plants were put out in the borders in mid-June, and in August were shapely little bushes from eighteen inches to two feet in height, completely covered with their soft, pure bloom. They seemingly can be moved at any time, and can take the place in the borders of waning zinnias or defunct poppies." No matter how often I go through already much underlined and very dirty files of *Garden Gossip*, I find bits that I have missed.

In spring, in Miss Edna Maslin's garden, I came upon bold shoots of an exotic-looking plant with reddish leaves newly un-

furled and stiff stems jointed like bamboo. "That," Miss Edna said, "is the Chinese bamboo." "But it couldn't be a bamboo." "Yes, Elizabeth, it is the Chinese bamboo." It proved to be a polygonum, a valuable one for fall bloom. It is cut to the ground in winter, and in spring sends up strong, bamboo-like shoots with wide, decorative, heart-shaped leaves. The shoots grow to fifteen feet by September, producing great sprays of fine, rosy red flowers. Some of the polygonums are hard to eradicate. Among these are two coarse and weedy autumn-flowering perennials known in the trade as *P. compactum* and *P. oxyphyllum*; both are to be avoided. The flowers are inconspicuous and the roots are nine lived. I do not think that there will be any difficulty of this kind with Miss Edna's Chinese bamboo, for it is so slow of increase that there is a waiting list for the offsets.

When October comes, and even fall flowers are beginning to pale, the bright buds of the dwarf pomegranate, *Punica Granatum nana*, grow more intense in color. In warmer climates this is an evergreen growing to five feet in height. With me it is cut back to the ground in winter and comes up tardily in spring, making a shapely bush to three feet. The numerous branchlets are covered with narrow, shimmering leaves and are tipped from September to frost with clusters of waxen, scarlet buds that open to display flounces of crinkled petals of an even more intense scarlet. The dwarf pomegranate is very drought resistant, blooming quite gayly in an unwatered garden. Its preference is for neutral soil and full sun.

Anisacanthus, a small shrub native to Texas, blooms a little in late summer, and more in late October. I found it in a list of shrubs described as climate proof and thought it would be a good thing for us. The small, tubular flowers in terminal spikes are not conspicuous, but they are a rare and lovely color, a tint of red-orange that is called grenadine. The small leaves are pale and shining, round at the base, and sharply tapered. It is described as a shrub from two to five feet, but here it seems unlikely to be more than three. I have not discovered any particular requirements for it except that it needs full sun.

In the woods, when the leaves are falling, the native witch-hazel, *Hamamelis virginiana*, blooms. I used to know where to find it, and I would go there in November with my grandmother to gather branches bare of leaves and fringed with sulphur-colored flowers. Now there are houses and gardens where the woods used to be. But a few nurserymen still grow the witch-hazel, and it finds a place in cultivation in the damper, shadier parts of the shrubbery, or in woodsy plantings of native shrubs and wild flowers. It is not an ornament in seasons other than fall.

In this part of the world, the broad-leaved evergreens are the choice shrubs for each season, and there are some in flower at all times of the year.

That the tea plant, *Thea sinensis*, from whose leaves is made the tea we drink, grows in the garden always seems to me as improbable as the possession of a breadfruit tree. In more favorable climates it is a sizeable shrub, and it blooms all through the winter. Here it is small, to about four feet, and blooms from late September until almost Thanksgiving. The fragrant white flowers and the pearly buds appear in quantities when the roots are in moist soil. The flowers are like those of the Franklinia: five concave, crinkled petals, cupped about the numerous pale gold stamens; but they are smaller, being less than two inches across, and are set on curved pedicels. This is a less hardy relative of the Camellia, requiring the same culture: an acid soil well supplied with humus, part shade, and in summer a mulch of peat moss.

The tea plant can be tucked into a small garden, but the tea olive, *Osmanthus Fortunei*, needs space. Instead of being crowded into a narrow planting, or huddled against a building, it should be set out in the open where it can grow into a shapely bush to fifteen feet (or more) tall, with a spread equal to its height. In fall, and again in spring, there are bunches of small, unbearably sweet, cream-colored flowers among the dark holly leaves. Fortune's tea olive is a hybrid, of Japanese origin, between the sweet olive and the holly-leaved tea olive, *Osmanthus ilicifolius*. It grows in sun or part shade and likes a rich soil.

After the fall rains, the damnacanthus blooms again as in spring. The twiggy stems are covered with the small white flowers and purple-tipped buds that continue to appear until well into November.

Fall-Fruiting Shrubs

The most decorative of the fruiting shrubs present, in autumn, wide areas of positive color. Some of them color late, and their fruits are all the more brilliant against dark leaves or grey stems. Others begin to glow in orange or red before summer is fairly over. These must be planted with careful regard for the flowers that are apt to be in bloom at the time. It will not do for the deepening orange of the berries of Laland's firethorn to appear with the red-violets of the late flowers of crape-myrtle or butterfly-bush.

Later spikes of two buddlejas, the near magenta Charming or the rosy Ile de France, are a good note with the bishop's purple of the Japanese beauty-berry, *Callicarpa Japonica*, especially against a background of grey—either of foliage or a stone wall. This is for September. The berries begin to color in August, and by October they have fallen. The Chinese beauty-berry, *C. dichotoma*, has smaller fruits and smaller leaves. Both the Japanese and the Chinese species are rather small, bushy shrubs to about four feet in height. The pretty but not conspicuous pink flowers come in midsummer. The more tender native species, called—for some unknown reason—the French-mulberry, *C. americana*, is even more magnificent than the Asiatic kinds as to fruit, though it is a coarse-leaved shrub, not attractive in habit. It is taller, too, being from six to ten feet. The blue flowers in summer are soon followed by cymes of large, bright, violet berries, bead-like and shiny. This grows in rich woods from Virginia south. In cultivation it grows in wet or dry places, in sun or part shade, and in any soil.

Japanese persimmons, *Diospyros Kaki*, are adapted to planting in the cotton belt, but they are not planted in the Middle South as generally as one would expect from the decorative value of their fruits. Dr. White says that several varieties are hardy at Boyce, and that the fruits of one have matured. There are several fine ones in Raleigh gardens. The persimmons are very large, to more than three inches across. In the named varieties they vary in shape from round to oval, and in color from yellow to scarlet. In Japan and China this is a large tree, but in cultivation in this part of the country it is a small or medium-sized shrub.

Several of the deciduous Oriental viburnums bear conspicuous red berries in the fall. One of the most striking in fruit is the tea viburnum, *V. theiferum*, of China. In October, the berries, like big holly berries without lustre, turn to nopal red. They are hung in drooping corymbs along the stem, and they persist well into the winter. This is a large, vigorous shrub to ten feet, with coarse, leathery leaves to five inches long. Another large, coarse-leaved species is *V. Wrightii*, from Japan. The fruits are dark red.

The best known of the native deciduous hollies is the native winterberry, *Ilex verticillata*. It grows in swamps and needs moisture. It thrives in shade in acid soil, and unlike most hollies, is easy to transplant. The large berries thickly clustered along the beautifully mottled, grey stems ripen in September. They are vividly scarlet in the woods after the leaves have fallen, and they hang on and keep their bright color until after Christmas. The fine-tooth holly, *I. serrata*, of Japan is more graceful in habit than the winterberry; it is about the same height, eight to ten feet, or a little taller. The leaves are small; the fruits are bright red and very shiny. The possum-haw, *I. decidua*, another native species, occurs only in the southern states. This is also a swamp holly, but it is amenable to adverse conditions and will thrive in dry soil. It grows in clumps, to a height of about fifteen feet, but spreads slowly. The bright orange red berries persist on the pale grey stems until spring.

Of the evergreen hollies with colored fruits, only the American holly is generally hardy in the North. In the South both the native and Asiatic species are among the shrubs most valuable for persistent fruits. The beautiful English holly, *I. Aquifolium*, is hardy too, but it is at its best only where there is plenty of moisture.

In the Far South, yaupon, *I. vomitoria*, is as common as privet. In our section it is all too rare except along the coast where it is native. Allowed to grow into its natural contours, it makes a charming small tree, with small oval leaves and small translucent berries, like red glass, in thick clusters along the silver grey stems. The berries do not color until November, and they persist until spring. For sheared plants to use in formal designs, or for clipped hedges, there is no better evergreen for this part of the country. The hedges are berried even when clipped, because the fruits grow low on the branches, and the flowers are on second-year wood. Nurseries offer both male and female plants, the berried plants being more expensive. Yaupon is easily transplanted, not choice as to soil, and grows equally well in sun or shade. The grey-green leaves turn purple in winter.

Dahoon holly, *I. Cassine*, grows in cypress swamps, but will do in ordinary garden soils. It is native to southern Virginia, and it is not hardy much farther north. Unlike most hollies, it is not dioecious but has perfect flowers. All plants are fruiting. They begin to bear when young, and the small, spectrum red berries are produced in quantities on the new wood. They color in summer and persist until the following spring. The spineless, unhollylike leaves are very long ovals, three or four inches from tip to tip. This is one of the hollies recommended for hedges, but the leggy plants are not nearly so good for clipping as the more compact, small-leaved yaupon. The closely allied myrtleleaf holly, *I. myrtifolia*, usually listed as a variety of Dahoon, is the best species for low, wet soils. It is of very open growth, small in leaf and small of stature.

The Chinese horned holly, *I. cornuta*, makes the most perfect of clipped hedges, but it is too expensive for most of us to use in that way. It can be kept to any size as a sheared specimen, and if left to its own devices, it grows slowly into a compact, shapely shrub, ten or fifteen feet high. The berries are very large and very red. The curious rectangular leaves with horn-like spines are a bright green and beautifully polished.

Hollies like an acid soil rich in humus, and those not native to swamps require good drainage. It should be remembered that with most of them the staminate and pistillate flowers are on different plants, and that pollen-bearing plants should be near the berry-bearing ones.

Cleyera ochnacea is another evergreen with red fall fruits and dioecious flowers. The descriptions of these flowers as "small, delightfully fragrant, creamy white blossoms" suggest to the imagination something similar to the characteristic and lovely flowers of other members of the tea family. But the gardener who expects anything like a gordonia or camellia will be much disappointed. The flowers are almost invisible greenish disks. The specimen in my garden bloomed several seasons before I knew that it had bloomed at all. And it is to be remembered that the fruits appear only when there are plants of both sexes. As to foliage and habit, this species is one of the most desirable of the broad-leaved evergreens. The leaves are crisp and polished, and the new ones, like those of the photinias, are bright red. In habit it is compact and shapely. It can be clipped in a formal shape, or grown with a single stem and round head like the little laurel trees you see pictured in old garden books. Left to grow naturally, it gets to be an enormous tree on the coast. There is one at the tea gardens in Summerville, South Carolina, that is more than seventy-five years old. Inland, it eventually gets to ten or twelve feet, but it is very slow growing. As to hardiness, it will stand at least to southern Maryland. It will grow in sun or shade, but requires an acid soil. This is a Japanese species.

The evergreen cotoneasters are many and varied. Most of them are not too hardy; these are well adapted to planting south of Washington. Several of the more vigorous species are particularly conspicuous in fruit. The willowleaf cotoneaster, *Cotoneaster salicifolius floccosa*, is a magnificent shrub where it is grown properly in the open with plenty of space to spread to its natural size. It grows to ten or twelve feet with a spread at least equal to its height. It is beautiful even in seasons when the drooping, willowy branches are not hung with bright corymbs of small, shiny, red berries. The flowers of this species are also showy. The wrinkled leaves, of a dark color, are long and leathery. *C. lacteus* belongs to the same group as the willowleaf cotoneaster and is similar to it in habit and size, but the leaves are wide and dull. The red fruits grow in very large corymbs, color late in the fall, and persist until freezing weather. This is one of the showiest species.

Franchet's cotoneaster, *C. Franchetii*, is interesting because of its very large, orange-red fruits that color in October and keep their color all winter. The flowers are pinkish and not at all conspicuous. It is like the willowleaf cotoneaster in size and habit, but does not keep its foliage so well in winter. The leaves are small and grey. All three of these species are native to China. Cotoneasters are difficult to move and are best bought in pots; they grow very rapidly. Unlike most of the evergreens, they prefer a sweet soil. They are at their best in the sun, and will grow in heavy soils that are soggy in winter and baked in the summer.

The best of the firethorns is the one that is least known. When I first saw it in the distance at the Wormsloe gardens, near Savannah, Ga., I cried out at the poignancy of the color. I said I had never seen such poinsettias, and Mrs. Du Renne said, "but that is the Formosa firethorn, *Pyracantha formosana*." I brought a small plant home from Georgia in January, and by fall it had shot up to nine feet. There were berries the first year. The berries are scarlet red, very large, and in heavy bunches. They begin to color in October when the early trees are turning, and they first take on the tender coral of the leaves of dogwood and maple. The berries are the most persistent of any species, and they keep their bright color until long after Christmas. I had thought that this firethorn, coming from the warm island of Formosa, might be tender, but it was not affected by the severe cold of last winter, and it is hardy at least to southern Virginia. The Formosa firethorn is a most vigorous species, making an erect, angular shrub twelve or fifteen feet tall. The foliage is good at all seasons.

Another red-berried firethorn, *P. Gibbsii yunnanensis*, is more spreading, not so tall, and sometimes thornless. The leaves are large and very long—to three inches—and very shiny.

P. crenulata, from the Himalayas grows to be a small or medium-sized shrub with us. The berries are a color between orange and red and are very small, but they are produced so copiously that they cover the branches and almost hide the narrow leaves. There is a variety *Rogersiana* with yellow berries.

The firethorns need sun, but they are not particular as to soil. The warm red and orange berries keep winter from the garden, and in fall they are delightful with the strong, late colors of marigolds and chrysanthemums.

Butchers broom and the Alexandrian laurel, shrubs of the hardy-to-Washington group, belong to the lily family. New shoots appear in spring to take the place of the old ones, but there is never a time when there is nothing to show above ground in the more or less herbaceous clumps. The glittering foliage of the Alexandrian-laurel, *Danaë racemosa*, said to be the true laurel used to wreathe the brows of the poets, is not made up of leaves, but of leaf-like branches. The solitary berries are as large and as brilliantly colored as cherries. They do not redden until November, and they last until spring. They appear on the new shoots, so the old shoots may be cut down when the new ones are grown. The poet's laurel is native to Asia Minor and Persia and has long been in culture in the southern part of this country. It was one of the shrubs of the Colonial gardens.

Butchers broom, *Ruscus aculeatus*, so called because of being used in England as a brush to clean the meat blocks, is similar to the poet's laurel, but the foliage is dull and dark and it is not so certain to fruit. With me a single clump of the poet's laurel fruits regularly, while long-established clumps of butchers broom have never borne a berry. I have read that even when both sexes of the latter are planted close together, they do not fruit freely. But the butchers broom is one of the most reliable shrubs for troublesome places. It will grow in the driest places, even under trees, and in all degrees of shade. It does need a good mulch of cow manure in the fall. When the plants are starved some of the new spring shoots become colorless by summer. The poet's laurel is more fastidious; it requires a moist rich soil and some shade.

The year begins and ends with evergreens. They are to southern gardens what the perennial border is to parts of the country where the summers are cooler and more moist, and the winters more severe. Always in planting a garden I would think first of the shrubs for it, and my first choice in shrubs would be the broad-leaved evergreens.

Frost—and the Garden Year Begins Again

*T*oday is the fourteenth of November. I have been sitting in the sun eating my lunch and staring at the barbaric scarlet of *Tithonia* Fireball against the cold blue sky. The low retaining wall of the terrace is a study in values: bright silver leaves of *Veronica incana*, dull grey mounds of santolina, scattered flowers of white verbena against dark foliage. The path to the summer house, framed in a green arch, is as gay as ever from a little distance, even though the edging of *Zinnia linearis* and sweet alyssum proves, on closer view, to be a little ragged. Against the dark temple fir the scarlet berries and glossy foliage of the Formosa firethorn have assumed the brilliance that they will carry well into the winter. Along the fence there are still a few pale butterfly flowers on the climbing rose, Mermaid. The flowers of the tall yellow crotalaria and of the dwarfer bronzed one have become discolored during the cold nights, but one plant—protected by the hedge—still lifts tender yellow spires against the green. Throughout the garden the ageratum volunteers have come into their own, covering bare beds with the intense blue that they take on with the first cool weather. The strawberry pink reflection of a neighboring maple lies on the black water of the pool. Already the leaves are falling from the trees.

Any night now frost may blacken the last crotalarias, zinnias, marigolds, and chrysanthemums. But, when the dead branches have been cleared away, there will still be the green of the ivy, the grey of santolina, and the scarlet fruit of the firethorn. Already sweet violets are in bloom, and before long there will be buds on the paper-white narcissus and the Algerian iris.

Further Notes, 1967

Winter

Since this was written a great many more winter flowers have bloomed in my garden. I never did find *Saxifraga ciliata*, but the search continues, and each year some plant that I did not know about before turns up to bloom between Thanksgiving and St. Valentine's day.

Narcissus bulbocodium monophyllus, which now appears in the Classified List (1965) as *Narcissus cantabricus subsp. monophyllus* (Durieu) Fernandes, proved to be transitory; but the variety *foliosus* is one of the most dependable flowers of the season of frost and snow. I have now had it for seventeen years, and its blooming is free and almost unfailing, though somewhat erratic. The small deliciously fragrant flowers sometimes bloom before Christmas and sometimes afterward, but whenever they come they linger for a month or more. Nylon is the only one of the hybrid white hoop-petticoats that I can count on. The name belongs to a strain rather than an entity, and the clones vary in performance.

It is no longer true that *Crocus sieberi* is the only species that blooms for me in January. *Crocus Imperati* improved upon acquaintance. It is usually in bloom soon after the New Year, and I have even found flowers before Christmas. *Crocus laevigatus* 'Fontenayi' blooms on sunny days all through the winter. I have known it to bloom from the first of December to the first of February, and it has bloomed at times before Thanksgiving. The flowers open wide in the sun. They are small but gay, and almost unbelievably indestructible.

The Algerian iris is the only winter-blooming species that I have found to be permanent and dependable. When I came to Charlotte, Helen Mayer gave me a clump from her garden. It begins to bloom around Thanksgiving, and there are flowers in

175

mild spells throughout the winter and sometimes even on frosty days. The flowers are rather small and the foliage rather tall, but this form is much more free-flowering than the one with larger flowers that I had in Raleigh and brought along when we came here. *Iris vartani* proved to be hardy but not permanent. It bloomed for Christmas, and that was the last I ever saw of it. I finally acquired a bulb of *Iris alata*, but it disappeared without blooming at all.

Omphalodes verna lived on in the Raleigh garden for five or six years, but it never again bloomed in December; after the first year the flowers appeared at various times between the middle of February and the first of April. Reading about it makes me want to grow it again, and I have put it on my list of plants to be ordered in the fall.

I have now had *Adonis amurensis* in my Charlotte garden for eleven years. I cannot say that it has improved with age, for it has never been vigorous, and it seldom blooms before February, but even so I am glad it stays with me. The flowers are double. A few years ago I found the single form, but so far it has not proved to be any earlier.

I cannot, as English gardeners do, call *Eranthis hyemalis* New Year's Gift. Over a period of twenty years it has often bloomed before February, but never before the eighth of January. If it is not overrun by stronger plants, it will seed itself in an ever-increasing carpet of gold. When the bloom is over, the foliage quickly disappears—that is when there is danger that other things will move in and crowd it out.

I have planted corms of *Cyclamen coum* a number of times since I came to Charlotte, but I still have no luck with it. I must try again.

When I wrote about two months of winter I did not know *Sternbergia fischeriana*. Now that I know, I find the bulbs are seldom available in this country, and when they are imported they deteriorate from being so long out of the ground. Out of nine bulbs planted on Christmas day only one bloomed. It produced two flowers at the end of February, and after that bloomed early in January, and after that ceased to bloom at all. Once established, however, they flourish and increase, and

bloom for Billy Hunt, at Laurel Hill, from the end of November to the end of January. Even when the flowers are killed, the buds survive near-zero temperature and open their golden petals as soon as it warms up. And now I know the Lenten rose is more suited to the South than the Christmas rose. Some Southern gardeners can grow the Christmas rose and grow it well, but I am not among them. Anyone can grow Lenten roses; they grow and seed themselves like weeds. As they are hybrids of *Helleborus orientalis* and several other species, they vary greatly in flower and leaf and in season. Most of them bloom long before Lent; my earliest date is the eighth of January. A clone with almost pure white flowers and just a touch of icy green is always first. Others follow with plum-colored petals, or white or pinkish or greenish or violet flecked and violet spotted, and last of all a white one that usually begins to bloom in Holy Week. The best clones make clumps nearly a yard across, with leaves a foot across. The leaves stay green all winter and are in themselves a handsome ornament for the garden.

I have never yet found a source for the winter-blooming violet, 'Prince of Wales,' but I now have it under the kitchen window where it gets the winter sun. Mrs. Jacob van Staaveren sent it to me from Alexandria, Virginia, and it bloomed in bitter weather from the last days of December into January. The flowers are large, very dark violet, and very fragrant. The leaves are small and round. Mr. Fowler, who took over Mr. Tong's Nursery, still lists 'Governor Herrick.' 'Rosina,' another variety of *Viola odorata* (not *Viola rosina*), which I put down in the blooming dates as in bloom the first of March, has bloomed in December and January. In favorable spots it is very free of its small rosy flowers. Mrs. Alexander Gibbes (who gave the yellow hoop-petticoats to Mrs. Bullitt, who gave them to everyone in Chapel Hill, and to me, and to everyone else) has a small, pale, and fragile violet that blooms in Columbia, South Carolina, in January.

Primulas bloom in winter (more or less), but not for me. Stray flowers often turn up in books: the poet John Clare wrote in his diary, "Found a cowslip in flower, December 12, 1841."

I was thinking only of its name when I included *Petasites* among the shrubs called *fragrans*. It is an herb, less than a foot tall, beloved by Mr. Darnell and Mr. Bowles, but banned by most gardeners as an ineradicable weed—the underground roots run for yards in all directions, going on from strength to strength, Miss Rohde says. Mr. Darnell says "The flowers may be termed dingy by those who can only see beauty in gaudy color, but it has a quiet beauty and delicious fragrance." Mr. Bowles liked to add the muted lavender spikes to the "pickings of tufted pansies" that he grew in a cold frame and arranged in a purple glass finger bowl. *Petasites* is not in the trade, but I have found it in old gardens in Virginia and North Carolina. It did not spread unduly in Raleigh, where it grew for five years, but I am beginning to think I may rue the day that I planted it in Charlotte. The flowers are called winter heliotrope. They shed their fragrance at the end of January or in February—if at all. The buds are frequently killed by frost.

For the last ten years winter-sweet (which should be called *Chimonanthus praecox*, not *Meratia*) has bloomed for me before Thanksgiving or very soon afterward, and sometimes if the weather is not too wet or freezing it continues well into

January, all the while filling the air with intense and delightful fragrance. I brought from Raleigh the one Miss Janet rooted for me so long ago. As it is squeezed into a narrow space between the house and a wall of ivy, it has grown taller than most—to at least twenty feet.

The Chinese say that the three friends of winter are the pine, the bamboo, and the flowering plum. The flowering plum is *Prunus Mume*. Last year borers killed the *Mume* that I planted in my garden when I first came to Charlotte. I was not as grieved as you might think, for it had become old and ungainly and was taking up more space than I wanted to give it, and one of my seedlings had already begun to bloom. I have come to the conclusion that the *Mume* is not a tree of graceful old age and that it is well to have young ones coming along, especially if they are on their own roots. *Prunus Mume* does not fruit often in this climate, but in a mild season it does, and so far the seedlings have been very like the parent, with double, pink-tinted, wonderfully fragrant flowers. They bloom very early in the year or, if the winter is severe, some time in February.

When frost catches the flowers of *Prunus Mume*—as it always does sooner or later—they hang on dismally for some time, but the pale bells of the autumn cherry quickly disappear. A few are found hanging on the thin twigs when the leaves are down, and more appear in mild intervals in winter, but the real bloom is in the spring. When the branches are leafless, the silver and gold coloring of the multiple trunks is beautiful enough, even though there are no flowers.

Twenty-five years ago there were not many camellias growing outside in Piedmont North Carolina. By the time we came to Charlotte gardens were full of them, and now they are going back into the greenhouse. Even so we all want a few in the winter garden, and I consider 'Berenice Boddy' the best variety of *Camellia japonica*. I would not be without *Camellia hiemalis* 'Dawn' even though the ivory flowers are often blackened by frost, and I am also fond of the small delicately scented flowers of *Camellia saluensis*.

Two shrubs and a vine, which I did not know about before,

should be included in any discussion of winter flowers, no matter how brief. *Erica carnea*, the spring heath, is at its height in February, but from Christmas on—and sometimes even earlier—I can find a few sprigs of tiny violet bells, for they are indifferent to all kinds of weather.

Viburnum fragrans now bloom in my garden from mid-November to March, and the little bunches of creamy, pink-tipped, heliotrope-scented flowers are almost frost proof. As it is a tall and awkward shrub with no beauty other than the flowers, it is best grown in an inconspicuous place. Recently *Viburnum bodnantense*, a hybrid between this and *Viburnum grandiflorum*, has been made available in this country. There are several forms, and Dawn is said to be the best.

Clematis cirrhosa has now bloomed for me for nine winters, but I had to search for many years before I found it. It is a slender vine with small, shiny, prettily cut leaves, and greenish creamy flowers that bloom steadily from early October through February; this year I even found a few in March. The fluffy, silvery fruiting heads develop as winter progresses, and they are almost as pretty as the flowers. The vine is practically evergreen, but has a curious way of shedding its leaves in midsummer. When the leaves first turned brown and began to fall, I thought it was dead and I almost pulled it up.

I like to leave flowers in the garden when the weather is pleasant, but in winter I bring them in out of the cold. On many chilly days I cut little bouquets of winter-sweet and spring heath, a blue viola, perhaps a paper-white narcissus, a camellia, an iris, and a few spikes of the pale blue flowers of rosemary. My rosemary blooms all winter.

Spring

Spring still comes with the early trumpets, and I watch for the daffodil man who sells them on the street. I think it is now agreed that they are forms of the Lent lily, *Narcissus pseudonarcissus subsp. major*, which is extremely variable. The ones I had in Raleigh were a particularly good form. I cannot

remember where I got them, for they were planted before I learned to keep records, but I think they came from an advertiser in *Garden Gossip* in the days when it was edited by Violet Walker. They are advertised in the Southern market bulletins under a variety of names. One name is buttercups.

The white swan's-neck daffodil called Silver Bells is not 'William Goldring.' So far as I know it has never been identified. The flaring crown distinguishes it from another old white trumpet that has long been in Southern gardens and that Mr. George Heath imported from England as *Narcissus cernuus*. *N. cernuus* is now considered a synonym of *Narcissus pseudo-narcissus subsp. moschatus*. Several of these little white trumpets are found in various parts of the South. Their ancestors were listed in Hartland's catalogue for 1887 (*The Little Book of Daffodils*) as *Narcissus pseudo-narcissus variiformis*. "To speak too highly in terms of praise of these most beautiful and varied forms of Pseudo-Narcissus is impossible," Hartland said. "They are all colors from nearly snow-white to bicolor. Some having dog-eared perianths like 'William Goldring,' and some short and stiff as obvallaris. If we could only be allowed to give them names, what a list we could make."

The white trumpets are still my favorite among the modern daffodils, but as a rule they are not persistent with me. I still

consider 'Beersheba' the best and the most dependable variety for the garden.

All of the snowflakes in my Raleigh garden turned out to be the summer snowflake, *Leucojum aestivum*. The tall, late-flowering one is the variety 'Gravetye Giant.' Nurserymen seldom list the spring snowflake, *L. vernum*, because the bulbs deteriorate as soon as they are taken out of the ground.

Scilla siberica taurica is seldom listed nowadays, but the variety 'Spring Beauty' appears in the fall catalogues, and it is a better bulb. The gentian blue flowers are sterile and therefore long-lasting. I have known them to be in bloom for nearly two months, and my earliest date for the first flower is the nineteenth of January.

Anchusa myosotidiflora must now be called *Brunnera macrophylla*. It does not really matter what it is called in Latin, but forget-me-not flowered anchusa is prettier than big-leafed brunnera. It is one of the very early perennials. Blooming dates now kept over a long period show its earliest date as the fifteenth of February, though the first week in March is more usual. The flowers are a deep tint of pure blue.

And the Japanese quince is *Chaenomeles lagenaria*, not—as we used to call it—*Cydonia japonica.* The most beautiful varieties are 'Apple Blossom' and the beautiful white one that

Mrs. Bullitt grew in Chapel Hill and divided with all her friends. Mine came with us to Charlotte. It blooms very early, and I have even found flowers on New Year's Day.

Botanists now recognize five species of shadblows in the Carolinas. They consider *Amelanchier laevis* as a variety of *A. arborea*. The lovely pink-flowered forms are now available.

It distresses me that I was ever so foolish as to say that *Iris albicans* is much too common. It is not half common enough, and it is not true that the buds are almost always caught by frost, though I must say that this year I had not a single bloom. That has never happened before, so far as I remember.

The crab-apples have been switched from the pears (*Pyrus*) to the apples (*Malus*), which seems a sensible thing to do. I might have said more about the crabs and cherries, but I did not have a chance to study them until later on. I have tried several crabs in my Charlotte garden, where they have been plagued with fireblight. But I am sad to think that I lived so long without Japanese cherries. The popular ones are the rosebud cherry (*Prunus subhirtella*), 'Yoshino,' and the double-flowering 'Kwansan' and 'Naden.' *Prunus sargentii*, a magnificent tree of forest size, is little known. It has dark bark marked with golden lenticels and amaranth pink flowers. It is supposed to be the finest of all trees for fall color, but mine is planted on the parking strip, where it does not get enough moisture, and the leaves fall before they color.

Although *Viburnum tomentosum* prefers a rich moist soil, it is not so sensitive to drought as I have implied, and if it does begin to droop is worthy of a good soaking. It is more than worthy, for it is one of the most beautiful of flowering shrubs. The variety *mariesii* is superior to the type in flower and in fruit; the sterile form is the least attractive.

When we came to Charlotte we left the old collection of bearded irises behind and planted new varieties in the new garden. I still think with regret of 'Princess Beatrice,' 'Lord Lambourne,' and the powder-blue flowers of 'Souvenir de Loetitia Michaud.' 'Loetitia Michaud' is a thing to remember. I like the recent introductions less and less, and do not feel that I can ever cherish such advanced varieties as 'Flaming Heart,' a "porcelain textured intense blend of pink, salmon, and tan" or 'Flapperette,' "a change of pace and a pleasant departure" in melon-pink with a tangerine beard. But before long these too will be forgotten.

Siberian irises are better suited to the garden than the bearded varieties of the present day, which are bred for the collector and the show table and need to be grown in rows like vegetables. The Siberians are practically free of disease, and they grow and bloom for years without being divided. Although they like moisture they must be well drained. There are better varieties than 'Emperor,' 'Snow Queen,' and 'Perry's Blue,' and there is a promise of more to come as breeders have turned their attention to this group. I have two that I hope will always hold their own. One is 'Caesar's Brother,' a splendid perennial that endures and increases and blooms freely in April or early May. The flowers are a brilliant color, close to spectrum violet. The other is 'Tycoon.' Its large flowers of soft dauphin's violet come into bloom a little later than those of 'Caesar's Brother.' I have had some difficulty in getting 'Tycoon' established, but it has made a respectable clump at least, and this year it bloomed beautifully.

The Delta irises belong to the South, and we must make more of them. The Dormons and their friend, Inez Conger (who lives in Arcadia, Louisiana), have sent me the cream of the hybrids and selected forms. I have not had equal success with all of them, but 'Lake Charles Blue,' 'Sunny' (a pale, pale yellow), and 'Royal Velour' (a magnificent purple velvet) give me pleasure year in and year out. 'Mac's White' and 'Wood Violet' are dependable dwarf varieties.

When I tried to straighten out the names of the spiraeas, or filipendulas, I decided it is not really worth while, for few gardeners will want all of them. The best of these are the Japanese species, *Spiraea palmata* (*Filipendula purpurea* is not a good name, for the flowers are not at all purple; they are pink mist) and our native 'Martha Washington's Plume,' *Filipendula rubra* variety *venusta*, which came to me as *Spiraea venusta*. I am glad to have a chance to correct a mistake I made about the climbing jasmines. They came to me with their names reversed. It is *Jasminum stephanense* that is so lovely. *Jasminum Beesianum* is not worth having and is difficult to control or get rid of. *Jasminum stephanense* is like its parent, *Jasminum officinale*, except that the fragrant flowers are pink tinted. It does not get out of hand. It begins to bloom in early May, lasts for several weeks, and sometimes repeats.

When I wrote about the black locust I had never had one in my garden. I had just sniffed their honeyed fragrance in the little lane in Raleigh where I used to take the dogs to walk. When we came to Charlotte, one of the first things planted was *Robinia Pseudoacia Decaisneana*, a pink-flowered form that turned up in France more than a hundred years ago. It grows even faster than the type. At the end of its first summer it had reached a height of sixteen feet, and we could breakfast in its shade. Now that it is some thirty feet tall, it spreads a light and welcome shade over the terrace without making the house dark and damp. When it is in bloom—usually on May Day—I look up at the pale pink honey-scented flowers against the blue sky of late spring and do not wonder that it is considered one of the beautiful flowering trees of the world. But after it had been with me for about twelve years I began to wish I had never heard of it, for the roots have run all through the garden, forming an underground network, and sending up shoots everywhere—in the paths, the borders, and the shrubbery.

I would not now say that yellow-wood is more satisfactory than the black locust. It does not sucker, but it is often short-lived in cultivation; it does not flower until it has been established for well on to ten years, and it does not flower freely every season.

When Elsie Hassan was living in Birmingham, Alabama, she and I made an exchange. She sent me a pretty little shrub that she called *Serissa foetida*, and I sent her a pretty little shrub that I called *Damnacanthus indicus*. They proved to be the same thing, and there was no doubt that Elsie's name was the correct one, for the leaves when bruised are fetid. And no wonder that it never bore any coral berries. It has grown in Southern gardens for a long time, and I have an idea that it is sometimes mistaken for myrtle. I have never been able to get hold of damnacanthus. Dr. John Creech collected plants in Japan and sent some to Mr. Dan Coleman and several other Southern nurserymen. I wrote to Mr. Coleman, who says he thinks it would be hardy in South Georgia if it were once established, but his plants were killed by a hard freeze that came before they were dormant.

When I wrote with such enthusiasm about the cross-vine I had never grown it in my own garden. I had admired it on Elizabeth Dortch's studio, where it must have grown for nearly a hundred years, and I never heard that it gave any trouble. But I rue the day I ever planted it in Charlotte, for I have never been able to get rid of it. And it is *not* evergreen—at least not in my garden. I read that in a book.

Two species of clematis should be added to the spring-flowering vines. *Clematis texensis* is like our bluebell (*Clematis crispa*) but it is a stronger vine, and the urn-shaped flowers are larger and are rose red. It usually begins to bloom during the last half of April, and if it is watered it sometimes blooms until frost. It dies to the ground in winter, and in very early spring the new shoots come up and grow very quickly to fifteen feet or more.

Clematis armandii needs plenty of room to ramble and a strong support to grow on. As to foliage, the long, tapered leaves are the most decorative of any evergreen vine; as to bloom, the flowers are a white shower in March or soon afterward. Armand's clematis is said to be hardy to Philadelphia. I cannot promise that, but it has never been in the least damaged by cold here, so I should think it would stand much farther north than Charlotte.

Summer

I must confess that there is no such day-lily as 'Golden Eye.' That is the way Miss Nannie pronounced it, and it never occurred to me that that was not the way to spell it: Golden Eye is 'Goldenii,' and I still think it one of the best. So is 'Hyperion,' but most of the day-lilies I grew before the war have been replaced by newer varieties that are not always an improvement over the older ones.

Achillea 'Coronation Gold' is a much better perennial than its parent, *Achillea filipendulina*. It is smaller and more compact; the flowers are clear lemon yellow, the foliage is silvery grey, and it is equally dependable. It blooms from mid-May through July, with a few flowers later on.

Lysimachia clethroides did not prove to be as desirable a perennial as I thought when I saw it at the lily show. In the garden it was weedy and invasive.

Catherine Taylor's Japanese aster still blooms in my garden all summer. It is *Asteromoea mongolica* (Franchi) Kitam.

Wherever there is shade, *Begonia evansiana* is indispensable for bloom in August and September. The flowers are showers of delicate pink, and the leaves are large, bright green, and handsome.

I do not know why it took me so long to discover that *Impatiens sultana* is also indispensable for shady places in summer. It is a tender perennial that seeds itself freely, but the volunteers do not begin to bloom until midsummer. Park lists them in separate colors, which is fortunate because the colors range from scarlet to red-violet, and an assortment is not always agreeable. Park says they grow well in full sun, but they do not. In hot sun they droop very quickly.

The Amaryllis family becomes more and more important in Southern gardens as more species and hybrids are introduced. Professor Claude Davis in Baton Rouge, Louisiana, and Dr. T. M. Howard, San Antonio, Texas, list crinums, hymenocallises, rain lilies, and all sorts of delightful things. Mr. Davis and Dr. Howard garden in Zone 9 and can therefore grow some amaryllids that are too tender for us, but many of their bulbs have proved to be hardy in my garden and there are more to be tried.

I have never been able to keep either pancratiums or sprekelias for more than a season or so, but *Amarcrinum howardii*, which is now called *Crinadonna corsii*, clone Fred Howard, has been with me twenty-five years and grows in grace. It flowers freely in August and September and sometimes puts up a scape in October. Lon Delkin is equally hardy, but does not bloom so well. Dorothy Hannibal is splendid.

Several white crinums growing in gardens from North Carolina to the Gulf Coast are all much alike, but have local names. Lester Hannibal says they are all crosses between *Crinum bulbispermum* and *C. americanum*. Mr. Davis lists 'Catherine' (which was found in a garden in Natchez), 'Miss Elsie,' one that I got from a friend in Atlanta, and 'Seven Sisters' from Grace Primo's garden in Mobile. I have another from Mrs. Parsley's garden in Charlotte. They all have a delicious scent of water lilies.

The introduction of more summer-flowering species of *Lycoris* has been a great thing for the South. Mr. Giridlian lists two that bloom in July. The finely wrought flowers of *Lycoris cinnabarina* are the color of ripe apricots, and those of *L. sanguinea* are dragon's-blood red. Some years ago Wyndham Hayward sent me the only yellow-flowered lycoris that has proved hardy with me, *Lycoris caldwelli*. After the middle of August the tall stiff scapes appear; they are crowned with pale gold. Sam Caldwell has found two hardy Chinese species that have flowers of a deeper yellow, but these are not yet available. He and William Lanier Hunt are making crosses, and they promise fine things for the future.

Now that it is grown in containers, *Gordonia lasianthus* is not difficult to establish. I have lost those that I planted in full sun, but I know of several that grow in shady gardens in Charlotte and bloom in July and August.

I am still unable to grow *Stewartia pentagyna*, now called *S. ovata*, but perhaps that too would take hold if it came out of a container. In Charlotte I have *Stewartia koreana*. After fifteen years it is nearly twenty feet tall; it blooms in July, and the bark has begun to peel in a delightful manner. It is in shade, but I think it would be better off in sun.

In Charlotte, *Erythrina crista-gallii* grows in sun on the south side of the house, blooms all through June and July, and continues to produce a few spikes until frost. It seldom sets seed, but some years there are a few, and once I even had a seedling that bloomed the second summer. It is listed in Texas nurseries as well as in California, and is sometimes advertised in the market bulletins.

Rhododendron prunifolium should be added to the summer-flowering azaleas. Although it grows in wet places in Alabama and Georgia, it blooms freely in a dry shady place in my garden in July and August. The flowers are said to vary from pure yellow through orange to red. Mine are vermillion.

I seem to have neglected the summer-flowering vines, a very important group of plants for Southern gardens. In Raleigh I could never get Confederate jessamine started, and so I did not realize that it blooms all summer and fills the garden with fragrance. Chapel Hill and Raleigh are near the northern limit of the Chinese species *Trachelospermum jasminoides*, but *T. asiaticum* (usually listed as *T. divaricatum*), from Japan and Korea, is considered hardier. *Kadsura japonica* grew on the summerhouse in Raleigh, but it was years before we knew that it flowered, for we were away in July and August. It belongs to the Magnolia family, and the flowers are like tiny magnolias of the palest yellow, with what looks like a small red raspberry in the center. They hang on thin pedicels nearly three inches long. I have never seen the fruits, which are described as showy heads of red berries. I think they must fail to mature. The vine was not really evergreen in Raleigh or Charlotte, though the leaves would hang on in mild winters.

Fall

Now, in addition to the red spider lilies, we have lovely creamy white flowers that open with a flush of delicate coral. These are considered more tender than *Lycoris radiata* and will probably not bloom much in gardens north of us, but the ones that have come to me as *Lycoris albiflora* and *L. albiflora carnea* have flowered well in my garden. When I say flowered well, I

mean they flower well when they flower at all. Like all other species, they are temperamental and may skip a season. Billy Hunt gives a good report of these and of *Lycoris elsiae* at Laurel Hill.

The oxblood lily is no longer called *Amaryllis advena*; it is *Rhodophiala* × *huntiana* Traub, hyb. nov., and it is from Argentina, not Chile. Dr. Hamilton Traub and Billy Hunt discovered that it was not a species because when they raised it from seed of the red one they got both pink and red seedlings. Dr. Traub then named these hybrids in honor of William Lanier Hunt, who has a notable collection of amaryllids at the Hunt Arboretum, which he has given to The University of North Carolina to be a part of the North Carolina Botanical Garden. The site is Laurel Hill, where native rhododendrons cover a hillside above Morgan Creek and mountain wildflowers mingle with those of the Coastal Plain. We can no longer say that nothing is being done for Southern gardens.

The name now valid for *Tithonia speciosa* is *T. rotundifolia. Hedychium gardnerianum* never did flower in Raleigh.

I tried it again in Charlotte, where it bloomed once, in mid-August, and then disappeared.

One more little autumnal flower must be mentioned because it is so charming and because it is so easily grown (in light shade) that any one can have it. It is the miniature cyclamen, *Cyclamen neapolitanum*. For some years seedlings have been appearing in my garden near the original tubers and even at some distance from them. The first flowers usually come in August, and occasionally I find a few stray ones early in December. The marbled leaves come up in October. *Cyclamen neapolitanum* is naturalized in the Hunt Arboretum, and Billy says *Cyclamen repandum* grows equally well and blooms from February to April.

I should not have said that Japanese anemones are doubtful in this climate. They are among the most dependable perennials, and the common pink one of gardens increases so fast it is a give-away plant.

The valid name for *Clinopodium caroliniana* is *Satureja georgiana*.

Miss Edna's Chinese bamboo is *Polygonum Spaethii*, a plant with spreading roots that is apt to become a nuisance if planted among other shrubs, but makes a fine large specimen when given plenty of room. It is sometimes advertised in the Southern market bulletins.

Pyracantha formosana, now *P. koidzumii*, does suffer in some very severe winters, but it recovers quickly and, as it blooms on new wood, will fruit as usual in the fall. *Pyracantha yunnanensis* is now *P. crenato-serrata*.

That must have been a very mild winter when the berries of the Alexandrian laurel lasted until spring. They color in October and are wizened by the first severe frost.

I now have the fruiting form of butcher's broom. The berries of this do remain all winter, and they keep their brilliant red color. A number of plants have been raised from seed sent from England by Clarence Elliott, and I hope in time they will be in the trade.

The tea plant is listed in *Camellia Nomenclature* (1964) as *Camellia sinensis*.

Cleyera ochnacea is no longer a valid name; it should be called *Cleyera japonica*. Moreover there seems to be some question as to whether the plant in the trade under that name even belongs to that genus. Whatever it is, it is one of our best broadleaved evergreens.

Blooming Dates

For many years my mother has kept a record of the first flowers of each season, writing down the bloom in the garden day by day in a series of small black diaries. She also takes note of the weather and some of the events of our lives. Turning the pages one finds:

January 23:
Cold and Cloudy
The Gatling's spiraea
Japan quince
White hyacinths
John's funeral

January 25:
Fair, Colder
Winter aconite
Christmas-rose
Stoker installed

February 9:
Fair and Warm. Lunch and tea out
Scilla taurica
Narcissus Grand Monarque
Forsythia
Ellen's birthday

I keep an alphabetical list on index cards. We check with each other to be sure that we have put down everything. I also put down the first bloom of the flowering trees and shrubs in the neighborhood: Miss Ellen Durham's magnolias, Mrs. Williams' lilacs, Miss Isabel Busbee's viburnums. Some of the daffodil dates came from Miss Loulie, the Persian buttercup from Isabelle Henderson. I have kept this list for six years. Since in that time we have had two extremely forward seasons, and two extremely late ones, I think the list covers the fluctuation in bloom. Miss Isabel's dates for flowering shrubs bear this out. She has kept records of bloom for twelve years, and over the longer period I find that there is little if any wider difference between the earliest and latest dates of the first bloom.

In the following list of blooming dates, the earliest date for the first bloom of each plant is recorded in the first column. The latest date for the first bloom is recorded in the second column. Where the dates vary but a few days I have set down only the earliest date. An asterisk before the name of a plant indicates that I have taken the date for only one season. The dates in the third column are for the latest bloom on record, or for the season or length of bloom. Except where otherwise noted, the dates are for Raleigh. The plants on the following lists are not necessarily recommended for this part of the country. I have included the blooming dates of all of those that I have been able to check, and that I have thought gardeners in the South might want to refer to.

Annuals

Scientific and Common Names	Time Sown (Ss = self-sown)	Earliest Date of First Bloom	Latest Date of First Bloom	Length of Bloom
Ageratum mexicanum	Ss	June 1	June 18	Late fall
Anchusa capensis,				
Cape alkanet	Nov. 15	May 22		3 weeks
Arctotis grandis,				
African daisy	Ss	April 30		Spring
Argemone grandiflora,				
prickly-poppy	Feb. 12		June 6	
var. Isabel	Ss	May 4	May 21	Nov. 25
	April 18		June 29	
	Ss	June 2	June 23	Nov.
platyceras rosea,				
crested poppy	Ss	Late May		Nov.
Browallia elata				
(*B. americana*)	Ss	June 10	July 11	Late summer
Calliopsis: Coreopsis				
Centaurea Cyanus,				
cornflower	Ss	April 11	April 27	End of May
Centranthus				
macrosiphon	Oct. 14	April 18		End of May
*Cleome lutea	March 23	July 10		Sept. 30
spinosa	Ss	July 1	Late fall	
Collomia coccinea				
(*biflora*)	Ss	April 28		End of May
Coreopsis				
Drummondii,				
calliopsis	Ss	May 15	June 3	End of June
var. Golden Crown	April 30	June 24		4 weeks
	Ss	May 26		June
Cosmos, Extra Early				
Express	Spring	July 9		To fall
Orange Flare	Ss	June 1	June 21	Late fall
Crepis rubra	Feb. 23	May 31		2 weeks
	Ss	April 15		
*Crotalaria argyraea	April 14	Sept. 9		Nov. 28
* *juncea*	April 14	July 10		Nov. 20
retusa	March 9	Aug. 2		Nov. 25
spectabilis	{ Late June / May 27	{ Early Oct. / Sept. 8		Nov. 20
usaramoensis	Ss	July 28	Aug. 9	Nov. 25
Cuphea purpurea	Late spring	July 28		Summer

197

Annuals

Scientific and Common Names	Time Sown (Ss = self-sown)	Earliest Date of First Bloom	Latest Date of First Bloom	Length of Bloom
Cynoglossum amabile, Chinese forget-me-not	Ss	April 28		Late May
Datura Wrightii (*D. meteloides*) angel's trumpet	{ March 6 Ss	{ Aug. 18 June 15		Sept.
Delphinium cultorum, larkspur				
Single	Ss	April 23	May 12	4 weeks
Imperial	Fall	May 24		Mid-June
Stock Flowered Rosamond	Fall	Mid-May		Late June
Dicranostigma Franchetianum, rapid celandine	March 25	July 4		Nov.
Dracocephalum Moldavica, dragonhead	Feb. 23	July 1		Summer
Eschscholzia californica, California-poppy	Late Oct. Ss	April 1 March 25	April 23	{ Into June
Gilia capitata, thimble flower	Oct. 10	May 26		June
Helianthus cucumerifolius	Spring	June 22		Fall
var. Lilliput	Spring	June 22		Oct.
Primrose	Spring	June 23		Oct.
Hibiscus Manihot Sunset	April 30	July 26		Summer
*Incarvillea variabilis	Spring	July 2		2 weeks
Lallemantia canescens	Feb. 23	June 20		All summer
Larkspur: Delphinium cultorum				
Leptosyne Stillmanii	March 6	May 13		2 weeks
Limnanthes Douglasii, meadow-foam	Ss	April 3	March 17	Into May
Lupinus subcarnosus, Texas bluebonnet	Nov. 15	April 1		Spring

Annuals

Scientific and Common Names	Time Sown (Ss = self-sown)	Earliest Date of First Bloom	Latest Date of First Bloom	Length of Bloom
Mesembryanthemum criniflorum	Feb. 23	May 18		Summer
Myosotis sylvatica, annual forget-me-not	Fall	March 28		Spring
Nemophila insignis, baby blue-eyes	Late Oct. Nov.	Feb. 22 March 12		May 7
Oenothera acaulis, dandelion-leaved sundrop	Nov. 20	May 29		Summer
Drummondii	Ss	May 6		Fall
Papaver Rhoeas, Shirley poppy	Dec. 19	May 12		Into June
somniferum, opium poppy	Late Feb.	June 12		June
Phacelia campanularia, California blue bell	Early spring	May 9		Fall
Phlox Drummondii, Drummond phlox	Ss	April 17		Spring
Portulaca grandiflora, rose-moss	Ss	June 8		To fall
Rudbeckia bicolor	April 27	July 1		All summer
Kelvedon Star	April 27	July 12		All summer
Salvia carduacea, thistle sage	Feb. 23	May 20		2 weeks
Horminum var. Blue Beard	Ss	May 14		Late June
Silene Armeria, catchfly	Oct. 20	May 19		Late June
pendula	Spring	April 9		Spring
Tagetes signata pumila, dwarf marigold	May 8	July 21		Fall
Tithonia speciosa, Mexican sunflower	Spring	July 23		Frost

Annuals

Scientific and Common Names	Time Sown (Ss = self-sown)	Earliest Date of First Bloom	Latest Date of First Bloom	Length of Bloom
Torenia flava (*T. Baillonii*), wishbone flower	Sown under Glass	Aug. 4		Into Nov.
Fournieri	Ss	May 6	July 15	Into Nov.
Zinnia elegans	April 26	July 1		
linearis	April 18	May 20		Nov. 25

Bulbs

Scientific and Common Names	Earliest Date of First Bloom	Latest Date of First Bloom	Length of Bloom
Agapanthus africanus var. *Mooreanus,* Lily-of-the-Nile	June 25		
Allium albopilosum	April 14	April 28	2 weeks
* *caeruleum* (*azureum*), blue garlic	May 5		June 7
flavum	June 13	June 16	Late June
montanum A. senescens			
neapolitanum, daffodil garlic	April 9	April 21	2 weeks
* *odorum*	May 27		2 weeks
Porrum, leek	June 1		End June
Schoenoprasum, chive	May 5		2 weeks
senescens	May 22		Until Aug.
sphaerocephalum	June 10	June 15	Late June
tanguticum	June 16	July 7	End July
triquetrum	March 30	April 5	End May
unifolium	Early May		
*Alstroemeria aurantiaca, golden Peruvian lily	June 22		
Amaryllis advena (*Habranthus*), Ox-blood lily	Aug. 24	Sept. 19	End Sept.
* *Belladonna* (*Callicore rosea*), Belladonna-lily	Aug. 18		
Belamcanda chinensis, blackberry-lily	July	Aug.	Into Sept.
Brodiaea Bridgesii	March 24	April 17	3 weeks
capitata, blue-dicks	March 23	April 3	
coronaria (*B. grandiflora*), Harvest brodiaea	May 22	May 31	Nearly a month
laxa	May 4		
uniflora (*Triteleia uniflora*), spring star-flower	March 1	March 15	
Calla: Zantedeschia			
Callicore rosea: Amaryllis Belladonna			
Calochortus Vestae	May 16		
Camassia Leichtlinii	May 30	April 18	4 weeks
alba	April 22	May 4	2 weeks
Quamash	April 18	April 20	
Chionodoxa Luciliae	Late March		
sardensis	Feb. 9		
Chlorogalum pomeridianum, soap-plant	May 21	March 19	

Bulbs

Scientific and Common Names	Earliest Date of First Bloom	Latest Date of First Bloom	Length of Bloom
*Chrosperma muscaetoxicum (Amianthium), crow poison	May 25		June 5
*Colchicum autumnale	Aug. 25	Sept. 25	Oct. 4
Cooperia pedunculata, prairie-lily	April 27		End July
Crinum erubescens	June 6		To July 1
Kirkii	June 9	June 23	Again July 8 Aug.
Kunthianum	May 24	June 6	Again in Oct.
longifolium (C. Capense)	April 24	May 24	Through May
Moorei	July 5	Aug. 11	No repeat
Powellii album	May 27	June 8	To July 15
species unknown, Milk-and-Wine Lily	Aug. 3		Nov. 10
Cecil Houdyshel	June 12		Aug.
* White Queen	May 30		
Crocus etruscus	Feb. 4		March 12
* Fleischeri	Feb. 4		
* Korolkowii	Feb. 1		March 12
* sativus, saffron crocus	Oct. 9		Into Nov.
Sieberi	Dec. 27	Jan. 13	Until Feb.
speciosus globosus	Oct. 8		2 weeks
susianus, cloth-of-gold	Feb. 4	Feb. 19	Mid-March
Tomasinianus	Jan. 16	Feb. 17	Mid-March
*Cyclamen coum	Feb. 2		
*Cyrtanthus lutescens, white Ifafa lily	May 21		
* parviflorus	May 17		
Eranthis hyemalis, winter aconite	Jan. 21	Feb. 18	End of Feb.
Erythonium albidum, white dogs-tooth violet	March 30	April 9	
americanum, common dogs-tooth violet	March 30		
Oregon species	March 30		
*Galanthus byzantinus, Byzantine snowdrop	Dec. 31		
Elwesii, giant snowdrop	Dec. 27	Jan. 27	Mid-March

Bulbs

Scientific and Common Names	Earliest Date of First Bloom	Latest Date of First Bloom	Length of Bloom
nivalis, common snowdrop	Feb. 14		March 14
var. *Scharlokii*	Jan. 29	Feb. 22	Late March
Galtonia candicans (Hyacinthus), summer-hyacinth	July 4		
Gladiolus	June 1	June 15	Summer
Habranthus: Amaryllis, and *Zephyranthes*			
Hedychium coronarium, butterfly-lily	Aug. 27		Nov.
Hippeastrum Johnsoni (Amaryllis Johnsoni)	May 19		
Hyacinthus azureus (Muscari azureum)	Feb. 14	March 10	Until April
candicans: Galtonia			
orientalis albulus, Roman hyacinth	Jan. 6	Feb. 11	Until March
single blue	Feb. 15	March 15	
hybrid King of the Blues	Feb. 27	March 25	Until April
Queen of the Blues	Feb. 21	March 19	4 weeks
Hymenocallis calathina (Ismene), Peruvian daffodil	June 29	July 15	End July
Sulphur Queen	June 11	June 24	
Iris, *see* Perennial list for bulbous iris			
Ismene: Hymenocallis			
Leucojum aestivum, summer snowflake	April 1		Mid-April
vernum, spring snowflake	Late Jan.	March 4	End of March
Lilium auratum, goldband lily	June 20	July 24	Aug. 10
candidum, Madonna lily	May 9	May 25	June 5
Grayi, Roan-lily	June 7†		
Henryi	June 13		
philippinense	Aug.		Fall
regale, royal lily	May 24	June 8	
speciosum, showy Japanese lily	July 23		To Sept. 1
speciosum var. *album*	July 30		Sept. 3
tigrinum, tiger lily	June 23		Aug. 20
Willmottiae (L. warleyense)	June 8		July 6

† Mrs. Lybrook, Winston-Salem, N.C.

Bulbs

Scientific and Common Names	Earliest Date of First Bloom	Latest Date of First Bloom	Length of Bloom
Lycoris aurea, hurricane lily	Sept.§		
incarnata	July 12	Aug. 9	
radiata, red spider-lily	Sept. 9	Sept. 17	Oct. 12
squamigera, Hall's amaryllis	July 8	July 17	Aug. 12
Milla biflora, Mexican star		Sept. 10	
Montbretia: Tritonia			
*Moraea glaucopis, peacock iris	June 6		Late June
Muscari azureum: Hyacinthus			
azureus			
botryoides, grape hyacinth	Feb. 18	March 10	3 weeks
Narcissus biflorus, twin sisters	March 27	April 16	
Bulbocodium var. *citrinus*		April 16	
conspicuus	March 25	April 12	2 weeks
monophyllus	Jan. 12	Feb. 15	
canaliculatus	March 23	April 3	
gracilis	April 15		
Jonquilla var. *simplex*	March 8	March 29	3–4 weeks
* *moschatus*	March 20		April 2
odorus: Campernelle	Feb. 13	March 2	
poeticus, poet's narcissus	March 17	April 15	
recurvus	March 21		
triandrus	March 6	March 19	
Alcida	March 20	April 5	
Barri conspicuus	March 19		
Bath Flame	March 9	March 23	1 week
Beersheba	March 5	March 21	3 weeks
Bonfire	March 20	March 30	
Brightling	March 20		
Croesus	March 20		
Emperor	Feb. 27	March 15	
Empress	Feb. 27	March 15	
Early Trumpet	Jan. 15	March 2	
Golden Sceptre	March 7		
Golden Spur	Feb. 9		
Grand Monarque	Jan. 20	March 15	
Haemon	March 9	March 18	3 weeks
Homespun	March 20		
Horace	March 22	April 12	1 week
King Alfred	Feb. 7	Feb. 20	

§ Mr. Jacques Busbee, from spring planting.

Bulbs

Scientific and Common Names	Earliest Date of First Bloom	Latest Date of First Bloom	Length of Bloom
Laurens Koster	March 16	April 3	2–3 weeks
Lucifer	Feb. 8		
Marmora	March 18	March 24	10 days
Mrs. Prentiss	April 3	April 6	
paper-white	Nov. 15	Winter to	Early spring
Queen of Spain	March 25		
Queen of the North	March 19	March 28	
Robert Sydenham	Feb. 27	March 17	
Silver Bells	Feb. 9	March 9	4 weeks
* Silver Chimes	April 21		
Silver Salver	March 23	April 15	1 week
Silver Spur	March 10		
Sir Watkin	Feb. 14	March 4	3 weeks
Soleil d'Or	Dec. 15		
Thalia	March 14	April 12	
Vanilla	March 17		
White Emperor	April 7		
White Nile	March 15		2 weeks
White Sentinel	April 2		10 days
White Wedgewood	March 28	April 5	
Yellow Poppy	March 19	April 3	
Ornithogalum arabicum	April 14	April 26	Into May
nutans, starre-flower of Naples			
pyramidale, virgin's spray	May 21	May 27	
umbellatum, star-of-Bethlehem	April 1	April 28	
Oxalis (common pink)	March 19	April 12	Nov. 20
(common white)	April 9	April 27	
*Pancratium maritimum, sea daffodil			
(planted in March)	July 23		Aug. 5
Polianthes tuberosa, tuberose	July 23	Aug. 12	Oct. 27
*Puschkinia libanotica (*P. scilloides* var.)	Feb. 22		
Ranunculus asiaticus, Persian buttercup[1]	Late April		

[1] Isabelle Henderson.

Bulbs

Scientific and Common Names	Earliest Date of First Bloom	Latest Date of First Bloom	Length of Bloom
Scilla bifolia, two-leaved squill	Feb. 26	March 10	
hispanica (S. campanulata),			
Spanish bluebell	March 26	April 11	
* *italica,* Italian squill	April 22		
peruviana, hyacinth of Peru	April 16		
pratensis, meadow squill	April 9	April 18	
* *siberica,* Siberian squill	Feb. 28		
siberica, var. *taurica*	Feb. 8	March 10	
*Sisyrinchium grandiflorum	Feb. 27		
*Sprekelia formosissima, St. James-lily	June 8		
Sternbergia lutea	Late Aug.	Sept. 17	Oct. 10
Tigridia Pavonia, tiger-flower	June 20[2]		
Triteleia uniflora Brodiaea uniflora			
Tritonia crocosmaeflora var.			
aurantiaca	July 1	July 12	4 weeks
Tulipa Clusiana, lady tulip	March 17	April 5	
Fosteriana	April 5		
var. Red Emperor	March 27		
Kaufmanniana, waterlily tulip	Early March		
sylvestris (T. florentina odorata)	March 18	March 31	
Single Early	March 15	March 21	
Avalon	March 24	April 7	
Bronze Queen	April 9		
Clara Butt	April 5		
Dom Pedro	April 8	April 17	
Feu Brilliant	April 12	April 20	
Golden Rod	April 8	April 13	
Madame Mottet	April 12		
Monsieur Mottet	April 2	April 15	
Pride of Haarlem	April 7		
Scarlet Beauty	April 7		
Wallflower	April 9	April 17	
*Watsonia mixed hybrids	May 28		End June
Zantedeschia albo-maculata, spotted			
calla	June 19[3]		

[2] Miss Isabel Busbee.

[3] Dr. Coker's garden.

Bulbs

Scientific and Common Names	Earliest Date of First Bloom	Latest Date of First Bloom	Length of Bloom
Zantedeschia Elliottiana, golden calla	May 29	June 3	2 weeks
Rehmannii, pink calla	May 24	June 6	
Zephyranthes Ajax	Aug. 4		Oct. 23
Atamasco, atamasco lily	March 26	April 19	4 weeks
candida	June 20	Aug. 8	Oct. 31
carinata (Z. grandiflora)	May 30	June 15	Repeats later
citrina	June 25	Aug. 7	Oct. 3
robusta (Habranthus)	June 12	Aug. 8	Aug.
rosea	Aug. 19		Sept. 1
texana (Habranthus)	June 21	July 21	Sept. 15
Treatiae	April 16	May 5	
*Zigadenus Fremontii	March 6		

207

Perennials and Biennials

Scientific and Common Names	Earliest Date of First Bloom	Latest Date of First Bloom	Length of Bloom
Achillea filipendulina, fernleaf yarrow	May 22	June 13	July 31
impatiens	June 11	June 17	Late summer
Millefolium var. rosea	April 23	May 21	Late fall
nitida impatiens			
Ptarmica var. Pearl	June 6		July
siberica	April 3	April 19	
tomentosa	April 11	May 10	End June
umbellata	April 5	April 15	May 31
*Actinea herbacea	April 5		
*Adonis amurensis	Feb. 14		
Aethionema cordifolium, Mt. Lebanon candytuft	Late April		
persicum, Persian candytuft	April 3	April 30	2 weeks
Ajuga reptans, carpet bugleweed	March 23	April 11	End May
Althaea rosea, hollyhock	May 14	June 16	End July
Alyssum argenteum (*A. rostratum*)	April 28	May 7	3 weeks
creticum	March 13	April 6	Into June
saxatile	March 17	April 13	Mid-May
Amsonia Tabernaemontana	March 30	May 1	2 weeks
Anchusa italica (*A. azurea*)	April 17	April 30	June
myosotidiflora (*Brunnera macrophylla*), forget-me-not-flowered anchusa	March 6	March 19	End May
Anemone japonica	Aug. 26	Sept. 26	Nov.
Anemonella thalictroides, rue-anemone	March 19	March 28	All summer
Anthemis tinctoria, golden marguerite	May 2	May 26	End June
*Anthericum ramosum	May 30		
Antirrhinum majus, snapdragon	May 10	May 17	Fall
Aquilegia caerulea, Colorado columbine	Early April		
canadensis, wild columbine	April 3	April 13	Into May
chrysantha, golden columbine	April 15	May 10	June
flabellata nana-alba, fan columbine	March 23	April 30	
longissima	April 21	May 10	June
vulgaris, European columbine	April 16	April 29	4 weeks
vulgaris var. *nivea*	April 16		2 weeks
long-spurred hybrids	April 19		May
Arabis alpina, mountain rock-cress	Jan. 23	Feb. 24	Late April
procurrens	Jan. 23		Mid-April
*Arenaria montana, mountain sandwort	April 15		

Perennials and Biennials

Scientific and Common Names	Earliest Date of First Bloom	Latest Date of First Bloom	Length of Bloom
Armeria: Statice			
Artemisia lactiflora, white mugwort	June 22	July 10	Aug.
Asclepias tuberosa, butterfly-weed	June 2	June 10	To fall
*Asphodeline lutea (Asphodelus), asphodel	March 29		
*Aster alpinus	May 29		
novae-angliae and varieties	May 29	June 15	Late Oct.
novi-belgii var. Queen Mary	July 7	End of summer	
tataricus	Sept. 1	Sept. 20	Late Oct.
dwarf hybrid Victor	June 7		Through Aug.
Astilbe hybrids	Mid-May	May 31	
Baptisia australis, false indigo	April 23	May 8	2–3 weeks
Bocconia cordata: Macleaya			
Boltonia asteroides	Mid-July	to Mid-	Sept.
latisquama	Mid-July	to Mid-	Sept.
Brunnera macrophylla: Anchusa myosotidiflora			
Callirhoë involucrata, poppy mallow	April 16	May 29	Mid-summer
Calystegia pubescens: Convolvulus japonicus			
*Campanula carpatica, Carpathian harebell	July 7		July
garganica	May 19		Into June
latifolia macrantha	Late May		Into June
* *Medium*, Canterbury bells	May 25		
persicifolia, peach bells	April 20	May 10	May
Poscharskyana, Serbian harebell	April 22	May 12	End May
rapunculoides, European bellflower	April 20		Nov.
Carex Fraseri, lilyleaf sedge	Jan. 10	March 30	
Centaurea dealbata	Late May		
macrocephala	Late May		
* *ruthenica*	May 26		June 4
Centranthus ruber, red valerian	April 17	April 30	End May
Cerastium tomentosum, snow-in-summer	Late March		Mid-May
Ceratostigma plumbaginoides (Plumbago Larpentiae), leadwort	June 10	Mid-July	Into Sept.

209

Perennials and Biennials

Scientific and Common Names	Earliest Date of First Bloom	Latest Date of First Bloom	Length of Bloom
Cheiranthus Allionii (*Erysimum asperum*), Siberian wallflower	March 7	April 10	Into June
Chrysanthemum arcticum, Arctic daisy	June 15		
coccineum: Pyrethrum roseum coreanum	Sept. 26		End Oct.
Leucanthemum, improved elder daisy	Late April		End May Fall
maximum, Shasta daisy	June 20		July
The Swan	April 18		End June
Alaska	June 6		
Parthenium, feverfew	May 27		Summer
var. Golden Ball	May 30		
Korean hybrids	Early Oct.		End Oct.
Chrysogonum virginianum	March 15	April 14	Nov.
Chrysopsis mariana	Aug. 10	Early Sept.	Oct.
Cimicifuga racemosa	June 12		
* *simplex*	Oct. 13		
Claytonia virginica	March 29		
Clematis integrifolia var. *coerulea*	May 24		
Convolvulus japonicus (*Calystegia pubescens*)	Late May	June 15	Into July
mauritanicus	May 8	May 25	2 weeks
Coreopsis lanceolata var. *grandiflora*	May 2	May 15	All summer
Coronilla cappadocica	May 27	June 3	June 27
varia, crown vetch	May 14	June 7	June
*Crucianella stylosa	May 18		
*Cynoglossum grande	April 12		
* *nervosum*	June 30		
Cypripedium acaule	May 17		
pubescens	April 7		
*Delphinium Bellamosum			
cardinale, scarlet larkspur	May 23	May 9	End May
chinense (*D. grandiflorum*)	Late April	May 21	Fall
tricorne, rock larkspur	April 2		April
Dianthus Allwoodii	April 22		
arenarius	March 22	April 2	
barbatus, sweet William	April 12	May 8	
var. *nigrescens*	April 29	May 6	Mid-July
caesius, Cheddar pink	April 4	April 19	Late May

Perennials and Biennials

Scientific and Common Names	Earliest Date of First Bloom	Latest Date of First Bloom	Length of Bloom
chinensis var. *Heddewigii*	May 1		Dec.
deltoides, maiden pink	Late March	Early April	Into June
* *Grisebachii* (*D. viscidus* var.)	April 19		
* *Knappii*	May 24		June 20
plumarius hybrids	April 1		
* Little Joe	April 6		Into June
Dicentra Cucullaria, Dutchmans-breeches	April 1	April 12	
eximia	March 23	April 20	Fall
* *formosa*	April 14		Into June
spectabilis, showy bleeding-heart	March 19	April 21	2 weeks
Dictamnus albus	April 25		May 7
Digitalis ambigua	May 17		
lanata, Grecian foxglove	May 16		
purpurea hybrids	April 23	May 9	End May
Doronicum caucasicum, leopards-bane	March 17	April 9	Into May
Echinops Ritro, small globe thistle	July 21		Aug.
Epimedium macranthum var. *niveum*, long-spur epimedium	April 17		2 weeks
pinnatum var. *elegans*, Persian epimedium	March 30		2 weeks
sulphureum	March 27		3 weeks
Erodium Manescavii, Manescaut's heronsbill	March 26	May 1	Late May
Eupatorium coelestinum, mist-flower	Sept. 10	Sept. 23	2 weeks
Euphorbia corollata, flowering spurge	May 25	June 20	All summer
Filipendula: Spiraea			
Funkia: Hosta			
Gaillardia grandiflora, blanket flower	Late April		Fall
var. Goblin	May 18		Nov. 14
var. Sun God	April 19	May 18	Nov. 14
Portola hybrids	May 10		Nov. 14
Galium boreale, northern bedstraw	June 12		2 weeks
verum, lady's bedstraw	June 10		3 weeks
Gaura Lindheimeri	May 22		Fall
Gazania speciosa hybrida	June 1		Late Nov.
Gentiana Andrewsii, closed gentian	Oct. 15	Nov. 1	Late Nov.

Perennials and Biennials

Scientific and Common Names	Earliest Date of First Bloom	Latest Date of First Bloom	Length of Bloom
Geranium grandiflorum	May 28		
maculatum	April 5	April 20	
pratense alba	May 10		
Gerberia Jamesonii hybrida, Transvaal daisy	May		Fall
Geum coccineum hybrids	April 15		May
Glaucium flavum	May 7		Late June
* *flavum* var. *tricolor*	May 7		Late May
* *leiocarpum*	April 23		Late May
Gypsophila acutifolia	May 29		
pacifica	July 12	July 25	Oct.
paniculata, babys-breath	Mid-May		Early June
Helenium			
autumnale, Riverton Beauty	Aug. 10		
autumnale, Riverton Gem	Aug. 10		Into Sept.
hybrid, Crimson Beauty	July 30		Into Sept.
Helianthemum vulgare in var.	April 30	May 10	2 weeks
Helianthus angustifolius	Sept. 27		Oct. 18
orgyalis	Sept. 5		Early Sept.
Heliopsis helianthoides var.			
Pitcheriana	May 26	June 28	Late fall
Heliotropium amplexicaule	April 23	May 10	To fall
Helleborus niger	Dec. 1		To March
Hemerocallis aurantiaca, golden summer day-lily	April 10	May 5	5 weeks
Dumortieri, narrow dwarf day-lily	April 15		4 weeks
flava, lemon lily	April 19	May 4	2 weeks
		Repeats in fall	
var. major	April 19		
		Repeats in fall	
fulva, tawny day-lily	May 21	May 28	5 weeks
Middendorffii, broad dwarf day-lily	June 10	June 22	
serotina (*Thunbergii*), late yellow day-lily	June 10	June 22	5 weeks
Amaryllis	May 26	June 4	4 weeks
Anna Betscher	June 15	July 3	
Bay State	June 16		3 weeks
Calypso	May 26	June 7	2 weeks
Florham	May 24	June 6	4–6 weeks

Perennials and Biennials

Scientific and Common Names	Earliest Date of First Bloom	Latest Date of First Bloom	Length of Bloom
Gold Dust	April 18		3 weeks
Golden Dream	June 4	July 19	7 weeks
* Gypsy	June 19		
Hyperion	June 3	June 26	4 weeks
J. A. Crawford	May 23	June 12	6 weeks
J. R. Mann	May 26	June 7	
Kwanso	June 10		7 weeks
Lemona	May 30	June 12	4 weeks
Margaret Perry	June 17	June 28	4 weeks
Mikado	May 26	June 3	6 weeks
Mrs. W. H. Wyman	June 16	June 26	5 weeks
Ophir	June 3		4 weeks
Queen of May (van Veen)	June 2	June 6	3 weeks
* Radiant	June 10		
Sir Michael Foster	May 23	May 29	4 weeks
Sovereign	April 4	April 29	5 weeks
The Gem	May 25	June 16	5 weeks
Hepatica triloba	Dec. 31	Feb. 19	
Hesperaloe parviflora, pink yucca	May†		
Hesperis matronalis, sweet-rocket	April 30		End May
Heuchera sanguinea, coral-bells	April 11	April 30	End May
Hibiscus coccineus	July 19		Sept.
Moscheutos, mallow marvels	June 19	July 3	Late July
* Golden Bowl	Aug. 15		Sept. 20
Hosta caerulea (*H. ovata*)	June 15		2 weeks
japonica (*H. lancifolia*)	Aug. 1		Aug.
plantaginea (*H. grandiflora*),			
August lily	Aug. 8	Aug. 16	End Aug.
Sieboldiana (*H. glauca*)	June 2		June
Iberis sempervirens, perennial			
candytuft	March 6	April 1	Late April
Iris cristata, crested iris	April 1	April 16	Late April
dichotoma, vesper iris	July 9		To frost
seed planted in Jan.	July†		
ensata	March 30	April 18	Into May
foliosa (*I. brevicaulis*), leafy blue			
iris	May 14	May 24	June 10
fulva, copper iris	April 16	May 7	End May
giganticaerulea, big blue flag	April 21		3 weeks
hexagona, Dixie iris	May 14	May 22	June

† William Hunt, Chapel Hill.

Perennials and Biennials

Scientific and Common Names	Earliest Date of First Bloom	Latest Date of First Bloom	Length of Bloom
Kimballiae, Miss Kimball's blue flag	Early May §		
ochroleuca	May 6		
persica, Persian iris	Feb. 15		1 week
Pseudacorus, water iris	April 12	April 22	Into May
reticulata	Feb. 19	March 7	2 weeks
* *reticulata* var. *histrioides major*	Jan. 21		
tectorum, roof iris	April 11	April 29	
* *tuberosa* (*Hermodactylis tuberosa*), snakeshead iris	Feb. 13		
unguicularis (*I. stylosa*), Algerian iris	Dec. 13	Feb. 11	
* *verna*	March 26		
versicolor, blue flag	April 25		
vinicolor, winecolored iris	April 16	April 27	
Dutch Iris	April 12	April 26	Mid-May
Siberian Iris			
Emperor	April 21	April 29	Until May
Perry's blue	May 2		
Snow Queen	April 18		
Delta hybrids or forms			
A. H. Nichols	May 21		Into June
Dorothea K. Williamson	April 26	May 12	End May
imperialis	May 6	May 19	10 days
oenantha	April 27	May 17	
Japanese Iris	Mid-May		Mid or late June
tall single purple, first to bloom with me	May 11	May 30	
* Mahogany, last to bloom with me	June 13		
Pogon Iris			
Early Dwarf			
Orange Queen	March 6	April 3	
The Bride	March 6	April 4	
Intermediates			
albicans	March 17	April 13	
Bluet	March 16		May 11
Kochii	March 27	April 20	
Nymph	March 9	April 19	
Porcelain Blue	March 31	April 18	End April
Purple King	March 22	April 19	

§ Mr. Jacques Busbee, Jugtown, N.C.

Perennials and Biennials

Scientific and Common Names	Earliest Date of First Bloom	Latest Date of First Bloom	Length of Bloom
Tall Bearded			
Alcazar	May 2		
Ambassadeur	May 4	May 15	End May
Black Wings	April 24	May 2	
Blue Jay	April 27	May 20	
Buto	April 27	May 8	
Coronation	April 26	May 10	May 28
* Dauntless	May 10		
Frieda Mohr	April 27	May 10	
* Happy Days	May 5		
Harmony	April 17	May 6	
Henri Rivière	May 1	May 7	
Isoline	April 11	May 2	
Jean Cayeux	May 6	May 12	
Lord Lambourne	April 15	April 24	
Magnifica	April 19	May 2	
Mother of Pearl	April 11	April 26	
pallida (of Southern gardens)	April 13	April 28	
Purissima	April 6	May 6	
Quaker Lady	April 15	May 8	
Sindjkha	April 19	May 10	
Souvenir de Loetitia Michaud	April 23	May 11	
Souvenir de Mme. Gaudichau	April 18	May 6	
Titus	April 1	April 22	
Western Dream	April 20	May 9	
* W. R. Dykes	May 10		
Isatis tinctoria, woad	April 11		
Kniphofia Pfitzeri (*Tritoma*), torch-lily	May 20		Repeats in fall
Towers of Gold	July 1		Repeats Oct.
Dwarf hybrids	June 12		Summer
Lamium maculatum, dead nettle	April 28	May 3	May
Lavandula Spica (*L. vera*)	June 14		2 weeks
Lepachys pinnata	June 20	June 27	Late July
Limonium: Statice.			
Linaria dalmatica	May 1		Mid-Aug.
Linum flavum, golden flax	March 28	April 25	June
perenne, blue flax	March 26	May 2	
Liriope Muscari (*Ophiopogon*), lily-turf	July 12	Aug. 12	Late Aug.

Perennials and Biennials

Scientific and Common Names	Earliest Date of First Bloom	Latest Date of First Bloom	Length of Bloom
Lithospermum prostratum	March 27		
Lunaria biennis, honesty	March 20	May 1	Late May
Lychnis Coronaria (*Agrostemma*), mullein-pink	May 8	June	Late June
Lysimachia clethroides, Japanese loosestrife	June 15	June 20	Into July
Lythrum Salicaria, purple loosestrife	May 29	June 15	Into Aug.
Macleaya cordata (*Bocconia*), plume-poppy	June 25	July 15	3 weeks
Malva Alcea	June 20		June
Manfreda virginica, false aloe	June 29		10 days
Matricaria: Chrysanthemum Parthenium			
Mazus Pumilio	Feb. 20	April 8	Spring repeats
Mertensia virginica, Virginia-bluebells	March 19	April 21	Into May
Monarda didyma, bee-balm	June 5	June 14	Summer
var. *alba*	June 15		2 weeks
Salmon Queen	June 14		Summer
fistulosa, wild bergamot	July 11	July 24	4 weeks
Myosotis palustris, true forget-me-not	April 22	April 29	To mid-June Repeats fall
Nepeta Mussinii, cat mint	April 21		Into June
Nierembergia gracilis, cup-flower	April 30		June
hippomanica (*N. caerulea*)	April 21	May 7	Fall
from seed sown Oct. 13	June 1		
rivularis	May 10	May 25	July
Oenothera fragrans	May 6		Into June
Fraseri	May 29		June 30
fruticosa	May 25		June 20
missouriensis	April 27	June 14	
speciosa (*Hartmannia speciosa*)	May 9	May 18	
var. *Childsii*, Texas windflower	April 17	May 6	All summer
Omphalodes verna, creeping forget-me-not	Dec. 10	Feb. 28	To April
Paeonia sinensis in var.	May 2	May 17	End May

Perennials and Biennials

Scientific and Common Names	Earliest Date of First Bloom	Latest Date of First Bloom	Length of Bloom
Papaver atlanticum (form of			
Rupifragum)	April 22		Into June
nudicaule, Iceland poppy	May		May
orientale in var., Oriental poppy	Early May		May
var. Olympia	April 30	May 10	
Penstemon barbatus Torreyi	May 15	May 31	Into June
hirsutus	May 21	June 2	2 weeks
Phlox divaricata, blue phlox	March 17	April 10	Into May
paniculata, garden phlox			Summer
* var. Augusta	July 7		
* Columbia	June 12	June 18	
Jules Sandeau	June 16		
Lilian	June 10	June 20	
Miss Lingard	May 10	May 29	Into June
Mrs. Jenkins	June 18		
Mrs. Milly van Hoboken	June 27	July 7	
Rheinlander	June 12		
R. P. Struthers	June 19		
Tigress	June 15		
subulata, moss-pink	March 20	April 3	End April
Physostegia virginiana	June 29	July 22	Until Aug.
var. *alba*	June 10		
Vivid	Aug. 1	Aug. 10	Oct. 1
Platycodon grandiflorus, balloon-			
flower	May 30	June 20	Fall
Plumbago: Ceratostigma			
Polemonium caerulum	May 6		End May
reptans	March 23		End April
Polygonum compactum			
(*P. cuspidatum*)	Aug.		End Aug.
oxyphyllum	Oct. 6		End Oct.
Potentilla Tonguei (*P. multifida*)	June 4	June 27	2 weeks
tridentata	April 19	April 29	Late April
verna nana	April 27	May 8	4 weeks
Warrensii	Feb. 18	April 6	Late April
Primula vulgaris, common primrose	Feb. 28	March 25	Late April
Pulmonaria angustifolia, blue cowslip	March 17		3 weeks
* *saccharata*, Bethlehem-sage	March 30		
Pyrethrum roseum (*Chrysanthemum*			
coccineum)	April 21	May 24	Into June
Ranunculus repens, pleniflorus	April 1	April 15	Mid-May
Rudbeckia Newmanii (*R. speciosa*)	July 1		Fall
purpurea, purple coneflower	June 1		Fall

Perennials and Biennials

Scientific and Common Names	Earliest Date of First Bloom	Latest Date of First Bloom	Length of Bloom
Sabatia angularis	Mid-July		2 weeks
Salvia azurea	June 29		All summer
farinacea, mealycup sage	May 28	June 19	Nov.
Greggii, autumn sage	April 13	May 3	Fall
* alba	April 23		Fall
leucantha, Mexican bush sage (not hardy)	Sept. 18	Sept. 30	Nov. 14
patens, gentian sage	May 21		Nov. 15
Pitcheri	Sept. 1		Nov. 13
pratensis	March 25	April 26	Late May
Sclarea var. *turkestaniana*, clary	May		Late June
* *virgata* var. *nemorosa*	March 20		Spring
Saponaria ocymoides, soapwort	April 5	April 10	Late May
Scabiosa japonica			Late June
Scutellaria baicalensis var. *coelestina*	July 1		Summer
Sedum pulchellum	May 29		June
sarmentosum	May 17		Into June
Sieboldii	Oct. 21		2 weeks
spectabile	Sept. 1		3 weeks
ternatum	April 17		Into May
Sidalcea malvaeflora var. Rose Queen	May 29		2 weeks
* Rosy Gem	June 2		2 weeks
Silene caroliniana, Carolina pink	March 30	April 17	End May
* *maritima*, sea campion	April 1		End May
Spiraea Aruncus (Aruncus sylvester), goats-beard	May 24	June	2 weeks
chinensis	May 27	June 7	2 weeks
* *Filipendula (Filipendula hexapetala)*, dropwort	May 18		2 weeks
lobata (Filipendula rubra), queen-of-the-prairie	June 16	June 20	3 weeks
palmata (Filipendula purpurea)	May 20	June 3	3 weeks
* *Ulmaria* var. *plena (Filipendula Ulmaria* var.), queen-of-the-meadow	May 28		Mid-June
venusta var. *magnifica (Filipendula rubra* var.)	June 16	June 24	Into July
Stachys grandiflora	May 18		Into June
* *lanata*, lambs-ears	June 9		2 weeks
Statice Armeria, common thrift	April 13		Nov. 14
latifolia (Limonium)			July
Stokesia laevis, cornflower aster	May 30		Into July

Perennials and Biennials

Scientific and Common Names	Earliest Date of First Bloom	Latest Date of First Bloom	Length of Bloom
Talinum calycinum, cherry sunbright	May 6		Aug. 6
Thalictrum aquilegifolium, meadow-rue	May 10		End May
dipterocarpum	May 27		Into June
glaucum	May 9	May 24	Into June
kiusianum	May 13	May 30	Mid-June
Thermopsis caroliniana, Aaron's rod	April 21	May 26	10 days
Tiarella cordifolia	March 31	April 15	2 weeks
Tradescantia bracteata var. *rosea*	April 17		Mid-May
brevicaulis	April 23		Late May
virginiana	April 21	May 10	Late May
var. *alba*	April 26	May 10	Late May
hybrida			
* Blue Stone	April 19		Into June
* Iris Prichard	May 3		Late May
J. C. Weguelin	April 11	May 9	Late May
* Leonora	May 5		Late May
* Pauline	April 21		Late June
* Purple Dome	April 21		Late May
Trillium cernuum	April 17		
Tritoma: Kniphofia			
Tunica saxifraga	May 14		All summer
Verbascum densiflorum	May 21	June 1	All summer
olympicum, giant mullein	May 18	June 3	Into July
Willmottiae	May 8	May 22	
* Cotswold Gem	May 2		June
Verbena bonariensis	May 9	June 15	Nov. 25
erinoides, moss verbena	May 1		Late fall
venosa	April 30	May 14	Fall
Veronica filiformis	Feb. 28		Early Apr.
incana	April 25	May 8	2 weeks
peduncularis	March 24	April 28	2 weeks
rupestris var. *alba*	April 30	May 12	1 week
* *saxatilis*	May 7		1 week
spicata var. *alba*	April 22	May 20	Fall
nana	May 17		Late June
Teucrium var. *prostrata*	May 14	June 1	Into July
Blue Spires	April 17	May 1	2 weeks
Vinca major	Feb. 21	April 3	
minor	Feb. 19	March 19	
var. *alba*	Feb. 19	March 11	

Perennials and Biennials

Scientific and Common Names	Earliest Date of First Bloom	Latest Date of First Bloom	Length of Bloom
Viola Gov. Herrick			March
incognita	April 1		
pedata, birds-foot violet	March 15	April 15	
primulifolia	April 18		
Rosina	March 1		
Yucca filamentosa, Adam's-needle	End May		Nov.

Shrubs

Scientific and Common Names	Earliest Date of First Bloom	Latest Date of First Bloom	Length of Bloom
Abelia grandiflora	May 25	June 29	Summer
var. *Sherwoodii*	June 17	July 1[†]	Summer
* *Schumannii*	June 16		Summer
Acanthopanax Sieboldianus (*Aralia pentaphylla*)	April		Spring
Aesculus Hippocastanum, common horse-chestnut	April 20		2 weeks
parviflora	Early June		2 weeks
Pavia, red buckeye	April 13[1]		
Albizzia Julibrissin, mimosa	May 31	June 10	June
Althaea Hibiscus			
Amelanchier canadensis, shadblow	March 20		March into April
Amygdalus: Prunus			
Andromeda: Pieris			
Anisacanthus Wrightii	July 29	Oct. 8	
Aronia arbutifolia, red chokeberry	March 20	April 19	April
Azalea amoena	March 20	April 1	
amoena var. *coccinea*			Mid-April
arborescens, sweet azalea	May 20	June 6	June
calendulacea, flame azalea	May 7	May 12	June
macrantha			May
Maxwellii	Late May		June
Vaseyi, pink-shell azalea	April 23[2]		
Hinomayo (Kurume)	March 20	Apr. 5	End April
* Mary (Kaempferi)	April 19		Into May
Benzoin aestivale, spice-bush	April 23		
Buddleja, butterfly-bush			
* Charming	July 1		Fall
Davidii	July 6	July 15	Fall
* Fortunei	July 7		Fall
Calycanthus floridus, sweet-shrub	May 27	April 25	Into May
Camellia japonica, single red	Jan. 20	April 25	
Sasanqua var., Snow on the Mountain			Nov.

[†] Coker, W. C., and H. R. Totten, *Trees of the Southeastern States,* Chapel Hill, 1937.
[1] Mrs. Godbey, Greensboro, N.C.   [2] Mrs. Totten, Chapel Hill, N.C.
[†] Coker and Totten, *op. cit.*

Shrubs

Scientific and Common Names	Earliest Date of First Bloom	Latest Date of First Bloom	Length of Bloom
Caryopteris incana, bluebeard	Sept. 1	Sept. 9	Sept. 30
Cassia corymbosa	July 29	Sept. 1	Into Oct.
marilandica, wild senna	July 6		Into Aug.
Cercis canadensis, redbud	March 6	April 7	April
Chaenomeles: Cydonia japonica			
Chionanthus virginica, fringe-tree	April 9	May 7	2 weeks
Citrus trifoliata: Poncirus trifoliata			
Cladrastis lutea, yellow-wood	May 5*	May 26*	
Clerodendrum trichotomum, glory-			
bower	Mid-July		Aug.
	(Berries	Oct. 15-20)	
Clethra alnifolia, sweet pepperbush	July 10	July 24	Aug.
Cornus florida, dogwood	March 22	April 14	2 weeks
Crataegus Crus-galli, cockspur thorn	May 19*		
Marshallii, blue haw	April 26*		
Cydonia japonica (*Chaenomeles*			
lagenaria), Japan quince	Jan. 10	March 15	Mid-April
Cytisus nigricans, spike broom	May 28		
scoparius, Scotch broom	March 25	April 29	Mid-May
Damnacanthus indicus	April 18	May 17	Nov. 13
Desmodium: Lespedeza			
Deutzia gracilis	April 15	May 20	
scabra	Late		
	March	April 18	Into May
Duranta repens, Mexican lilac	Aug. 1		Oct.
Erythrina Crista-gallii, coral-tree	June		July
Escallonia (species unknown)	May 21		
Exochorda grandiflora, pearl-bush	March 6	April 11	Late April
Forsythia intermedia	Jan. 25	March 20	Into April
suspensa	Jan. 25		Into April
Fothergilla monticola	April 17		April
Gardenia florida (*G. jasminoides*),			
Cape-jasmine			June
radicans	June 12		July
Gordonia alatamaha, Franklinia	Aug. 1		Frost
Lasianthus, loblolly bay			July

Shrubs

Scientific and Common Names	Earliest Date of First Bloom	Latest Date of First Bloom	Length of Bloom
Halesia carolina (*H. tetraptera*), silver-bell			Late April
*Hamamelis mollis, Chinese witch-hazel	Late June		
virginiana, witch-hazel	Nov.		Late Dec.
Hibiscus syriacus, althea	June 20		July
Hydrangea quercifolia, oakleaved hydrangea			June
*Hypericum aureum, golden Saint Johnswort	June 6		Summer
calycinum, rose of Sharon	May 27	June 6	June
densiflorum	June 16		Summer
Moseranum, gold-flower	June 17		June
Jasminum floridum, flowery jasmine	April 27	May 11	Into June
humile var. *revolutum,* Italian jasmine	April 17	May 24	Into June
nudiflorum, winter jasmine	Jan. 1	Feb. 16	Into March
primulinum, primrose jasmine	April 17		
Kalmia latifolia, mountain-laurel	May 13	May 17	Late May
Kerria japonica, single kerria	March 26	April 29	2 weeks
japonica var. *pleniflora,* double kerria	March 28	April 11	End April
Koelreuteria paniculata, goldenrain-tree	June 5		Late June
Kolkwitzia amabilis, beauty-bush	April 10	April 25	May 10
Laburnum vulgare (*L. anagyroides*), golden-chain	April 11	April 24	
Lagerstroemia indica, crape-myrtle	Mid-June	July 1	Sept.
Lespedeza formosa (*Desmodium penduliflorum*), purple bush clover	Sept. 1	Sept. 11	Late Sept.
Leucothoë axillaris	April 20	April 27	
Lonicera fragrantissima, Christmas honeysuckle	Jan. 1	Jan. 27	End Feb.
Lyonia lucida: Pieris nitida			

Shrubs

Scientific and Common Names	Earliest Date of First Bloom	Latest Date of First Bloom	Length of Bloom
Magnolia fuscata: Michelia fuscata			
grandiflora, bull bay	May 10		June
macrophylla	May 24†		Aug.[3]
purpurea	March 6	April 6	
Soulangeana, saucer magnolia	Jan. 29	April 1	
stellata, star magnolia	Feb. 15	March 15	Late March
tripetala, umbrella-tree	April 20		Early May
virginiana (*M. glauca*), sweet bay	May		Into June
Mahonia Bealei (*M. japonica*)	Jan. 10	March 1	2 weeks
Malus: Pyrus			
Meratia praecox (*Chimonanthus fragrans*), winter-sweet	Dec. 15	Dec. 20	Jan.
Michelia fuscata (*Magnolia fuscata*), banana-shrub	April 13	May 7	May
Neviusia alabamensis, snow-wreath	March 29	April 12	2 weeks
Osmanthus Fortunei, Fortune's tea olive	Oct.		Nov.
fragrans (*Olea fragrans*), sweet olive	Sept. 1	Sept. 24	Jan.
Oxydendrum arboreum, sour-wood			June
Philadelphus coronarius, mock-orange	April 10	May 10	Mid-May
Photinia serrulata	April 13		
Pieris floribunda (*Andromeda floribunda*)	March 23[4]		
japonica (*Andromeda japonica*)	Feb. 10		April 13
nitida (*Lyonia lucida*), angle-stem fetterbush	May 13		Late May
Poinciana Gilliesii (*Caesalpinia Gilliesii*), bird-of-paradise tree	May 31	July 13	Fall
Poncirus trifoliata (*Citrus trifoliata*)	March 20	April 11	
Potentilla fruticosa, shrubby cinquefoil	April 22		
Prunus americana, river plum	March 14†	March 27†	
angustifolia, Chickasaw plum	Feb. 16	March 20†	
cerasifera var. *Pissardii*, purpleleaf plum	Feb. 13	March 15	2 weeks

†Coker and Totten.
[3]Nik Nar Nursery, Biltmore, N.C.
[4]Duke Campus.

Shrubs

Scientific and Common Names	Earliest Date of First Bloom	Latest Date of First Bloom	Length of Bloom
glandulosa, flowering almond,			
white	March 22	April 7	
pink	March 10	March 31	
Persica (*Amygdalus Persica*),	Early		Late
double-flowering peach	March		March
subhirtella pendula, rosebud			
cherry			March
Punica Granatum, pomegranate	April 26	May 17	Oct.
Granatum nana, dwarf			
pomegranate	Sept. 20	Nov. 1	Nov.
Pyrus coronaria (*Malus coronaria*),			
garland crabapple	March 20	April 21	10 days
Sargentii (*Malus Sargentii*)	April 6		
Rhododendron catawbiense, rose bay	April 11	May 15	
maximum, great laurel			June
Rhodotypos tetrapetala (*R.*			
kerrioides), white kerria	March 18	April 14	
Rhus Cotinus (*Cotinus Coggygria*),			
smoke-tree	May 18		
Robinia hispida, rose acacia	April 21		Mid-May
Pseudoacacia, black locust	April 23		
Rosa Hugonis	April 18	April 29	3 weeks
Rosmarinus officinalis, rosemary	Feb. 19	April 1	3 weeks
Sambucus canadensis	May 24		Mid-June
Sorbaria arborea glabrata	June 19	July	2 weeks
Spiraea Bumalda var. Anthony Waterer	May 3	June 6	
japonica ovalifolia	April 29		
prunifolia var. *plena*	Jan. 28	April 1	3 weeks
Reevesiana	March 4	April 19	2 weeks
Thunbergii	Feb. 15	March 9	Late March
* *Vanhouttei*	April 1	April 24	Late April
Stewartia Malacodendron	April 5 [5]		
pentagyna, mountain stewartia			
* *Pseudo-Camellia*, summer camellia	June 11		
Styrax americana, American storax			Early May
grandifolia	April 26	May 17	May
japonica, Japanese snowbell	Early May	May 18	Early May

[5] Orton Plantation, Wilmington, N.C.

225

Shrubs

Scientific and Common Names	Earliest Date of First Bloom	Latest Date of First Bloom	Length of Bloom
Syringa persica laciniata, Persian lilac	Late March	April 17	Late April
vulgaris, common lilac	April 1	April 17	Mid-May
* Ludwig Spaeth	April 14		
Tamarix gallica, French tamarisk	April 2		Mid-April
hispida, Korean tamarisk			June[6]
Thea sinensis (*T. Bohea*), tea plant	Sept. 3	Oct. 13	
Viburnum acerifolium	April 26	May 15	Late May
Carlesii	March 23	April 15	2 weeks
Opulus var. *sterile*, snowball	April 5	April 24	3 weeks
plicatum, Japanese snowball	Late April		
prunifolium, black-haw	March 26	April 17	10 days
rufidulum, blue-haw	May 2†	May 12†	
Tinus, Laurestinus	Christmas	April 11	
tomentosum	March 24	April 20	2 weeks
Vitex Agnus-castus (var. *Macrophylla*), chaste-tree	June 6	June 21	July
Weigela rosea (*W. florida*)	April 1	April 28	May
Zenobia pulverulenta	May 8		

[6] Miss Edna Maslin, Winston-Salem, N.C.
† Coker and Totten.

Vines

Scientific and Common Names	Earliest Date of First Bloom	Latest Date of First Bloom	Length of Bloom
Actinidia chinensis			May
Akebia quinata	March 14	April 20	2 weeks
Antigonon leptopus, coral-vine	Sept. 1		Late Oct.
Bignonia capreolata, cross-vine *radicans: Campsis*	March 20	April 20	April
Campsis radicans, trumpet-vine	June 15		Summer
Clematis crispa, blue bell	April 18	May 8	June
paniculata	Aug. 12	Aug. 19	3 weeks
Mme. Edouard André	May 31		October
Gelsemium sempervirens, Carolina jessamine	March 17	April 12	
Jasminum Beesianum	May 5	May 31	Summer
officinale, star jasmine	Mid-May		
Kadsura japonica	June 29	July 10	July
Lonicera flava, coral honeysuckle	March 26		April
sempervirens	April 23†		
Polygonum Aubertii, Chinese fleece-vine	Aug.		Sept.
Rosa anemonoides, pink Cherokee	March 31	April 27	4 weeks
Banksiae, Lady Banks' rose	March 22	April 17	5 weeks
bracteata, Macartney rose	Late May		Nov.
laevigata, Cherokee rose	March 20	April 30	2 weeks repeats
rugosa repens var. Max Graf	May 9		Late May
setigera, prairie rose			June
Wichuraiana, Memorial rose	Mid-May	May 31	June
Climbing Killarney	April 15	May 12	2 weeks
Climbing Pink Daily	March 27	April 29	Dec.
Dr. Van Fleet	April 25	May 10	
Gardenia	May 13		May
Jacotte	April 4	May 16	3 weeks
Mary Wallace	April 27	May 15	Late May
Mermaid	May 8	May 17	Nov.
Silver Moon	April 22	May 12	3 weeks

† Dr. Coker's garden, Chapel Hill, N.C.

Vines

Scientific and Common Names	Earliest Date of First Bloom	Latest Date of First Bloom	Length of Bloom
Trachelospermum jasminoides, Confederate jasmine	June 29		
Wisteria frutescens, American wisteria			May
sinensis, Chinese wisteria	March 17		April
var: *alba*	March 20	April 15	Mid-May

Index

229

brids), 48; Kurume (*R. Kurume* hybrids), 48; *ledifolia* (*R. mucronatum*) var. *alba* (*Rhododendron* × 'Mucronatum') ('Ledifolia Alba'), 48; *macrantha* (*R. indicum*), 128, 221 'Mary', 48, 221; *Maxwellii* (*R. Maxwellii*), 221; (*R. Vaseyi*), 67, 221

Baby blue-eyes. See *Nemophila*
Baby's-breath. See *Gypsophila paniculata*
Bachelor's-button. See *Centaurea Cyanus*
Bacon, Lord, quoted, 4, 7–8
Balloon-flower. See *Platycodon grandiflorus*
Balsam. See *Impatiens*
Banana-shrub. See *Michelia fuscata*
Baptisia australis, 59, 209
Bay. See *Laurus nobilis*
Bean, xxxii
Bearded iris, 49–53. See also *Iris*
Beauty-bush. See *Kolkwitzia amabilis*
Bedstraw. See *Galium*
Bee-balm. See *Monarda didyma*
Begonia evansiana, 188
Belamcanda chinensis, 96, 138, 201
Belladonna-lily. See *Amaryllis Belladonna*
Bellflower. See *Campanula*
Bellis perennis, 36
Benzoin aestivale (*Lindera Benzoin*), 221
Bethlehem-sage. See *Pulmonaria saccharata*
Betony. See *Stachys*
Bignonia capreolata, 78, 227; *radicans*. See *Campsis radicans*

Bird-of-paradise shrub. See *Poinciana Gilliesii*
Blackberry-lily. See *Belamcanda chinensis*
Black-haw. See *Viburnum prunifolium*
Black locust. See *Robinia Pseudoacacia*
Blandy Experimental Farm, xxxii, 137
Blanket flower. See *Gaillardia*
Bleeding-heart. See *Dicentra*
Bluebeard. See *Caryopteris*
Blue bell. See *Clematis crispa*
Bluebell. See *Campanula rotundifolia; Scilla*
Bluebells. See *Mertensia*
Blue cowslip. See *Pulmonaria angustifolia*
Blue-haw. See *Viburnum rufidulum*
Blue phlox. See *Phlox divaricata*
Blue spirea. See *Caryopteris incana*
Bocconia cordata. See *Macleaya cordata*
Boltonia asteroides, 136, 209; *latisquama*, 136, 209
Bolton's aster. See *Boltonia asteroides*
Bongoume apricot. See *Prunus Mume*
Bottlebrush bush. See *Aesculus parviflora*
Bridal wreath. See *Spiraea prunifolia* 'Plena'
Brodiaea Bridgesii (*Triteleia Bridgesii*), 201; *capitata* (*Dichelostemma pulchellum*), 201; *coronaria*, 201; *grandiflora*. See *B. coronaria. laxa* (*Triteleia laxa*), 201; *uniflora* (*Ipheion uniflorum*), 201

Yew. See *Taxus*
Yucca angustifolia. See *Y. glauca.*
  filamentosa, 6, 220; *glauca*, 6

Zantedeschia albomaculata, 206,
  Elliottiana, 207; *Rehmannii*,
  207
Zenobia pulverulenta, 70, 226
Zephyranthes × 'Ajax', 123, 124,
  147, 207; *Atamasco*, 73, 207;
  candida, 147, 207; *carinata.*
  See *Z. grandiflora. citrina*, 123,
124, 147, 207; *grandiflora*, 122,
  123, 124, 147, 207; *robusta* (**Habranthus tubispathus**), 123,
  207; *rosea*, 124, 207; *texana*
  (**Habranthus texanus**), 123,
  144, 147, 207; *Treatiae*, 207
Zephyr-lily, 122–24. See also
  Zephyranthes
Zigadenus Fremontii, 36, 207
Zinnia elegans, 200; *linearis* (**Z.
  angustifolia**), 103, 109, 149,
  151, 173, 200